By Royal Warrant of Appointment to

HIS MAJESTY
KING GEORGE V

HIS MAJESTY
THE KING OF SPAIN

HIS MAJESTY
THE KING OF ITALY

Patronised by

HER MAJESTY THE QUEEN

THE PRINCESS ROYAL

H.R.H. PRINCESS MARY
VISCOUNTESS LASCELLES

H.R.H. PRINCESS VICTORIA

ETC., ETC.

And the Leading Angling Authorities
:: throughout the World ::

Makers of the Miniature Salmon Fly Rod displayed in the
Queen's Doll's House at the Wembley Exhibition, London, 1924

1924

REPORTS FROM "FISHING GAZETTE."

OLYMPIC GAMES.

ELEVENTH INTERNATIONAL

Fly and Bait Casting Tournament,

FRANCO-BRITISH EXHIBITION, LONDON,
1908.

HAROLD JOHN HARDY.   JOHN JAMES HARDY.   LAURENCE R. HARDY.

A SKILFUL TRIO.

There is an old saying that "the man who drives fat oxen should himself be fat," and, by parity of reasoning, the man who makes first-rate fishing-tackle should himself be able to use it in first-rate fashion. This certainly holds true of the "Hardys." Mr. J. J. Hardy's portrait, flanked by those of his two nephews, Messrs. L. R. Hardy and H. J. Hardy, is here reproduced.

THE BEST OF Hardy's Anglers' Guides

Compiled by
JAMIE MAXTONE GRAHAM

MACDONALD PUBLISHERS
EDINBURGH

Published by Macdonald Publishers
            Edgefield Road
            Loanhead
            Midlothian EH20 9SY

ISBN Paperback 0 904265 95 1
     De-luxe   0 904265 94 3

The Author and Publishers wish to extend their thanks to Hardy
Brothers (Alnwick) Limited for their permission to reproduce
the articles in this book, and for their kind help and
co-operation.
The front cover shows Mr William Hardy fishing near Alnwick;
photograph by G. S. Gilbert.
Cover design by Iain McKinlay after Hardy's catalogue style.

Printed in Scotland by Macdonald Printers (Edinburgh) Ltd.
                      Edgefield Road
                      Loanhead
                      Midlothian EH20 9SY

Introduction

It is well over a hundred years since Hardy Brothers started making sporting goods at Alnwick, Northumberland. During that time, their fishing tackle has taken its place beside the guns of Purdey, the cars of Rolls Royce, the jewellery of Asprey and the luxury of the Ritz.

Hardy's were inventive in design, accurate in engineering, and quietly irresistible in publicity. Almost every year they produced a catalogue, or "Anglers' Guide", showing off their wares to the world's fishermen. Some years it was free, but at most it cost two shillings. Today these catalogues are eagerly sought by fishing tackle collectors, an eccentric breed who have been known to pay hundreds of pounds for a rare reel.

I happen to be one of these, and I spend much of my time surrounded by mounds of fascinating old tackle which I must sort and identify. So I need catalogues, and have been lucky enough to acquire an almost complete set of Hardy's. But I know that other collectors, particularly overseas, cannot possibly do so—hence this book.

I have taken the best pages from 26 available catalogues between 1886 and 1954, and made a composite catalogue which will, I hope, be useful to collectors.

But if, like most people, you are sane enough not to collect old tackle but are still prepared to admire it, then you will enjoy seeing the multiplicity of gadgetry that Hardy's offered their customers.

In 1934, for example, you could choose from 9 different fly reels made in 40 different sizes; and you had all sorts of optional extras like line guards (9s 6d), auxiliary brakes (12s 6d) and silent check (no extra charge). There were split bamboo fly rods in astonishing quantities— 94 models and sizes of trout rods, plus 39 of salmon. Much Hardy tackle was designed by customers and bore their names: how proud of their catalogues must have been C. C. Bethune Esq of the elegant line drier, W. H. Hope Esq of the 2-piece 10-foot rod, and M. B. Davy Esq of the Davy reel!

You don't even have to be an angler to enjoy the supreme examples of Hardy inventiveness. Their landing equipment includes a shooting-stick/landing-net, a gaff/spring-balance, and a really astonishing Royde net-cum-steelyard. But the favourite composite gadget is undoubtedly the Curate, which is a small priest, tweezers, gut-cutter, oil-bottle, and bodkin—and has a roughened surface for striking matches on.

There is *nothing* like having the real old catalogues—but there are just not enough to go round, and they change hands at up to £100 a copy for the oldest ones. So I hope that you enjoy this facsimile—and that you might one day pick up an original Hardy's Anglers' Guide for a song.

80 High Street
Peebles
Scotland

JAMIE MAXTONE GRAHAM
October 1982

BY APPOINTMENT TO HIS MAJESTY KING GEORGE V.

Important to Sportsmen

Buy from Manufacturers who are expert anglers.

It is important, in order to obtain perfectly suitable equipment, to buy from a Firm the members of whom are *Anglers* **as well as Manufacturers.**

Adaptability.

Whether for salmon, sea trout, trout, coarse fish, mahseer or big game fish, etc. ; whether for fly or spinning, every rod must be perfectly adaptable to the particular purpose for which it is intended to be used.

Nearly Sixty Years' Angling Experience.

For nearly sixty years we have fished regularly in the British Islands, Ireland, Norway and other parts of Europe, and are familiar with most rivers.

Fifty-four years' Manufacturing Experience.

For fifty-four years we have given to the manufacture of fishing rods, reels, lines, gut, flies, etc., our whole attention, and the many important improvements introduced by us are well known and acknowledged.

The " Field " and " Fishing Gazette " Testimonies.

The " Field " says :—" **It ought never to be forgotten by anglers that it is to Messrs. Hardy of Alnwick we owe the supremacy which we have achieved as rod makers. They have left all competitors hopelessly behind.**"

The " Fishing Gazette."—" **What Messrs. Hardy do not know about angling is not worth knowing.**"

Our Manufactory.

Our manufactory is the most perfectly appointed in Europe. During the year 1926 we have considerably enlarged many of our departments, in order to meet the ever increasing demand for our goods. Tools and systems are in common use by us, which are absolutely unknown to the general trade. All work turned out is personally tested and guaranteed superior to any other.

The Secret of our Success.

In 1872 we commenced business, as engineers, **Fishing Rod and Tackle Makers,** and gun-makers. Seeing the scope which existed for improvement in the fishing tackle trade, we gave intensive attention to this department. Being able to supply superior mechanical knowledge to the construction of fishing rods, reels, lines, etc., and not being hampered by old-fashioned methods, we improved all departments.

**Enthusiastic
Anglers and
Manufacturers.**

As enthusiastic anglers for both salmon and trout from boyhood, we were able to bring the angler's practical knowledge to assist and guide the manufacture, and from this dual standpoint we produced the improved articles which we now have the pleasure to offer anglers.

**Information
Free to Clients.**

All we know of angling in various localities, such as the most suitable flies, rods, etc., is at all times freely at the disposal of clients.

**Largest
Producers of
High-Class
Work in
Europe.**

In split bamboo rods—the system of building—double building — steel centre — improved joints — " Bridge " rings, reversible spear and button, Pat. " Screw Grip " reel fittings, etc., are all our patents and registered designs, and are fitted to and supplied with " Hardy " rods only.

Our **latest and secret** method of building **" Palakona "** split bamboo rods is of the greatest importance, the work is absolutely mathematically accurate, with the result that our rods are perfectly built and balanced, and vastly superior.

All imitations of " Hardy " rods are valueless when compared with the real article, and this fact discriminating anglers appreciate. It is well known and freely acknowledged that **no firm in any country can produce equipment for angling equal in value to " Hardy's."**

Our premises (in Alnwick alone, not including our branches) are *by far the largest in Europe*. The most casual observer in comparing our work with that of others, will note that these latter are mostly spurious copies.

Mr. J. J. Hardy, our Managing Director, is the author of " Salmon Fishing " in the *Country Life Library of Sport,* also " Salmon Fishing and Salmon Fly Dressing "

**Superin-
tendence.**

and is one of the best known salmon and trout anglers in this country. His experience—which extends to many rivers in England, Scotland, Ireland, Norway, and other parts of Europe—is very valuable. The heads of all other departments are also keen and well-known anglers.

In tournament casting Mr. J. J. Hardy (who is the present Professional Champion Salmon and Trout Fly Caster) has **won more championship events than any**

**Championship
Casting.**

man in the British Empire, and at the tournament held at the Crystal Palace, 1904, distinguished himself by winning no less than *four* Championships—two for fly casting and two for bait casting—in one day, all in the Professional Class, a performance quite unique and unequalled at any Championship Meeting.

**Franco-British
International
Fly and Bait
Casting
Tournament,
London, 1908.**

The most extraordinary results were obtained with Hardy " PALAKONA " rods at the Great International Fly and Bait Casting Tournament held at the Stadium, London. Mr. J. J. Hardy won the Professional Salmon Fly Casting, and also won the light Dry Fly Casting. Mr. H. J. Hardy won the Amateur Salmon, Trout, and Dry Fly Casting. Mr. L. R. Hardy won the Professional light bait casting, using a " Silex " reel. The " Silex " reel won *five* Gold Medals ; no other make of reel won more than *one*.

**Partnership
by Workers.**

As a reward for honest endeavour, the Directors of " Hardy's " have taken into partnership (by giving Shares in the business at original value), all workers who by diligent and conscientious work have helped to build up the world-famous business of " Hardy's." Thus the interest of Capital and Labour is made one, with but one desire, " *That the Firm of ' Hardy's '— their firm, shall and will be first.*"

No good workman ever leaves " Hardy's " ; they mostly spend their lives there ; as an instance, the average number of years in the employment of the firm of eleven men in the " Palakona " Split Bamboo rod finishing department is well over thirty.

The workers have generous wages, Sick and other Clubs to which the firm contribute, and at death their heirs are not left destitute. Thus it is that the business is a smooth and happy one.

It is interesting to quote the remarks of one of our greatest authorities in the angling world when shewn over our works at Alnwick :

" I am told you have no slackers among your workers, and I quite believe it from what I have seen to-day. Apparently you treat them well, and that is the secret."

We desire Sportsmen to take advantage of this co-operation, which creates a desire on the part of all to give of their very best to reduce cost and produce the very highest possible value. Purchasers of these super qualities obtain their requirements at the first cost, direct from the inventors, designers and actual manufacturers.

February, 1927.

B 2

A Famous Northumberland Manufactory.

[Reprinted from the " Newcastle Daily Journal," May 29, 1890.]

(GENERAL VIEW) LONDON AND NORTH BRITISH WORKS, ALNWICK.

Few of the implements which man has made in order to facilitate an indulgence in sport afford more pleasure to those who are expert in its use than a fishing rod. Yet how few of the disciples of Izaak Walton have any conception of the numerous and delicate processes through which the material must pass before the perfect rod is revealed ; how few have any idea of the careful and judicious selection of material required, and the severe tests by which its quality is proved, or the mathematical accuracy with which the numberless parts must be fashioned and fitted together, in order that a strong, reliable, and useful rod may be placed in their hands. A visit to a manufactory would astound most followers of the gentle craft, and would inspire them with a respect for their instruments in other senses as well as that of a means to the enjoyment of a gentlemanly, exciting, and healthy recreation. " It takes ten men to make a pin," so the school books of twenty and thirty years ago informed us, and that was the marvel of the juvenile minds of a generation ago. To make a complete fishing rod of the best type ready for use it requires as many men, and they must be skilful and able to work to the most minute precision.

We have experienced nothing so interesting for a long time as a visit paid to the new manufactory of Messrs. Hardy Brothers, rod, reel, and tackle makers, Alnwick, who in the course of a comparatively short career have established a reputation and a connection which is world-wide, and made the name of the little Northumbrian town in which they are located familiar to all who whip the waters in pursuit of their finny denizens.   Scarcely twenty years ago Messrs. Hardy opened a factory for making guns, fishing rods, reels, and gear in Paikes Street, Alnwick, thus introducing to that neighbourhood an entirely new industry.   They had an uphill task at the outset to establish themselves, but north-country determination, a prolific inventive faculty, and sound workmanship carried them through, and in time enabled them to force themselves to the front.   As business increased they were obliged to seek larger premises, and they, therefore, entered new workshops in Fenkle Street in the same town.   These in turn were subsequently found too cramped for a constantly increasing demand upon their resources, and recently they erected entirely new and extensive premises in Bondgate Without, where now a large staff of workmen are actively engaged in turning out fishing materials to meet orders from far and near.

Messrs. Hardy Brothers served their time as engineers, and afterwards learned the business of gun makers.   An inherent love of sport, and all connected with it, impelled them to enter upon the manufacture of the instruments required for shooting and fishing, the former of which, although a good county business (supplying most of the gentry and sportsmen in North Northumberland), takes a very second-rate place to their fishing rod and tackle business, in which they have displayed an aptitude which has done much to advance the trade and promote the interests of rod fishermen everywhere.   In their earlier career they made the ordinary wood rods, but subsequently, struck with the superiority of cane, took up the cane-built work, and we believe we are correct in stating that they are now the largest manufacturers of cane-built rods in the world, and have transactions with all parts.   The excellence of their workmanship, as well as the improvements they have invented and patented, have constituted a lever by which their work first forced itself into notice, and then into great demand.   Among the customers of the firm may be numbered Prince Albert Victor, Mr. C. Pennell, Major Turle, Mr. G. Selwyn Marriott, Mr. H. S. Hall, Mr. W. Senior (*Field*), Mr. R. B. Marston (*Fishing Gazette*), Mr. G. M. Kelson, Mr. F. M. Halford, and many other distinguished anglers at home, and also in France, Germany, Austria, Switzerland, India, New Zealand, Spain, America, and elsewhere.

The new premises, which are built in the Jacobean style, are situated in close proximity to the railway station, and form a striking contrast to some of the buildings in the neighbourhood that have long contributed their quota to the quaintness which is one of the charms of the old ducal town. All that modern progress could suggest towards rendering them suitable to the business for which they are intended, promoting the comfort of the workpeople, and securing the convenience of those who trade with the firm, has been worked into the plan of the building, and the result is eminently satisfactory.   Attention is first drawn to the handsome frontage, which is wide and striking, and the varied display of sporting implements in the windows of that part of the premises which does duty as a sale shop ; roomy and well-stocked without being overcrowded, the shop gives one a favourable impression of the place from the beginning of the visit.   Access may be had to the factory from the rear of the front or sale shop, or by a wide archway opening from the footpath.   We will conduct our readers there by the former way.   Behind the sale shop is the packing room, where the various consignments are made up and packed, and in due time sent out for delivery. Leading from this room is a spacious staircase, affording means of approach to the ground floor of the main part of the building, which is, of course, the factory, and which stands higher than the front premises, as the whole block is built on the side of a hill.

WOOD ROD-MAKING DEPARTMENT.

On the second floor of the manufactory is the office, which is so situated as to command through the glass panels of the partition almost the entire floor. In front of the office is an eight-horse-power cycle engine of the newest type, which works all the machinery of the establishment. It is on this floor that the wood rods are made. To facilitate this branch of the business there is a useful little machine, a sort of variety worker, which does sawing, planing, grooving, and a number of other operations with the utmost celerity. One man is occupied the whole of his time at this machine selecting and cutting material. Another man spends his time in putting handles on rods. Throughout the place there is an endeavour to keep one man, or one set of men, always to the same operations. Messrs. Hardy have found, as others have, that work is done quicker and better when men are kept to one thing than when they are required to turn their hands to anything and everything. Especially is this the case in some of the finer work connected with the building of fishing rods. After the material of the wood rod is cut, as stated, it is then rounded and taken to a lathe which describes about 2,700 revolutions. Then it is passed to another man who finishes and balances it.

The next step is to send it upstairs, where the silk tyings and rings are put on and affixed, and where it is varnished. Lastly it goes back to the finisher to be finally finished off and made ready for use. An ordinary wood rod goes through about seven different hands before it arrives at the complete state. The rod itself is made of greenheart and the handle of cork, &c. So far we have only referred to the wood portion of the instrument, but Messrs. Hardy make the whole implement right from the ground, and on the first floor is found all the essential equipment for brass work, brazing, making of reels, and packing boxes, &c. Here it is that notice is first attracted to the fact that no fires are used. Fires are dirty and dangerous, and the work can be done equally well, if not better, with the aid of gas. The heating of the shops for the comfort of the workpeople is effected by pipes through the entire building.

ROD-TYING AND VARNISHING DEPARTMENT.

Another flight of stairs conducts one to the second floor, where cane-built work is done. Here it is that one is most struck with the commanding strides that have been made in the manufacture of fishing rods during the past twenty years. Two decades ago the making of fishing rods used to be a rough and ready art. Now things are quite different. The rod which satisfied the last generation would be regarded with a feeling akin to contempt by the present. Great mental activity and manual skill have been brought to bear upon this branch of industry, and now we have angling appliances that it would seem difficult to further improve upon. In this progress Messrs. Hardy Brothers have taken a large share, and indeed their fame has grown with the progress which has been made in the trade, and this would seem to be conclusive evidence that the latter has received no small portion of its impulse from their endeavours to get established and afterwards to maintain a front place in the market. The medals they have gained fully corroborate this idea, and shows how much the angler is indebted to this firm for many of the improvements which have been effected in fishing appliances.

India supplies the best bamboo for the cane-built rods, and the number of bamboos imported by this firm is simply astounding. On the occasion of our visit to Messrs. Hardy's factory we saw no less than 10,000 bamboo canes waiting for the processes of manufacture on the fourth floor, which, as well as the third floor, is devoted to cane-built work. Of these, we are informed, probably only 30 per cent. would be fit for use. At the other end the agents satisfy themselves that the bamboos look serviceable, but it is impossible from the outward appearance to judge with anything like accuracy. A consequence of this is that a considerable number are received which are of no use. When a cane is being selected a portion is cut off the thick end, and then it can be seen whether there is sufficient fibre to warrant its being further dealt with. One out of ten, on an average, are found ultimately to justify the hope that they may come unscathed out of the test to which they are subjected. But only a very small portion of the cane is available, as for a considerable distance from the top the material is unsuitable, and only part of the remainder actually goes into the rod. The portion of the selected canes which are fit for the purpose is rent into strips, and then it has to withstand the severest test, or it is cast aside as useless.

CANE ROD-FINISHING DEPARTMENT.

About twenty-five canes that have stood the test are needed to furnish the material for one 18 feet salmon rod. In the case of the double-built cane rod, which this firm introduced, 48 different strips of cane are required. Each section of the rod is composed of six strips forming the outer portion, and six other strips forming the inner portion, so that they are really two rods, one within the other. The accuracy with which these strips are cut and fixed together is really wonderful. Right to the minute end of the tapering rod the double set of strips are continued and fixed with the same exactitude as if they had grown that way. The more expensive cane rods have steel centres. Within the inner rod of cane a steel rod is introduced, which adds greatly to the power.

It is in the fourth or top storey from which, over the roofs of adjacent buildings, a fine view of the surrounding country is obtained, that the bamboos are stored, and they are selected and tested, rent into strips, cut to the proper size. straightened, and have the knots removed. The rod has to be thoroughly balanced before the parts are fitted together, as to interfere with the hard enamel of the cane would greatly impair the serviceability of the instrument. The strips are fitted together and secured by cement.

CANE ROD-BUILDING DEPARTMENT.

Ordinary glue would be valueless for this work ; something more adhesive and less susceptible to wet is required, and Messrs. Hardy have invented a cement which answers the purpose admirably, and which has never failed to give satisfaction. Next the rods are finished and bound and tied down in

REEL-MAKING DEPARTMENT.

order that they may dry straight. Afterwards they are sent downstairs to have the handles put on, and then on to the joint maker who makes the joints to fit. Next they go to the tying shop and the varnishing shop, and finally back to the finisher, who completes them ready for sending out.

Hardy's patent lock-fast joint is one of the specialities of the firm, and one that has given the greatest satisfaction all round. Its advantages are simplicity, quickness, strength, and the impossibility of putting the joints together without being locked. When the old clumsy and ineffectual devices are remembered, fishers will readily admit the importance of this invention. The point of contact between the cane or wood and the metal wnich forms the joint is the weakest part of a rod, as the unyielding nature of the metal throws the whole strain on the cane or wood. To obviate this Messrs. Hardy have extended and split the end of the ferrule and tapered it down so that there is no sudden arrest of the vibration and less susceptibility to strain at that particular point. Since adopting this plan they have never heard of a rod breaking at the joint. But this is only one of the inventions of Messrs. Hardy. They began to win medals in 1881. At the Fisheries Exhibition, London, 1883, they won the gold medal for the best

FLY-TYING DEPARTMENT.

trout rod, and were awarded £10 for the best collection of trout rods against 45 competitors. This signal success they have followed up by winning 31 medals, diplomas, &c., since for improvements in rods and reels. Besides manufacturing these, they also make artificial flies, and this is a very pretty work, and also a delicate work, as the variety of types, of colours, and shades of colour needed in order to suit the requirements or whims of fishers are legion. Gut cast-lines and almost every kind of tackle are also made in this department, including artificial baits, &c., too numerous to mention.

A much more extended notice of these works is given in the *Fishing Gazette* of June 14th, 1890, whose representative personally inspected them.

☞ FOR FLIES, SEE PAGES 37 TO 46.

Dry=Fly Fishing for Trout

The great favour with which our " Houghton " dry-fly specialities have always been received is very gratifying ; it is a real pleasure to us to feel that our efforts have satisfied the present needs of dry-fly anglers. Without doubt, dry-fly fishing is becoming more popular, and is now practised in the North of England and Scotland, not only in river fishing but also on lochs, as well as on the typical dry-fly south-country rivers, which are the home of the dry-fly man. In Ireland and in Wales the trout have reason to fear his skill. On the Continent, in America and the Colonies the dry-fly is now a popular method. On most rivers the angler frequently reaches a quietly-flowing pool, or a glassy glide at the head of a stream, where the upright split-wing floater, fished dry, is the lure par excellence ; indeed, if properly presented to a rising fish in any such situation it is nearly certain to prove successful. It must not be forgotten that it is not the fly but the angler that succeeds ; and that he must be properly equipped.

10LB. KASHMIR TROUT KILLED BY LT. COL. ALBAN WILSON ON A 10FT. 7IN. "HARDY MARSTON" ROD.

We would emphasize the fact that an ordinary wet-fly outfit is not suitable for dry-fly fishing ; a special build of rod, a special weight of line, a suitable reel, and a very evenly tapered cast are absolutely necessary if the angler wishes to become an expert,—of course, the flies must be dressed to float. We have been asked so often by would-be dry-fly fishermen to give a few practical hints on the art of manipulating the " floater," that we make no apology for doing so. We have already expressed our thanks to the experts who have been good enough to approve the appliances manufactured by us ; to the beginner only, " who wants to know," do we address the following remarks.

Briefly, then, the art of dry-fly fishing is to present a fly that floats,—and floats perfectly,—to the notice of a rising fish in such a manner that it is mistaken for the natural *ephemera* which is hatching out, and in the result is accepted as such by the fish. To lure *Salmo Fario* successfully after this manner it is necessary that the angler should have skill ; be very observant, and have the patience of Job.

Worm Fishing for Trout.

This style of fishing has its charms as well as any other, and although we quite agree with those who protest against it as permitted on some waters (*i.e.* from early Spring till late in the Autumn) yet an angler would feel very stupid after walking several miles to the seat of his intended sport to find the water was too heavy, or the sun too bright for fly-fishing, and he minus his worms. Indeed we should never think of going out for a day's sport without a few, from June to August, more especially when the weather is bright and the water low and clear. They are easily carried, and make sport more of a certainty.

Your fly-rod, if good, will, at a pinch, answer the purpose, but the rod *par excellence* for this work is one we have added to our list, exactly similar to one we used successfully many years ago on the wide shallow waters of the Coquet. These rods are made 12ft. to 16ft., and are very light, see pages 248 to 259. The secret of success in this kind of fishing lies in presenting your bait from a distance so great that, even in shallow water the fish cannot see you. With a short rod, say 11ft., this cannot well be done, but with a long light and fine rod the matter is quite easy. The reel should be light and free running, with fine check and a large barrel. The most suitable is one of our patent "Silex" reels, *pages* 126 to 131, say 3¼ or 3½in., which is also equally useful for spinning or any kind of float fishing. The running line should be of very fine dressed silk, and the gut trace not less than four or more than six feet long, according to the state of the water. This should be mounted with either a round bend single hook, a

☞ IN ORDERING FROM THIS LIST PLEASE QUOTE LETTER Q.

three-hook Stewart's, or two-hook "Pennell," which latter we prefer. The hooks best adapted are (as single hooks) our new pattern Needle Point, and our Special Round Bend Fine Wire, which are made in three sizes, *see Plate page* 134, *Figs.* K, L, Lx *and* M.   As a two-hooked tackle, either Major Ilderton's or Mr. Pennell's are good and certain in hooking, *Figs.* N *and* I, page 134.   Our Stewart worm tackle, made with fine eyes instead of whipping, *Figs.* H and P are certainly for bright water (as a Stewart Tackle), the best extant.

Lead in some form is required in order to steady the line; more or less being applied at the discretion of the angler, when by the waterside he ascertains the rate of the current, (See our "Simplex" Leads, page 152).

The question of bait is most important.   Undoubtedly the best worms for colour and toughness we have ever seen or used, are those obtainable in the neighbourhood of Edinburgh (called the "Edinburgh Pink Tails") which can always be had by return of post, from our Edinburgh house, 5, South St. David Street.   See page 151.   Many anglers, of course procure their own.   The worms best for trout fishing are the marsh-worm, red-worm, button worm, and the brandling.   All these worms should be scoured, a process which consists of starving them in damp moss for three or four days before use.

Having procured the necessary apparatus, the angler then, with his wading boots on, if he uses them, quietly wades into the water; or, if preferring *terra firma*, he keeps as much as possible out of sight of the fish upon a part of the bank suitable for his purpose, and below the water to be fished.   The worm in all cases should be cast up stream, and suffered to float down, for reasons which will be clear enough when explained as follows :—1—The trout lie head up stream, and, therefore, do not see the angler; 2—The bait floats gently down without injury, which is liable if dragged against the stream; 3—In striking a fish the hook is much more likely to hold in this way than if struck in the line of the axis of his body; and fourthly, the water is not disturbed by the wader till it has been already fished.   The angler swings or casts his worm gently as far up stream as he can, using as long a line as he can easily manage, and suffering the bait to float down with the stream until within a short distance of where he is standing, when it should be lifted and re-cast.   He should gather in all slack line with his left hand, and so keep it taut.   When a fish is felt to bite, wait a few seconds until he is done nibbling; and the moment he is running off with it, strike smartly but tenderly with the wrist—with "Stewart" or "Pennell" tackle strike as soon as you feel the fish, and proceed to land him with as little delay as possible.   In striking, the point of the rod should be lowered as near the surface of the water as possible, and the stroke made in the opposite direction to which the fish is going.

In shade fishing, a short line should be used, and the rod pushed through between the bushes, &c., allowing the bait to fall gently on the water, with sufficient slack line to allow it to sink.   The principal baits are :—Dung Beetles, Grasshoppers, Natural May Fly, Caddis Fly, Bumble Bee, Blue Bottle Flies, and many Larvæ, or Grubs, the principal of which are Flesh Maggots, Caddis, Caterpillars, Wasp and Dock Grubs.

☞ FOR WORMS, SEE PAGE 151.

PRACTICAL HINTS ON FLY-FISHING FOR TROUT, &c.

(BY HARDY BROS., ALNWICK.)

Fly-fishing for Trout is perhaps one of the most enjoyable sports practised on the waters of this country. In the perfect casting and delivery of the fly, as much enjoyment is experienced as falls to the lot of the most clever shot or most skilful billiard player, who prides himself on the true and perfect working harmony of hand and eye. But this is all the comparison, for besides the pleasure of perfect casting and eager expectation, there is the excitement of stalking and ultimate capture, while the great uncertainty of the latter adds not a little to the charm. Then if we take into consideration that the angler is necessarily something of an entomologist and a naturalist in general, we may fearlessly say, that angling is one of the most truly enjoyable sports a man can indulge in.

To proceed to such a general description and direction as may be of some little use to the tyro, we may first observe that he should confine himself to a single-handed rod, of from nine to twelve feet, according to the water to be fished. Two-handed rods were once commonly used for this class of fishing, more especially on wide rivers, but these are now almost things of the past ; as the shorter and lighter rods, working with finer tackle, gain in dexterity and delicacy of delivery, more than they lose in the area of water under control. It is most important that the rod should be correctly balanced with a suitable reel and line, and this should be carefully seen to, as no one can make good work with badly-matched tools. The advice and assistance of some older hand should be asked.

CASTING THE FLY.

To make an ordinary overhead cast correctly, the tyro should begin with a gut line not more than two yards long and with two flies. Supposing then the rod and line correctly balanced, and mounted with a suitable gut line and flies ; he should draw off from the reel as much line as once and a half the length of his rod, holding the end fly between the finger and thumb of the left hand, grasping the rod a little above the reel with his right, and waving it gently a few times, until he gets the required momentum to carry out the line, when he should release the fly, making at the same time a cut with the rod, over or in line with the spot where he intends his flies to alight, care being taken in doing this, that the point of the rod should not be allowed to drop further than at right angles to himself. He will do well at first to fish down stream, as should he not have made the first cast correctly, the stream will put the matter right, and float the line and flies out straight. Then he should raise the point of the rod gently upwards, in order to get as much line clear of the water as possible, and also to give the flies a little life-like motion before making the back stroke ; in fact all but the flies should be clear of the water. Then with a smart stroke back over his head, slightly inclining the rod point to the left, he should lift his line clear behind him, at the same time avoiding all elbow work, as much as possible, and without allowing the rod point to go back further than an angle of 45 degrees to the body. Having done this, a moment's reflection will tell him, that as the line went back in a curve, it will take an instant to straighten after the rod is thrown back into the required position. This is very important, as the line should have exact time to straighten out before making the return cast. If he does not, it is possible he will hear a slight crack, signifying that the flies have gone. Bear in mind, that the throwing the flies back correctly is as important as laying them straight and fine across the water. Now it only remains to drive the line and flies forward, by smartly bringing the rod down into a horizontal position again, and in doing this, he should aim at a point, say two or three feet above where he intends the flies to fall (as they should not be thrown at, but above), so that they may alight softly on the water. There are three movements and a pause. 1. Raise the rod point in order to get as much line clear of the water as possible. 2. Make the backward sweep, then pause until the line gets time to straighten, but not so long as to allow the flies to drop and catch the grass, &c. 3. Make the cast as described over the place intended.

It is very simple and yet we have seen amateurs very much troubled and in despair, simply because they had not tried in a simple and systematic manner to attain the art.

Having in some degree mastered this, he may let out a little more line, about a yard at a time, until he finds he can fairly command the water he is fishing, but on no account more than is absolutely necessary.

WHERE AND HOW TO FISH.

He must now choose where and how he will fish, and in this only experience will guide him, keeping in view that the wind at his back is an advantage, and that he should always fish up and across stream ; never (unless unavoidable) down.

We will suppose the seat of his intended sport is on one of our sharp gravelly north-country streams. Begin at the bottom or tail of the pool, and fish all the likely parts across and up stream, wading gently and fishing every yard of likely water to the neck of the stream. As soon as a fish is hooked, it should be brought down past the angler, and played in that part which has been fished, so as not to alarm the other feeding fish. Of course where the water runs quick, he will require to make frequent casts, as the stream so quickly carries the flies down. Use as short a line as possible. It is often a very deadly plan to let the flies sink a little, and simply be guided by the running line, striking when it stops.

The idea of fishing up stream is this : The fish lie with their heads up stream, and do not see the angler until his flies have well covered them ; secondly, they take the drowned fly in a perfectly natural manner, as it floats down the stream, and, lying with their bodies in a direct line from the rod, are much more liable to be hooked. Fishing down stream, although easy and often adopted by anglers from the bank, is a very poor business, and six fish will be missed for every one hooked. Let your maxim be, "Fish up and fish fine." The foregoing hints only apply to wet fly-fishing ; the instructions to casting hold good for either wet or dry fly. The art of dry fly-fishing we cannot in the small space at our disposal go in to, and would refer those anxious to learn this, the highest branch of the angler's craft, to such works as Mr. Halford's "Dry Fly-Fishing in Theory and in Practice," which we keep in stock, price 25s., and others of a like nature.

STRIKING AND HOOKING.

Besides throwing the fly, there is a great art in striking and hooking the fish. When a fish is seen to rise, the rod point should be smartly raised with a motion of the wrist only, care being taken not to do this in any degree harshly, as a very little, in fact the mere tightening of the line, is sufficient to fix so sharp an instrument as a small fly hook in the mouth of the fish ; and in this he must be careful, as the momentary excitement generally causes young anglers to strike too hard, and the consequence is a smash unless our new patent regulating check reel is used. The object of striking is simply to fix the hook before the fish has time to discover his mistake, and prevent his blowing out the fly from his mouth, which if left to himself he would generally do.

LANDING THE FISH.

Having hooked your fish, it now remains to land him, and here much discretion must be used. Small fish may generally be dropped into the net as soon as you can shorten line sufficiently, but if large, say over ½ lb.,

caution must be used. Keep a firm strain on him at all times, and if he rushes wildly off do not attempt to stop him, but the moment he eases at once commence to put on more pressure, and in a few minutes, if you are fortunate enough to hold and keep him away from snags and the like, he will be exhausted. Then by winding in your line, and advancing the butt of the rod and so using its flexibility as a safety spring, he may be brought sufficiently near to be dropped into the net, after which he should be at once killed by a blow on the head. Fish killed at once after landing are always better for table, besides it is more humane.

CHOICE OF ROD.

Small wooded streams are easiest fished with 9 to 10 ft. rods, but fairly open ones require a somewhat longer weapon. The correct thing is 10 ft. 6 in. or 11 ft., certainly nothing over 11 ft. 6 in. It should be sufficiently fine in the point so as not to break the finest gut in striking just a little hard, and the other parts should be in proportion, so as to carry itself without the least top-heavy feeling. See article page 82.

It is almost impossible to describe the correct rod, as balance is a very subtle thing, and more a practical than theoretical one. Our choice for all round fly-fishing, spinning a light minnow, or one of our "Halcyon" spinners on fine tackle, is one of our 10½ to 11 ft. cane-built steel centre rods which will tackle a 5 or 6 lb. fish if required.

Loch Fishing   By the late HAMISH STUART

MR. J. J. AND MISS FANNY HARDY OFF CASTLE ISLAND, LOCH LEVEN.

It is now admitted that to describe the loch as the " Duffer's Para-
dise " is an abuse of terms. Lakes differ as much as rivers, and though
there are lochs in which no great skill is required to kill fair baskets,
there are others which make as great a demand upon the intelligent
use of skill as any river. Our angling fathers used to consider a
breeze essential to sport on lakes ; now our ideas are different, and,
by the use of fine tackle and improved gear, there is no sort of condition under which trout and sea-trout may not be killed with the
fly in lakes. Into the history of this change, it is unnecessary here
to enter.

The principle on which the modern loch fisher proceeds is, that
loch trout worth catching must be treated with precisely the same
respect as is shown by the river fisher for his quarry. Regard must
be had for the cunning, the moods and habits of the fish, and the loch
must be treated as a large still pool in a river. It is a mistake to
suppose that preserved or almost virgin waters holding large trout
can be fished successfully by the " duffer " or by the man of skill who
declines to study their peculiarities, and employs the same methods,
uses the same flies, and generally " fishes in the same way " in all
sorts of lochs, in all states of water, wind and weather, and at all
seasons of the angling year, times of the day, and moods of the fish
The real secret of success in loch fishing, apart from mere manual
skill, lies in an *intelligent study of the conditions*, in leaving no method
untried, and " in using the head " freely and fully. Unless you are an
opportunist and cultivate the faculty of observation and deduction

IN ORDERING FROM THIS LIST PLEASE QUOTE LETTER B.1.

you will miss half the charm of loch fishing, and your successes will be limited to " good days."

In the matter of the proper rod or rods for loch fishing for trout, sea trout and salmon, one is necessarily forced to take refuge in a generalisation, and within certain limits the proper rod varies with the angler, for all anglers do not possess the same strength and the same temperament. As I have said elsewhere, " go to a good rod maker who also is an experienced angler, trust him, and do not grudge the initial expense." Let him choose the rod best suited to your personal peculiarities. Any rod with which you cannot cast continuously for a day is too heavy for loch fishing. Use is not everything in a rod but it counts for much, and it is better not to be under any necessity to change your rod when you pass from brown trout to sea trout fishing. For this reason a first-class split bamboo rod of from 9½ to 11½ ft. (pages 232 and 233) will be found to exactly fulfil all the requirements of a rod suitable to every sort of fly fishing from a boat in lochs. For an angler who confines himself to trout fishing, or who prefers like the writer to use one rod, for both brown and sea trout, there cannot possibly be a better rod, and there is certainly no cheaper rod of the same quality, than the split bamboo rods of Messrs. Hardy Brothers. For fishing in lochs I never use any other rods, and I have never fished with any rods which gave me the same satisfaction, the same sense of security (a great gain), and the same pleasure as an 11 ft. one of this class which I possess. In twelve days with one of these rods in a weedy loch holding good trout I killed 93 fish running from 1½ lbs. to 2¾ lbs. and landed in six days almost every fish that rose. The conditions were of the most varied kinds, from dead calm and hot sun to a gale of wind and rain.

The reel is important and it should be one of the quick winding ones, i.e. much contracted and with regulating check, called the Hardy's " Perfect " (page 130) for this reason. Fish so often on being struck run towards the boat that you must wind very quickly. Besides, in general use a reel of this sort saves a great deal of labour in winding up, as with half the number of turns you can do the same work,—a great saving certainly.

As to tackle for loch fishing, the finer you fish the better will be your sport ; though here again, as in the matter of rods and " the stiffness " of your reel, a great deal depends upon the temperament of the angler. In any case every angler should endeavour to fish as fine as he dare, and as the varying conditions compel him to fish. Flies should vary in size and pattern with the lake and with the day. It is quite unnecessary to use large flies in any lake either for brown trout, sea trout, or salmon, and, as a general rule, flies dressed on three sizes of hook (Nos. 8 and 9 Limerick and 4 sneck bends) will satisfy all the conditions. Flies imitating surface flies should be used as top droppers, while those imitating subaqueous insects should be used as tail and middle flies.

The angler should have a very large landing net and the best known to the writer is Hardy's " Collapsing " net (page 308), the grilse or salmon size. The shaft should be long and strong and the angler should land his own fish. The reel and line must balance the rod.

FOR " LOCH BOAT " LANDING NET, SEE PAGE 315.

As a rule loch trout must not be struck too quickly. The secret of success is to wait until the fish is " felt," though every rise must be treated on its merits. Large loch trout are generally as " slow " takers as sea trout, and this is particularly true of good fish rising in a calm or a very slight breeze. To determine to strike late generally results in the angler schooling himself to exercise the necessary restraint, which prevents too quick or too hard striking,—faults to which the loch fisher is peculiarly liable. Sea trout cannot be struck too late, and the angler is always the most successful who determines *not to strike at all.* He rarely " misses " large fish and he is ready for all sorts of fish, from a half pound " brownie " to a six or seven pound sea trout. In playing large loch and sea trout, as well as salmon, the great aim of the angler must be to keep the fish under control and parallel with the boat. In open water it is very easy to follow a fish and to " play " him with the boat, but in lochs with reed beds delicate coaxing is often necessary to persuade the fish into the open, when all his attempts to get away from the boat may be met by judiciously heading him off. In landing a good fish the stock of the net should be brought under the elbow and lie along the arm. This gives leverage in lifting. The strain at the last moment should be even and steady. The boat should be suffered to come slowly back on the fish, and the net allowed to glide under him.

In most lochs frequented by salmon the fish may be taken with the same flies, and landed on the same " gear " as sea trout. The same rod and reel may, on a pinch, be used for all three fish, salmon, sea trout, and brown trout, and it is for this reason that the writer recommends all loch anglers to use Hardy's split bamboo rods.

MR. J. J. HARDY FISHING A DEVONSHIRE STREAM FOR SALMON,
WITH SINGLE HANDED ROD.

Salmon Fishing with the Fly

THE LESSON—"HE PULLED TOO SOON."

Fly Fishing is undoubtedly the form *par excellence* of angling for this game fish. *Salmo Salar* is far and away the best of all fish for sport. Possessed of great strength and vigour, he affords when hooked a vast amount of play and excitement to the angler.

No branch of the art of making rods and tackle has received more careful attention and study by us than that of making suitable gear for this form of sport. The introduction of so light a material as bamboo, with its great toughness and strength, the system of doubling the enamel, and the introduction of a centre of highly tempered steel, has enabled us to produce lighter rods of greater power, so that one can now fish comfortably and without the fatigue consequent on the use of the heavy greenheart rods.

The length of rods used for fly-fishing for salmon vary from 10 ft. to 18 ft. The more general length is from 15 ft. to 17 ft. The 14½ ft. to 16 ft. is perfectly suitable for small rivers or larger where a boat is used. As all-round rods, 16 and 17 ft. are the most popular.

The reel and line should be carefully selected to match the rod in order to give the best results in casting. The gut trace may be partly twisted or plaited, and partly single (see page 85); the thickness

FOR " PERFECT " REELS, SEE PAGE 108.

should be regulated by the state of the water and the probable size of the fish. It is a mistake to use too thick gut, unless the water is heavy. In choosing a fly, always select one on the small side. Flies up to 2/0 may be either single or double ; but larger sizes are generally single.

Suppose, then, that the ghillie has put into the hand of our young angler such an equipment as above, and directed him where the fish lie, and where to fish ; he should begin by casting his fly across the stream at an angle of about 45 degrees, working it (as it sweeps round with the stream) to his own side. A very good measure for covering the water effectually is to step a yard and a half between casts. Do not dwell at any particular place unless you have seen a fish, or know of one lying there, but get over the water at a regular and moderate pace. Then, if you are not going on to a fresh pool, rest the one you have already fished, put up another fly and try it over again. In this, as indeed in most other things, remember that perseverance brings success. Therefore, keep pegging away, and sooner or later you will be rewarded with a pull which sets every fibre of your being in motion ; you need not be told to strike, instinctively you will do this, but avoid doing it too rashly, and yet it should be firmly done. It is seldom that on hooking a salmon he goes off with a rush, more generally he seems puzzled and undetermined what course to take, and this gives you a moment to breathe. See that your line is clear, but at all times carefully look to this, as you never know when you may hook a fish, and to have the line caught round the handle or under the reel means disaster, for which you will hardly forgive yourself, as it may be that the one chance of your day has been lost, and you go home " clean " to tell people stories they never believe. Having hooked your fish, look to your reel to see that the line is clear ; don't touch it with your fingers, the friction on the rings and resistance of the check should be sufficient pressure if properly regulated. It is probable your fish will rush across and up or down stream ; do not be too hard on him, keep your rod well up and, as soon as possible, get op-posite him : keep on a steady pressure which must not be relaxed for an instant. Now you must have patience, as you cannot expect to kill him much under one minute to the pound. Carefully watching, be quick and prompt to act, either in following or taking in line the moment you can. If he leaps, drop the point of the rod at once to avoid his striking the line, then tighten again as quickly as possible, and keep your fish moving. If he is going for a dangerous place, where he may lie up or cut your gut line, use such discretion and means as occur to you at the moment to prevent him, but do not be afraid to ply the butt. As soon as he seems exhausted, work him in to the side, so that the ghillie may use the gaff or net. It is not likely he will be brought within reach the first time, as if he catches sight of the ghillie he will be off again into the middle, or possibly quite across the pool ; try him again until he is exhausted, when, if successful, your ghillie will get his chance. Personally, we always prefer to clip through the belly, as it does not destroy the fish so much as when done in the shoulder. Let the ghillie get down on his knee and place the gaff stretched out under water, then work your fish over it, when he cannot fail to gaff him.

It is curious to observe the different methods employed in working the fly, almost every man works differently ; one will cast his fly across stream and allow it to come round without moving his rod ; another will sink it deep and with long slow draws work it round ; while another will work his rod top quite vigorously.

In the very early spring and late autumn we prefer to sink the fly deep and give it a moderate movement. When the season advances, say into May, and comparatively small flies are used, they should be fished nearer the surface and a little quicker. When fishing a strange river, it is best to experiment a little, and having found the best method, stick to it.

The Patent Hardy " Oval " Wire Salmon Fly Hooks (see page 166) have solved the difficult problem of a perfect salmon fly hook, being much stronger in the bend and back of the barb, which in the usual round wire hooks is always a dangerous part.

In this hook the wire is **oval,** and consequently resists pressure more effectually as applied to its greater axis : we are therefore enabled to use wire of the same area of section, while increasing the strength where required, *i.e.* in the bend. The larger proportion of metal left after cutting up the barb, also adds greatly to the strength of the hook at that particular part.

In wading swift rocky rivers, or any river to which you are a stranger, you should be provided with a wading staff of some kind, after the manner of the wading staff and gaff (page 287). It is handy, saves many a tumble, and gives confidence. Should the water be discoloured, you can feel before you and so prove the depth. On hooking a fish, it practically serves the purpose of a third leg, as it enables you to get ashore quickly and safely.

Kendal, 26/6/23.

I am delighted with the flies—the best I have ever seen. I do not think anyone could beat you in fly dressing. I also like the hooks they are dressed on.

R. J. B.

Masterton, N.Z., 19/5/23.

I have never been let down with a " Hardy " Cast yet, they are simply steel in comparison with all other makers.

R. W. McMASTER.

IN ORDERING FROM THIS LIST PLEASE QUOTE LETTER D.I.

Hints about New Zealand.

By GEO. M. M.

(SOMETHING LIKE SPORT).

" I have just had a fortnight among the mountain streams of the interior in company with R. C. and E. B., both of this city, and a right good time we have had. We took two tents and provisions, and camped on the banks of a large stream, called the Waikaia. This stream has a gravelly bottom, with banks of clay and mould 6 to 8 feet high, with plenty of rapid runs into large deep pools. I have one of your 11 feet steel-centre cane rods, and I was glad I brought it with me. I was very nearly persuaded to leave it at home, as a gentleman who had visited this stream told me the fish were all large, and I would never be able to check them with such light gear ; but I found out from experience that such a rod is not to be beaten for these very active large fish, the extraordinary elasticity, combined with the great strength of the cane, we found was just the thing, for whenever the fish made a strong rush out into heavy water, we could put on any amount of strain knowing that the rod would not fail us, and how easy it was to strike the hook home when a fish rose ; the great elasticity of the rod never allowed you to bring up the slack with a jerk, and thus have a chance of breaking the casting line, but the strain being so equal from butt to point it was almost a dead certainty that you hooked your fish. All the settlers, (called cockatoos out here) were daily enchanted with the rods, and looked on in amazement to see us landing such big fish—and strong fish—with such light tackle ; they were used to heavy minnow rods, and fished with minnow only ; they had never seen fly-fishing like this. Our camp was quite the talk of the district, we being the first lot of Dunedin anglers who had had a successful time of it on this stream. A Runholder in the vicinity of our camp remarked to the farmer, who was kind enough to write to me and advise me to try this stream : " What on earth induced you to tell them to come out here ; why, they'll clean out the river in no time." If we had caught all the fish I saw in one pool, we should have had a bag the weight of which would have astonished the anglers of New Zealand. Why, the river was fairly alive with big fish, from 10 lbs. to 1 lb. in weight ; so that the runholder need have had no fear of our clearing out the river. I only wish some of your expert men were out here for the January and February fishing in these streams ; they would be astonished at the bags they would make. Bye-the-bye, I must say a word in praise of those tapered casts of yours. R. C. fished for five days with one cast and never lost a fish by breakage. I will give you a sample of his sport, fishing only for three hours in the morning—1st day, five fish, 14 lbs. ; 2nd day, four fish, 12 lbs. ; 3rd day, four fish, 10 lbs.; 4th day, six fish, 20 lbs. ; 5th day, eight fish, 21 lbs.; in Waikaia River. In the Pomahaka—Wednesday, five fish, 18 lbs. ; Thursday, eight fish, 23 lbs. ; Friday, five fish, 19 lbs. Myself—Wednesday, six fish, 22 lbs. ; Thursday, four fish, 18½ lbs. ; Friday, nine fish, 42 lbs. ; Saturday, in one hour, three fish. E. B.—On Wednesday,

☞ FOR "SILEX" REEL, SEE PAGE 126.

twelve fish, 52 lbs. E. B. left for home on Thursday, and R. C. and myself stayed on until Saturday morning. On this day, Mr. B., manager of the Clinton Hatcheries, came over with a buggy to take us back to catch the train for home. Having a couple of hours to spare, he took Mr. C's rod and went up the stream for about two miles, in that time killed four splendid fish, weighing 15¾ lbs. I went down stream, but having an old hickory minnow rod with me, I unfortunately broke it at the second joint, by striking a fish rather too hard; after splicing this break with flax and got fairly at it again, another big fish rose, and away went the top joint this time. I then gave up in disgust, vowing that I should not go out another year without a "Hardy's Steel-Centre Minnow Rod." Mr. C. had one and he could always kill his fish in half the time that I could with my hickory and greenheart rods. The fly rods of your make were too slender for using with heavy minnows, and besides, the reel would not carry enough line for such large fish in such heavy water. That is another thing I must have—a good light reel, easy running. I lost a big 6 lb. fish on Friday, the day I got nine, through the reel not letting the line off fast enough he broke me, taking cast and minnow with him. In the same pool our party killed seven big fish from 5½ lbs. (which I caught) to 3¾ lbs. each. In one run Mr. B. and I killed four big fish; as soon as he hooked one, I went and had a cast, and also hooked one, taking care to work it down quickly into the pool, in this way we caught four fish in the run, all large. The river is one series of cascades and pools, running alternately through gorges and open plains with nothing on the edge to stop casting as long a line as you like. Two can fish the stream, one on each side, facing each other, as it is so wide, and the stream cut up into runs through rocks, it is a perfect picture of a trout stream, and is just as full of fish as a plum pudding is full of plums. Angling people come from all parts of New Zealand to fish this stream. It is at its best in January, February, and the half of March, sometimes it is good right up to the end of March, then ducks are plentiful, and large herds of red deer are in the forest through which it runs; the season for shooting these begins when the fishing ends. The fee for fishing is £1, available for the whole colony, and the licence to kill deer is £2 for two months. The land is the property of the Crown, and is free to all licence holders. Trout streams have a chain reserve on each bank. Some of the small streams were sold out and out before the Act came into force, but all the best and largest rivers have the reserve for the public.

"Our best Otago rivers are the Waipahi, the Waikaka, the Mataura, the Waikaia, the Pomahaka, the Shag, and the Molyneux, a very large and deep river flowing out of Lakes Wanaka, Hawea, and Wakatipu. This river is full of big fish that take the minnow readily; perch are also very plentiful in it. In two lakes which drain into it, namely, Tuakitoto and Kaitangata, the perch are so numerous that an expert minnow fisher can catch 50 or 60 lbs. weight in a morning, wading out about ten yards and casting all around him. You need never shift if you strike a shoal. I killed, in a little creek that flows into the first mentioned lake, forty fish in four hours, from ¾ lb. to 2¼ lbs., and returned twenty more as I had no room in my basket for them."

The Waitaki, the large river that drains the best part of the
Southern Alps, Mount Cook included, has afforded splendid sport
this year; bags of 70 lb. and 80 lb. for one day's angling were not
uncommon in October and November. This is an early river—the
snow begins to melt in December, and then it is not much use fishing
until March, when the snow is all melted. At that date, however,
the stream is full of whitebait, but they do not take the artificial then
so readily as they would in October and November; as this river goes
off, our Southern streams come into form, and thus you will see we
have capital fishing the whole six-and-a-half months, ending with
unlimited duck, pigeon, kaka, pukaki, wild black swans, and deer
shooting. Wild goats are also very plentiful in the interior among
the mountains, which are quite easy to get to from this city.

The rod most suited for our rivers is one about 14 feet long, with
one top pretty stiff for minnow, and one top fairly fine that would do
for cricket and fly-fishing on the larger streams. The 11 and 12 feet
fly-rods are right for the ordinary streams, only the spare top should
be heavier than the fly-top, so that, if necessary, the heavier top
could be used for the minnow. An angler with two rods as above
would be set up for any of our rivers. If you are fitting up any one
for New Zealand rivers, give them a good stock of tapered casts from
stout lake to very fine drawn 3 yds., one or two dozen Soleskin
and Horn Phantom Minnows, and also some "Halswell" Devons, only
the belly to be silvered, and all the rest the colour parchment has
when it is wet; I killed one cwt. with minnows like this. Other
artificial minnows, fly minnows, Halcyon Spinners, &c., are good.
A gaff is better than a landing net for the big streams, and it has to
have a fine point or it will not go into the thick skin of our trout.

FLIES FOR TROUT FISHING.—Sneck hooks, Nos. 1 & 2.
Alexandra. Coachman. Hawthorne Fly. Hofland's Fancy. Francis.
Red and Yellow Tipped Governor. Irish March Brown. Grey
Spider. Red Palmer. Zulu. Hardy's Favourite. White and Brown
Moths. Black Quill Gnat, silver twist on body. Coch-y-bondhu.
Olive Dun. Whirling Dun. Blue Upright. Greenwell' Glory.
Alder. Red Spinner. Bradshaw's Fancy. Claret Spinner. Ruby
Drake, &c On gut, 2/- per doz.

Capt. G. D. Hamilton's Flies on his special pattern hooks eyed
or tapered.   Nos. 4.   5.   5A. wide.   7.   8.

2/-	2/3	2/3	2/6	on gut.
2/6	2/9	2/9	3/-	eyed.

The famous "R.A.B." Fly on No. 11 Limerick Hooks to gut 2/3
per dozen, eyed hooks 2/9 per dozen. Larger sizes dressed to order.

FLIES FOR RAINBOW TROUT.—Sizes, Nos. 5 and 6
Limericks. On gut, 3/6 per doz.; eyed hooks, 4/- per doz. Whitney's,
King and Queen, Green and Grey Drake, Scorcher, Alexandra,
O'Callaghan's Orange Grouse, Professor, Butcher, Cinnamon; also
Jock Scott's, Silver Doctors, Wilkinson's, &c. See page 90.

For Rods for New Zealand, see page 248.
For Reels for New Zealand, see pages 112 to 131.

W. H. Spackman, B.A., author of "Trout Fishing in New
Zealand," says—" . . . . If the angler does not object to a
little expense, split cane rods with steel centres are certainly preferable to any other kind . . . . Hardy Brothers, of Alnwick, make
special New Zealand rods."

HOOKED THROUGH THE BACK FIN.

We turned again to Tyn-y-cae just about lunch time, and I was setting my rod against the old toll bar, preparatory to going in to lunch, when my friend H. said, "Just try another cast over the tail of this pool, it is perfect." Just to please him I did so, and fished very closely for about ten yards, when my man said, "There, did you see that?" On enquiring what he had seen, he said a fish had made a boil at my fly. At that instant a fine salmon jumped right over the cast. I struck with all my might, hoping to get the fly in some part of him, but I missed. I tried three or four more casts, but he would not come again. David was sent to ask Mr. Hall to come and have lunch at the toll bar. After my man had gone I thought I would try just once more, and put a silver-bodied fly on. I commenced fishing a little above where the fish had risen, and had only made a few casts when I saw a boil. On tightening, I felt that I had him. The salmon was just at the tail of the pool, and, being afraid lest he should make a dash down the river, I brought him up quietly until he got opposite the little island, and then, with a rush, he bolted to the other side. With about sixty yards of line out, he jumped clean out, showing well. With the rocks at the bottom, I knew the danger of having so much line out, and slowly but surely got him to my side. My friend H., who was looking down into the water, announced that the line had got round the fish. This did not make me feel very comfortable, but in less than a minute I felt I had him unwound and secure, Then he made up the pool, and my man declared I had hooked him through the back fin; he could see the jungle cock feather. I was fishing with one of Hardy's cane-built, steel-centred rods, 18 ft. long, made specially to my order. It was stiffer than most men like, but when once used anglers were compelled to say of it 'What a beauty!'

The fish all along meant fight, so did I. For the next ten minutes my work was well cut out. Up the pool, down the pool, across the pool went the fish. Still I held on, allowing between five and six pounds pressure, which, from the length of the rod, was equal to ninety pounds on my arm. Flesh and muscle could not endure this long, and I said to my friend H., who had persuaded me to try for the fish, and was in some way responsible, 'It's not a question of my killing the fish, but rather a question of the fish killing me. My arms are almost paralyzed. Just put your hand under that rod and hold it up.' He did so, easing me a little, but only a little. In another five minutes the fish made up his mind to go out of that pool if he could. As I made up my mind that he was going to do nothing of the kind, when he got at what I considered a fair angle from the point of the rod, I dropped on one knee, keeping the rod perpendicular, throwing the butt into the hollow of my right foot, passed my hand rapidly up, and held on. Now it was a question of what was going to give, 'You will smash,' said my man. 'Smash away,' I replied. But it was no smash. Slowly but surely I felt the fish coming to the top, nearer and nearer, and at last the salmon lay athwart the stream, fully one third out of the water. But he sailed up the river once more, and putting on a good bit of presure I brought him in; he went under the bushes. I was as far back as I could get on account of the trees behind me, and, holding my rod nearly perpendicular, tried the risky game of pulling the line through the rings to bring the fish up to David's gaff. The fish objected, and I was determined. So, one pull, a second pull, and still a third pull, and then I saw David reach over the bushes, the steel of the gaff flashing through the air. The pressure was taken off the top of my rod, and a 25lb. salmon lay gasping on the bank, truly hooked through the back fin. My arms were so stiff that I could hardly raise or drop them. The time of landing the fish from the moment I hooked him was just thirty minutes. Fortunately, before starting out in the morning, I put a small box of Homocea in my pocket. I went into the toll bar, and before a nice warm fire I rubbed it in for the space of ten minutes, and was just as fresh as if I had never had this hard battle."—*The Field*, 1893.   RAQUETTE LAKE.

☞ FOR WADING STAFF & GAFF, SEE PAGE 220.

SILKWORM GUT DEPARTMENT.

VIEW OF GUT FACTORY IN MURCIA.

For many years we have been large importers of this article, working in conjunction with a syndicate for which we are the sole agents. Parcels have been and are largely sold to all parts of the world, a considerable portion of the choicest being retained for our retail trade. We are always open to deal liberally with merchants who can buy large quantities ; and invite enquiries. This season in consequence of favourable purchases, we have determined to offer small lots at very low prices, so that our clients who buy a few single bundles can now do so at practically wholesale prices. At the same time, in buying through us, they may be assured that no " Estriada," or common qualities, are offered them. All guaranteed to be the finest Spanish " Select."

For the guidance of our customers we give a scale of the different thicknesses, which is as exact to actual size as it is possible to engrave.

NOTE.—The thicknesses given are only approximate, as any single hundred will contain a variety of thicknesses, and even a single strand will vary sometimes two thousands of an inch.

☞ IN ORDERING FROM THIS LIST PLEASE QUOTE LETTER **G.**

Improved Line Drier

In Use

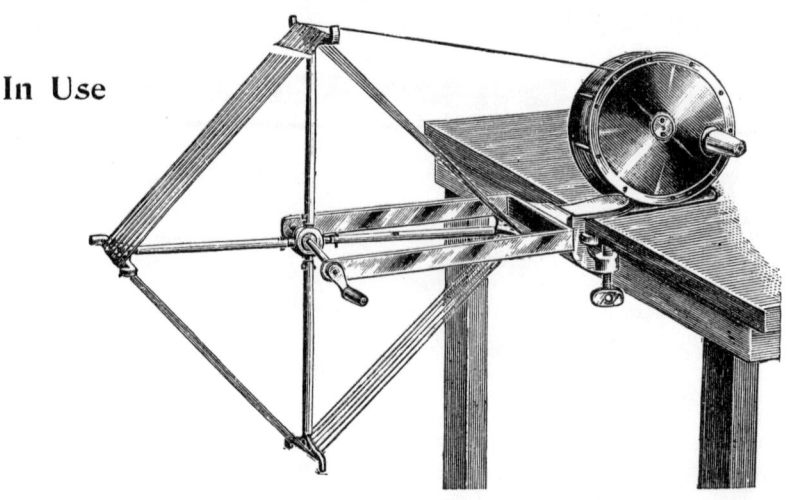

374L.—Can be screwed to a table and the line unwound from the reel in a few minutes. The drum is 11 inches in diameter. It takes to pieces and packs into small space. A splendid and practical winder.

Price, in box, complete, **15/6**.

The "Ward" Line Drier

COLLAPSIBLE.

Made to the idea given to us by Dr. Ozier Ward.

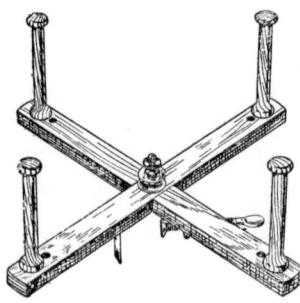

This is a strongly made and handy line drier, which can be fixed to a table by means of the usual screw clamp. The arms are of hickory mounted with detachable wood pegs, upon which the line is wound. A milled nut with cushion spring is fitted on spindle end, and allows the tension to be regulated when winding line on to reel.

Packed in neat box, size 12 in. × 4 in. × $1\frac{3}{8}$ in.

Price **6/6** each.

The New "INDIAN" Reel Lines.

These are intended for spinning in any climate.

Indian anglers and others well know the great difficulty in procuring dressed lines which do not turn sticky.

In the new "Indian" Line we believe we have one which will give most satisfactory results. So far they have been tested in various parts and all reports are satisfactory. We have stoved them at a very high and moist temperature, but they do not show the slightest inclination to tackiness. From the nature of the dressing it does not fill up and make a smooth level surface as in the best quality "Alnwick" Spinning Lines, but has a rougher appearance. The dressing, however, adds considerably to the strength, which is a most important item. Thicknesses are about the same as the "Challenge" Parallel on page 104, No. 18 being what we call Fine, No. 20 Medium, No. 22 Heavy, and No. 24 Extra Heavy.

	100 yds.	80 yds.	60 yds.	
Extra Heavy	18/6	15/-	13/6	The usual backing can be spliced to these to make any length, or two can be spliced together.
Heavy ...	16/8	13/4	10/-	
Medium ...	15/-	12/-	9/-	
Fine ...	13/4	10/8	8/-	

THE "FACILE" LINE DRIER.

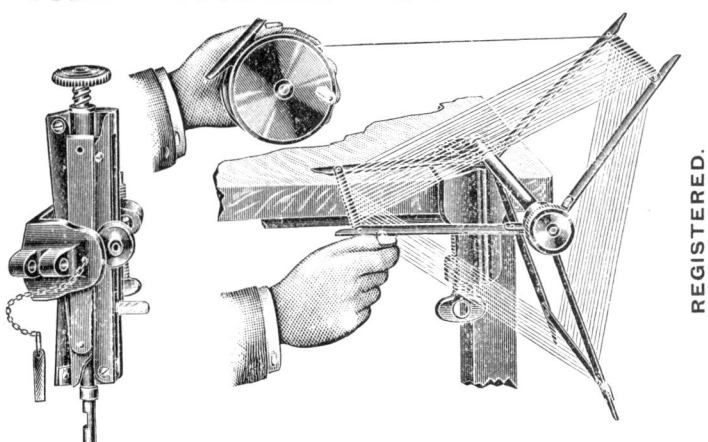

REGISTERED.

Fig. 2.   Fig. 1.

Illustration is the latest design in line driers and is most effective and complete. Fig. 1 shows the apparatus at work, Fig. 2 shows the arms folded ready for going into its case. The arms are hinged to the body and only require to be set up, and the attachment made to a bench by means of the usual clutch. Each turn of the winder takes up fully 2 ft. of line. The width of the frame being 3½ ins., the line may be spaced out, the coils being clear of each other, so that it dries quickly.

As may be seen, the line is simply attached to the bar and the wet part unwound when rewinding on to reel, a milled nut with cushion spring is fixed on end of spindle, by which the tension can be regulated. Extra bodies can be supplied, so that when one is filled, it can be removed and another substituted.

Complete in box .. **21/=.**   Extra per drum .. **10/6.**

The "Bethune" Line Winder.

(HARDY'S PATENT)

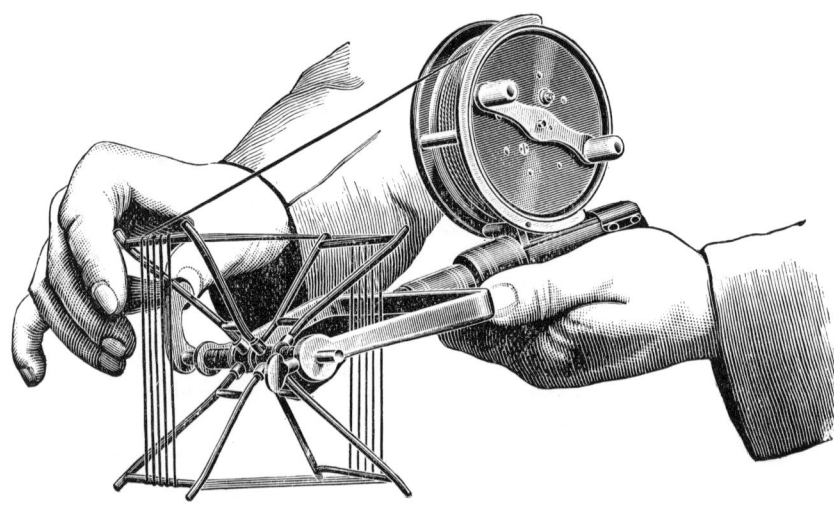

T HE invention of C. C. Bethune, Esq., and is one of the best and most compact yet invented. The illustration shows it in use. The reel is put on the handle, exactly as on a rod butt, the fittings being the same. The winder works between two spiral springs, and can be oscillated in winding, thus the line is not all wound in one place, but is evenly distributed.

In winding line off the reel, the small thumb screw should be eased. When as much line as desired has been wound off, this screw is then tightened, and keeps all taut. When the line is being wound back on to the reel again, the thumb screw should be eased a little to allow winder to travel steadily.

When line is wound off reel on to winder, both the reel and winder may be hung up until they are again wanted.

They are made in two sizes, Trout and Salmon, and packed in neat cedar wood boxes, with slide lids.

To PACK.—Simply unscrew arms and handle.

SIZES—TROUT—6 × 4 × 2½.   SALMON—6¾ × 5¼ × 3.

PRICES—   TROUT, 8/6.   SALMON, 10/6.

Suitable for 2 to 3¼ in. Reels.   Suitable for 3½ to 5 in. Reels.

☞ FOR LANDING NETS, SEE PAGES 285 TO 296.

Hard-Braided Tanned Flax Lines.

BEST QUALITY.

These make splendid backing lines for splicing to the "Corona" and Double-Taper Switching Lines for Salmon, or good Sea Lines.   We splice them free.

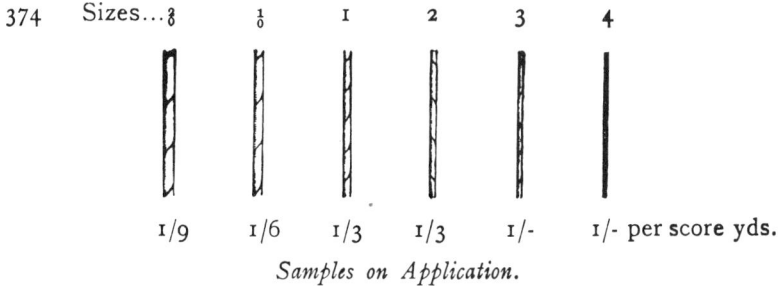

374   Sizes...⅜   ⅒   I   2   3   4

1/9   1/6   1/3   1/3   1/-   1/- per score yds.

Samples on Application.

The 1911 Model Line Winder.

COLLAPSABLE.

A most useful, convenient, and superior type of folding line winder.   The fittings are made of fine brass.   The frame and stand are of oak.

The spindle is fitted with an adjustable spring tension, with regulator.   The reel is held in brass clips, as shown in illustration.

By unscrewing the locking nut on the upright brass standard, and removing the two little holders, the whole winder folds up into a space of 12in. × 4in. × 2¾in.

Each turn of the winder takes up over 2ft. of line, while the width on arms is 4in. across, giving ample space to keep line fairly open.

Complete in box, **15/6** each.

The " Practical " Line Drier

This line drier can be used with all sizes of reels from the smallest trout to the largest.   It folds into convenient space for packing, and there are no loose parts to be mislaid.   Each turn of the winder takes approximately one yard of line, while the pegs are long enough to permit the line to be widely spaced to dry quickly.

The standard and arms are fixed to a stout wood base which is covered on the under side with a soft cloth, and on the upper side has fittings to hold the reel.

The illustration shows the line drier in use.   To fold for packing, pull the front arm forward so as to compress the spring at C, when the arms will close one over the other ; release the thumbscrew at the back of the standard opposite A ; raise the standard to clear the pin at A, and the whole (standard, arms and pegs) will fold neatly down on the wooden base.

The pegs to carry the line are removable and adjustable.   The holes in the arms are arranged to suit lines in the coil as they are generally sold, or for putting back, on the drier, coiled line while the slot at B permits of any necessary adjustment.

In stout Cardboard Box. Price

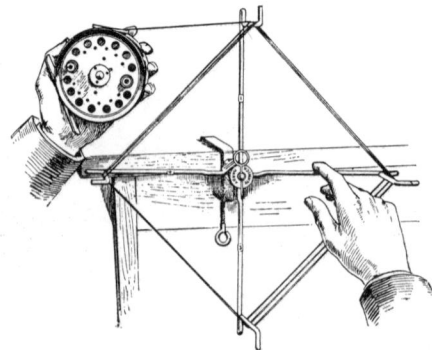

The " Hotspur " Line Drier

A useful line drier which is collapsible and packs into a small space.

To Assemble.—Place the spring and square body over the spindle on the clamp, then push the arms on to the square body, commencing with the arm numbered No. 1, then 2, and so on. Screw on lock nut, and then secure by passing the pin through the hole at the end of spindle.

Price

The " Compact " Line Drier

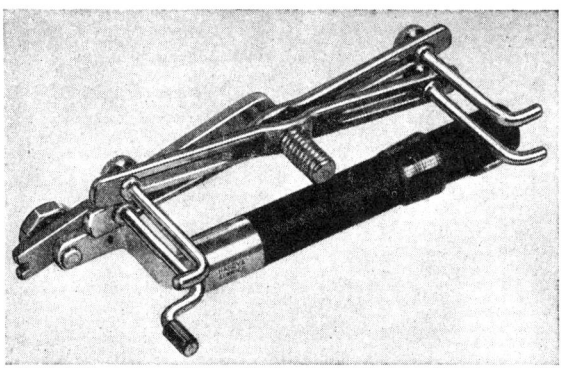

Fig. 1.—The Line Drier with Handle folded for packing

A light, compact and quickly assembled line drier with no loose parts to find and assemble.

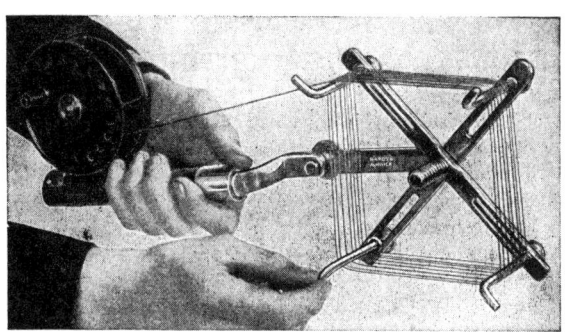

Fig. 2.—The Line Drier with Handle in use

Measurement across arms, 6 in.

Fig. 1 shows the Line Drier folded for carrying. To assemble, open the arms when they will snap into the open position, then slip the slot in the end of standard over the stud and secure with the thumbscrew. One of the cross arms is carried in a slot and may be locked in it in any position, therefore it is an easy matter to take off lines in coils and put the coiled line on to the drier again

Made either with a handle and reel fittings or with a bracket to secure to a table, shelf, etc., packed in a strong cardboard box.   Price   each.

ULVERSTON.

I am grateful for your quick response to my request.

The Nyking (6lb.) line has been in use and it is immeasurably superior to anything else in that line I have ever used. It does not saturate with water in a long day's spinning—not to speak of rain and easily gives me from 10—12 yds. measured range without effort. Regarding its B.S. during the first week's use I had five sea trout, one of 7 lb. 13 ozs., but once being held up in a snag I exerted much more than 6lb. in a steady straight pull intending to break. However, by great good luck I retrieved everything with no detriment to the line.

(CAPT.) T. M.

RTIFICIAL FLIES.

————o◦❁◦o————

TROUT FLIES.

THERE is, perhaps, no subject on which anglers differ so much as in selecting flies which may be the most successfully used during the different months. Nor is there any perfect certainty in the matter; for the insects being the production of nature, it follows that as no two seasons are ever alike, there will be no two seasons in which the same fly will appear at the same time, and when they do appear, they may not be exactly alike ; the chemical composition of the different waters, together with their different temperatures, making any absolute rule impossible. At the same time we have in our list, flies which are always found to kill their share in almost any river. They are marked †.

In compiling the following list, Messrs. HARDY were in part guided by "Ronald," "Ephemera," and other naturalists, while copying from nature as near as possible. To this end they have devoted considerable time, which has, however, been amply repaid by the very flattering testimonials received by them.

Any fly dressed from description given in any work on angling.

NOTE.—All trout and grayling flies are dressed on the finest quality of hooks, specially made for HARDY BROTHERS.

LONDON, S.W.

DEAR SIRS,—The flies received are perfectly satisfactory. We are quite agreed as to size, yours are smaller than London-made (see for ex. —— March Brown enclosed). I also enclose —— Greenwell. It appears I was right as to the dressing being wrong in these flies. Your tapered fly casts are the very best I have seen. I have had them from —— disgracefully bad, and so bad that I had to throw them away. Send me 1 doz. of your improved Taper Fly Casts, impossible to get in London, also impossible, I think, to get well made London Flies (trout), they are too thick (bushy).

Your prices are under the London prices, and I don't doubt for a moment but that the worth is more.   I am, yours truly,   J. H.

REFORM CLUB, PALL MALL, S.W.,
LONDON.

GENTLEMEN,—I am *very much pleased* with the pattern trout flies you have sent me. The hooks are not smothered with feathers and fur, which some London fly-dressers seem to consider necessary. I have a very large stock of flies, but shall certainly send you an order for some of yours, which I consider very cheap, considering the quality of the work.

I should like you to dress me some flies to my own patterns, for California, where I have had some really magnificent sport.

When I get back there again I will send you an order for myself, and also have no doubt many of my friends will order on my recommendation.

Enclosed is P.O. order for the 20 dozens received.—Faithfully yours,   F. T.

MILITARY EQUIPMENT STORES AND TORTOISE TENTS CO., LD.,

PRIZE MEDAL TROUT FLIES.

	MARCH.		APRIL.		MAY.
1	Black and Blea (large)	11	†Cairn's Fancy	26	Sand Fly
2	March Brown (male)	12	†Needle Brown	27	Teal Drake
3	†March Brown (female)	13	†Hardy's Favourite (large)	28	Willow Fly
4	†March Brown (spider)	14	Johnstone's Glory	29	Whirling Dun
5	†Greenwell's Glory	15	Blue Dun	30	†Francis Fly
6	Cinnamon Fly	16	†Fenwick's Favourite	31	Grouse and Peacock
7	†Woodcock and Hare's Ear	17	†Cow Dung	32	Dark Partridge
8	†Cock-y-bondhu	18	†Red Spider	33	Light Partridge
9	†Blue Upright	19	Dark Snipe and Orange	34	Black Palmer
10	February Red	20	Red Spinner	35	Bracken Clock
		21	†Gravel Bed	36	Yellow May Dun
		22	†Light Snipe and Yellow	37	†Light Woodcock & Yellow
		23	Grannom	38	†Dark Woodcock & Orange
		24	Hawthorne	39	Welsh Fly
		25	Sedge Fly	40	Coachman
				41	†Olive Dun
				42	Pale Evening Dun

	JUNE.		JULY.		AUGUST & SEPTEMBER.
43	†Hardy's Silver and Black	58	Red Ant	68	August Dun
44	†Hardy's Silver and Red	59	†Dotterell and Yellow	69	Jenny-Spinner
45	†Hofland's Fancy	60	Red Palmer	70	Black Spider
46	Little Park Spinner	61	Golden Dun Midge	71	†Hardy's Favourite (small)
47	†Black Gnat	62	Yellow Sally	72	Dun Midge
48	Black Midge	63	†Blea & Hare's Ear (small		Furnace Palmer
49	Water Cricket	64	†Woodcock & Hare's Ear	74	†Prince Charlie
50	†Black and Blea (small)		(small)		
51	†Red Hackle	65	Iron Dun		
52	Black Spinner	66	Sky Blue		
53	Golden Plover and Yellow	67	July Dun		
54	†Quill Gnat, Red, Black or Grey				
55	Green Midge				
56	Alder Fly				
57	Oak Fly				

The foregoing list of flies are dressed on the finest wires, and superior drawn gut ; price 1s. 6d. per dozen, in lots of not less than half-a-dozen of one kind. If smaller quantities are required they will be charged 2s. per dozen.

Any pattern dressed to order with the utmost despatch and correctness, but not less than half-a-dozen of any one kind ; price 2s. per dozen, Dressed on Eyed Hooks, 2s. per dozen.

(Notice of Great Fisheries Exhibition, London, 1883.)

MANCHESTER GUARDIAN.

The first place may be claimed for the absolutely perfect specimens of fly-tying sent by Messrs. HARDY BROTHERS. These are not only truthful, but also fashioned —and every fisherman will know the value of this extra quality—so as to give them just the right quantity of "work" in the water. They are undoubtedly the gems of the Exhibition.

ODD TROUT FLIES.

All the many flies we catalogue are useful in their place ; but there are still a few odd curious patterns not to be found in angling catalogues nor tackle shops as a rule, but which are most useful, and often prevent a blank day. Almost every angler has some pet fly which on occasions has stood him in good stead, and although some grudgingly give the fruits of a lucky hit, we are pleased to think the fraternity as a rule are glad to help each other to sport.

In a long experience (about thirty years) of fly-fishing, HARDY BROTHERS have, like others, found some curious patterns, which, although not previously stocked for sale, we would not be without, and of these we select a few which we know will be found useful. Some of these have been kindly given by friends, and we will be glad to add to the list any original pattern sent us after we have proved it.

"The Defiance." Wings, woodcock ; body, bright scarlet ; with one turn of gold at tail, which is composed of two red whisks ; red legs. This fly is not unlike Hofland's fancy, but much brighter, and kills well, especially when the March Browns are thick on the water, and although the trout are feeding well they will not (we presume in consequence of the number of naturals) take your imitation, and all you can get is a few small fish. This is the time for the " Defiance," for then it is most deadly, and the large trout take it well. Unfortunately, bull and sea trout kelts have a weakness for it, and if there is one about he will be almost sure to have it.

"Kingsley's Cock-tail Spinner." Blea wing ; tail end of body olive quill, other half bright green quill ; hackle, honey dun. We are indebted to that good angler the Rev. W. Kingsley for this pattern, who found it good on every stream and lake he fished. It is not unlike the blue upright, and kills well when that fly or any of the duns is on the water.

"The Ghost." White wings ; black body and hackle ; ribbed with silver. This fly is most deadly in the twilight. Just at the head of streams, large trout take it well, as also do sea and white trout.

"Never Fail." Blea wing ; dark green body ribbed with fine gold ; red hackle and legs. One of the best all-the-season-round flies which can be used. The pattern is little known, but we confidently recommend a trial.

"Scarlet-ribbed Hare's Ear." Blea wing ; scarlet and gold body ; with Hare's Ear picked out for legs. This is a most deadly fly in full water. It was invented by HARDY BROTHERS many years ago, and may always be tried when at a loss.

"Yellow Hammer." Blea wings ; primrose yellow silk body ; with yellow legs, and two white tails. The best imitation of the pale July Dun which is made. It is a useful fly at almost any time, and is the only one which will kill when the fish are feeding on these pale watery duns which defy the fly-tyers' skill.

"Little Favourite." Blea wing ; dark olive green silk body ; with blue legs and tail. A small clear water fly, and a grand killer.

"The Mystery " (No. 1). In dead low clear water with this fly many a good basket has been killed when it might have been said fly-fishing was impossible.

"The Mystery" (No. 2). To be used as a dropper to No. 1, only two flies being on the cast.

The dressing of these two last we do not give, but they may be ordered with perfect confidence ; for dead low water they have no equals.

The first six are on ordinary best sneck-bend hooks. The three last are on very fine wires especially made for them, and in using them care should be taken in striking or landing a good fish, as the wires are so fine. Price 2s. 6d. per dozen, not less than half-a-dozen of any one kind.

UPRIGHT SPLIT-WINGED FLOATING TROUT FLIES.

These are intended for use as dry flies, and float perfectly. They have also been found very deadly used as ordinary wet flies.

75 March Brown	86 Welsh Fly
76 Greenwell's Glory	87 Hardy's Silver and Black
77 Blue Upright	88 Pale Evening Dun
78 Cairn's Fancy	89 Hardy's Silver and Red
79 Hardy's Favourite	90 Hofland's Fancy
80 Blue Dun	91 Quill Gnat
81 Red Spinner	92 Iron Dun
82 Gravel Bed	93 August Dun
83 Teal Drake	94 Hardy's Favourite, small
84 Whirling Dun	95 Olive Dun
85 Francis Fly	

The above are finest quality, and on best very fine gut, price 2s. 6d. per dozen.

Tied to order on Mr. Hall's turned-up Eyed Hooks, or Mr. Cholmondeley-Pennell's turned-down Eyed Hooks, same price.

Not less than half-a-dozen of one kind.

Salmon Fly Department.

ALL RIGHT WHEN YOU GET THERE.

This important part of our works is under the most experienced and practical management. Our extensive personal knowledge of most rivers and lakes in all parts of the globe, places us in a position to advise and supply patterns which are not generally known, and this knowledge is always at the disposal of our customers.

The Best & most Popular Flies
For Salmon Angling on the following Rivers.

Avon (Hampshire).—Eagles, Popham, Jock Scott, Dusty Miller, Gordon, Wilkinson, Louise, and Major.

Alness.—Doctors, Jock Scott, and Childers (small).

Awe and Orchy.—Blue Doctor, Silver Doctor, Blue Charm, Sailor, Jock Scott, Childers, Black Doctor, Thunder and Lightning, Dunkeld, Dusty Miller, Durham Ranger, Claret and Mallard.

Annan.—Butcher, Jock Scott, Parson, Silver Grey, Grey Turkey, Red Turkey.

Beauly.—Snow Fly, Gordon, Jock Scott, Peacock, Silver Doctor, Silver Grey, Dunkeld, Black Doctor, Wilkinson, Childers, Thunder and Lightning, Ackroyd.

☞ IN ORDERING FROM THIS LIST PLEASE QUOTE LETTER Q.

Berriedale, Langwell, Wester Wick, Dunbeath.—Silver Grey, Childers, Jock Scott, Major, Black Doctor, Silver Doctor, Spirit, Wasps.

Brora and Blackwater.—Jock Scott, Childers, Ackroyd, McIntyre, Silver Grey, Fraser, Thunder and Lightning, Dusty Miller.

Exe and Barle.—Gordon, Jock Scott, Silver, Blue and Black Doctors, Parson.

Conon, Blackwater, and Orrin.—Wasps (black and blue), Sir Archibald, Silver Doctor, Sailor, Dunkeld, Black Doctor, Childers.

Dee (Aberdeen).—Grey Eagle, Yellow Eagle, Gordon, Dunt, Mar Lodge, Ackroyd, Black Doctor, Silver Doctor, Jock Scott, White Wing, Glentana, Blue Charm, Sailor, Jeannie, Jockie, Logie, Watson's Fancy, Green Peacock, Silver Blue, Sherbrooke, Tricolours.

Dee (Welsh).—Jock Scott, Butcher, Wilkinson, Black Doctor, Gordon and Grey Turkey.

Dionard, Inver, Kirkaig, Laxford, Hope, and Duartmore.— Wasp, Yellow Wasp, Sailor, Watson's Fancy, Claret and Mallard, Blue Charm, Blue Doctor, Black Doctor, Silver Doctor, Poynder, Butcher, Jock Scott, Green Highlander, Dusty Miller, Thunder and Lightning.

Don, Deveron, Ythan, and Ugie.—Eagles, Jock Scott, Silver Scott, Silver Grey, Silver Doctor, Dr. Forbes, Ackroyd, Glentana, Dunt, Black Wasp, Sir Archibald, Jockie, Black Doctor, Mar Lodge, Lady Caroline, Popham, Dusty Miller, Durham Ranger, Butcher, Bumbee, Gordon Cumming, Thunder and Lightning, Magenta Scott.

Eden.—Silver Grey, Jock Scott, Childers, Black Doctor, Butcher, Bull Dog, Sweep, Grey Turkey.

Findhorn and Nairn.—Evelyn, Gordon Cumming, Butcher, Jock Scott, Silver Doctor, Brown Dog, Childers, Thunder and Lightning, and lots of " collared " local patterns.

Forss and Halladale.—Eagles, McNicol, Red Sandy, Red Drummond, Canary, Murdoch, Jock Scott, Childers, Wilkinson, Silver Grey, Green Highlander.

Forth and Teith.—Jock Scott, Silver Doctor, Nicholson, Wilkinson, Childers, Durham Ranger, Poynder, Claret Wasp, Thunder and Lightning, Black Dog, Claret Scott, Popham, Blue Doctor, Black Wasp, Yellow Wasp.

Garry, Oich, and Moriston.—Jock Scott, Beauly Snow Fly, Red Sandy, Red Drummond, Murdoch, Silver Doctor, Wilkinson, Silver Grey, Childers.

Greeta and Derwent.—Turkey Brown, Silver Doctor, Butcher, Kate, Poynder.

Helmsdale.—Eagles, Red Drummond, Red Sandy, Murdoch, Canary, Silver Canary, Dawson, Silver Doctor, Yellow Doctor, Jock Scott, Popham, Coates, Helmsdale, Black Doctor.

☞ FOR WATERPROOF LINES, &c., SEE PAGES 104 TO 109.

Lochy and Spean.—Black Spean, Martin Spean, Lizzie, Captain Waugh, Irishman, Sun Fly, Peacock, Gled Wing, Jockie, Blue Charm, Amethyst, Black Doctor, Fort William.

Lune.—Silver Grey, Childers, Black Doctor, Blue Doctor, Parson, Jock Scott.

Lyon.—Blue Doctor, Silver Doctor, Jock Scott, Blue Charm, Sailor, Davidson, Dusty Miller, Childers.

Naver and Borgie.—Eagles, Childers, Jock Scott, Green Highlander, Murdoch, Silver Grey, Red Drummond, Greenwell, Wilkinson, Black Doctor, Silver Doctor, Red Sandy, Butcher, Durham Ranger.

North Esk and South Esk.—Silver Doctor, Silver Grey, Dunkeld, Dusty Miller, Jockie, Red Rover, Member, Carnegie, Dalhousie, Black Doctor, Gordon, Red Drummond.

Severn.—Eagles, Popham, Wilkinson, Parson, Dusty Miller, Gordon, Jock Scott.

Shin, Oykell, Cassley, and Carron.—Jock Scott, Blue Doctor, Wasp, Murdoch, Childers, Colonel, Silver Grey, Sailor, Black Doctor, Poynder, Golden Wasp, Glentana, Dallas, Dusty Miller.

Spey and Avon.—Green King, Purple King, Lady Caroline, Black Fancy, Jock Scott, Grey Heron, Black King, Gold Riach, Silver Riach, Dunkeld, Jockie, Blue Charm, Glentana.

Tay, Earn, and Tummel.—Jock Scott, Black Doctor, Black Dog, Claret Scott, Gordon, Dunt, Benchill, Butcher, Nicholson, Silver Doctor, Dusty Miller, Poynder, Wilkinson, Claret Wasp, Silver Grey, Smith.

Tees.—Butcher, Silver Doctor, Wilkinson, Poynder, Black Doctor.

Test.—Silver Test, Mystery, Butcher, Jock Scott, Gordon, Kendle, Dusty Miller, Silver Grey, Bruce, Baron.

Thurso.—Eagles, Canary, Childers, Wilkinson, Murdoch, Red Drummond, Silver Grey, Jock Scott, Enys, Rory Ross, Durham Ranger, Sir Richard, Wasp.

Tweed.—Jock Scott, Wilkinson, Silver Grey, Greenwell, Black Ranger, Durham Ranger, Sir Richard, Kelly, Green Peacock, Stephenson, Poynder.

Tyne.—Wilkinson, Poynder, Parson, Lovat, Butcher, Smith, Eve's Fancy, Nunwick, The Red Tag.

Usk.—Lion, Little Kelly, Leigh's Sun Fly, Lord Henry, Penpergwm Pet, Barrington's Favourite, Sir Herbert.

Wye.—Leigh's Sun Fly, Colonel, Britannia, Black Dog, Red Drake, Rocke's Fancy, Jock Scott.

We are much indebted to W. Murdoch, Esq., for assistance in compiling this list.

For best Norwegian patterns, see page 53.
    ,,   Irish   ,,   ,,   92.

☞ IN ORDERING FROM THIS LIST PLEASE QUOTE LETTER Q.

FLY MAKERS' TOOLS.

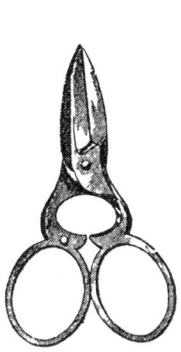

J.
Straight Blade
Scissors, 1/9 pair.

K.
Folding Pocket
Scissors, 2/3 pair.

L.
The "Gem" Scissors,
in case, 2/9 pair.

I.
Bent Blade
Scissors, 3/- pair.

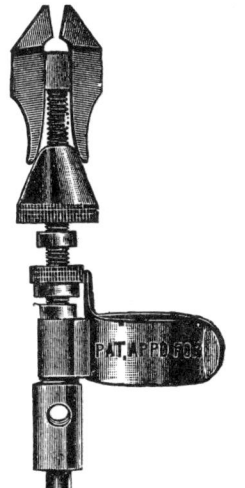
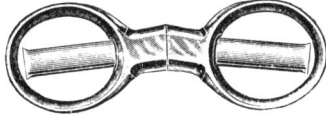

M.
Folding Scissors, best quality, 3/·
2nd Do., 1/6 per pair.

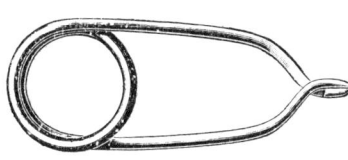

N.
Telescopic, best quality, 3/6 per pair.

Q.
Fly Vice, to screw in table
or use on thumb, as
illustrated, 7/6 each.

O.
Fly Tweezers,
1/6 per pair.

P.
File for Pointing
Dull Hooks,
1/- each.

Ditto, to screw on table with hook for looping, 6/- ; larger size, 12/6 each.

☞ The best Guide and Instructor for Salmon Fly Dressing is
"Salmon Fishing" by J. J. Hardy, 6/4 post paid.

Dry Fly Requisites.

Waistcoat Pocket Fly Oil Bottle.

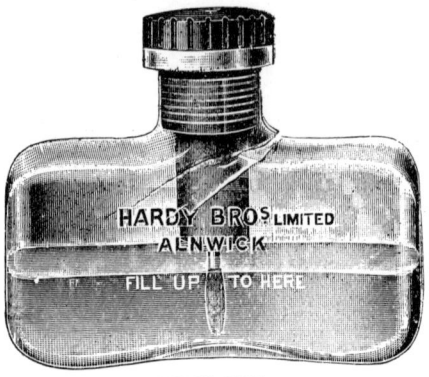

EXACT SIZE.

A convenient form for the waistcoat pocket. The interior is fitted with a long sleeve, which prevents the oil flowing back when filled to line mark.

Price 1/6 each.

Magnetic Stiletto.

Very useful for picking eyed-flies from a box. Any fly touched immediately adheres to the point, and may be removed without touching with the fingers. The forked end can be used as a disgorger, while the point is useful for opening gut loops, cleaning the eye of the fly, etc. Price 1/- each.

Magnetic Fly-Holder & Scissors (Combined).

Registered No. 520345.

This is a very handy little tool. A, is a magnetic steel holder. Any hook touched by it, immediately adheres, so that it can be lifted from the box without touching with the fingers. The hook may then be placed under the holder, and held in position by pressure of the left thumb while tying on the gut. The dotted lines show scissors in sheath. Price **2/6** each.

Lubricant for rod joints. In tins, 1/- each.

Odourless Paraffin for refilling waistcoat pocket bottle, 6d. per 4 oz. bottle, and "Vapourizer."

Preservative for rods and lines. In tins, 8d. each.

Dry Fly Oil Bottles

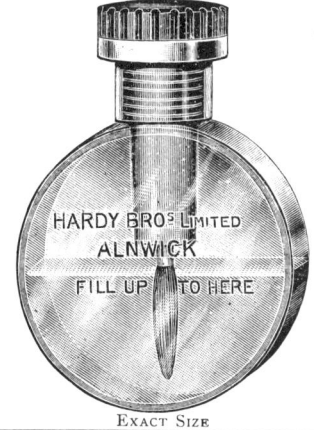

HARDY BROS LIMITED
ALNWICK
FILL UP TO HERE

EXACT SIZE

THE "WAISTCOAT POCKET" FLY OIL BOTTLE.

(MADE IN CELLULOID.)

A convenient form for the waistcoat pocket. The interior is fitted with a long sleeve, which prevents the oil flowing back. Care should be taken to fill only up to the mark indicated.

Price **2/6** each.

THE "ZEPHYR" POCKET BOTTLE.

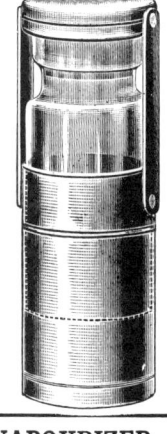

EXACT SIZE

Made of metal and designed for use with "Zephyr" (see page 81) or similar preparations, with which it is only necessary to prepare the fly by dipping it in the liquid. The stopper is detached by gripping the reservoir at the shoulder with the first and second fingers (one on each side) and pressing the bottom upwards with the thumb.

Price **4/6** each.

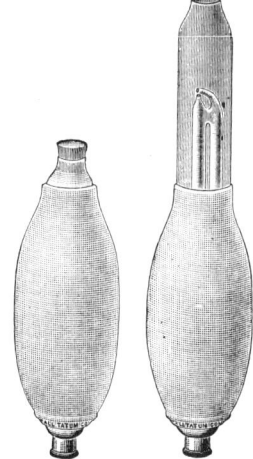

FIG. 1.   FIG. 2.

POCKET DRY FLY VAPOURIZER.

This vapourizer is of a convenient size, 3 ins. overall, when closed as Fig. 1. The glass reservoir is thoroughly protected by the rubber bulb and the vapourizer can be carried in the pocket. When required for use, hold the bulb firmly in the hand and press against the metal valve, this will start the glass reservoir, when it can be easily grasped and pulled out as far as the stop on its end will allow (see Fig. 2). The glass reservoir should never be filled more than one-third of its capacity.

Price **7/6** each.

Refills, Hardy's "Zephyr" Preparation
1/- per bottle

Odourless Paraffin, 1/- per bottle

Dry Fly Requisites

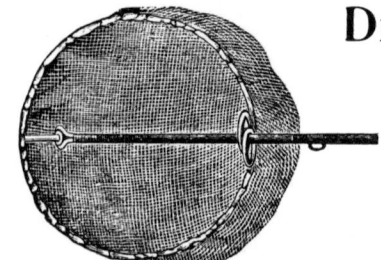

FLY CATCHER.

A useful little net, $3\frac{1}{4}$ in. dia. Can be quickly attached to the rod top to pick a fly from the water.

Price **10**d. each.

RED DEER FAT.

A specially prepared fat for rubbing the reel line. Will float the line a considerable time.

Price **6**d. per tin.

See also " Cerolene " (page 122).   **9**d. per tin.

POCKET LINE GREASER.

For fatting the reel line.   Price **1/-** each.

KNEE PAD.

Made of grained cowhide, with pad and two straps for buckling on. A great protection when kneeling on wet grass, gravel, or loose sand.

Price **6/-** each.

The "Curate."   Regd. **557672.**

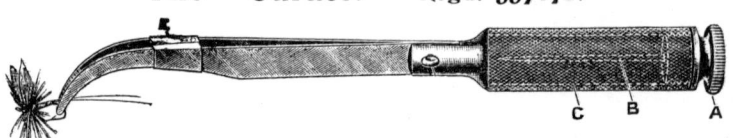

The " Curate " is an ingenious combination of angler's tools, comprising (1) Tweezers, useful as a disgorger or fly holder ; (2) Gut Cutter E ; (3) Reservoir C, to hold oil for dry flies or reels ; (4) Stiletto B, used to apply oil or clean the eye of the fly.   The handle is milled as a match striker or small " priest."   **Price 6/- each.**

FLY PAD.

A green felt pad (Size, $4\frac{1}{4}$ in. × 2 in.), with leather back and leather pocket to carry Stiletto, fitted with two clip hooks to attach to coat. A handy arrangement for carrying flies, **1/-** each. Stiletto, **1/-** extra.

Dry Fly Preparation

This preparation is perfectly clean, harmless to feathers and wax, and sweet to use—has no stickiness like the usual dry fly oils, and is an absolutely perfect preparation for floating flies. It does not discolour the fly in any way, therefore the fly is presented as it should be, giving full effect to all colour. Price 1/2 per bottle.

The " Drianoil " Fly Drier and Oiler

Made in metal, similar in form to a Hunter Watch, and convenient to carry in the waistcoat pocket. Fitted with Amadou (on which a water-logged fly can be dried) and felt which will carry odourless paraffin, etc., and into which the fly is pressed to proof before using.

Price, **6/6** each.

Exact Size.

Anti=Midge

A most excellent compound of essential oils. It is a clean, healthy preparation, not unpleasant in odour, and has no deleterious effect on the skin. Some form of midge preventative is a necessity for anglers, and this compound does all that is required in most places. The bottle is of a convenient form to fit the waistcoat pocket, and has a sprinkler stopper. Price **1/6** each.

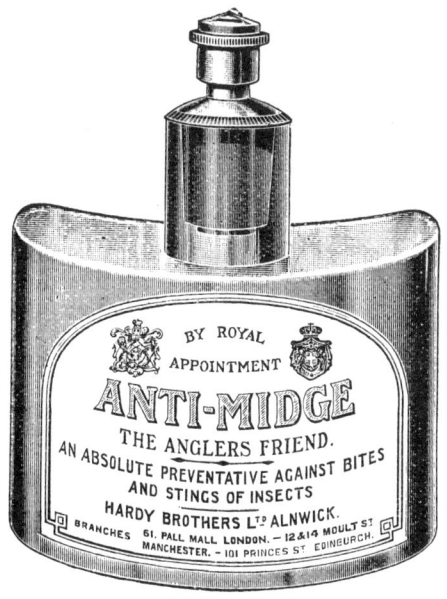

THE "DRIFLYDRESER"
(Pat. No. 19101/25)
Illustration exact size

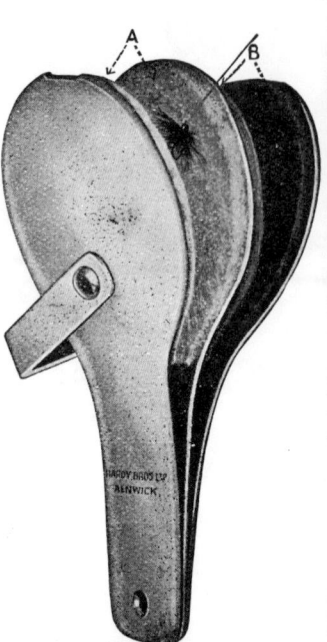

This novel arrangement is, without doubt, the handiest and most convenient form of dry fly dresser. It hangs from the coat, and consequently is always at hand when required, while it relieves the necessity for carrying bottles, etc.

It is shown in use. The leaves **AA** are fitted with pads of Amadou to dry a fly, and **BB** with prepared felt to proof it. All that is required is to place the fly between **AA** or **BB** as may be desired and press the leaves together with the finger and thumb.   Price **4/6** each.

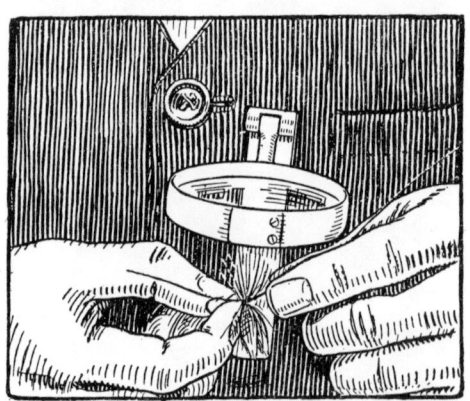

The "WARDLE" MAGNIFIER
Regd. No. 704251

We are indebted to Major Wardle for this excellent idea. The magnifier is carried by a safety pin fastening to the coat and is always handy for immediate use. When not in use it closes up against the body quite out of the way.

Price **10/6** each.

ANTI-MIDGE

A healthy, clean compound of essential oils, pleasant in odour, and without the slightest deleterious effect on the skin. Some form of midge preventative is a necessity for anglers, and this compound does all that is required. The bottle, which is fitted with a sprinkler stopper, is of a convenient form to fit the waistcoat pocket.

Price **1/3** each.

Fly Makers' Vices

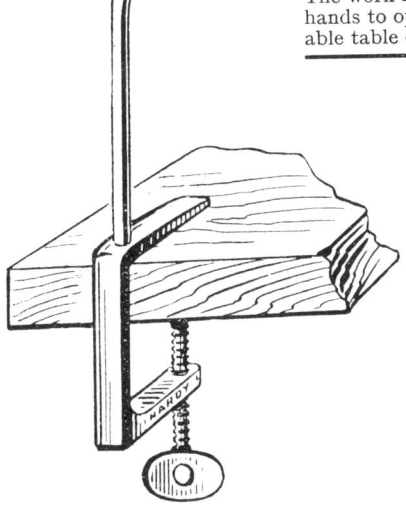

THE "HARDY-COULIN"
Suitable for Small Flies

In designing this vice we have been kindly assisted by Mons. E. Coulin, an ardent amateur fly dresser.

The vice and locking ring being perfectly plain there is no liability of the tying silk, etc., becoming entangled with parts of the vice whilst working. The work is held at an angle which permits both hands to operate with ease. Fitted with adjustable table clamp.   Price **9/-** each.

THE "AMATEUR"

Made with strong adjustable vice, operated by fly nut, and adjustable table clamp.

The hooked arm is made to screw in and a rubber washer is provided with a slot to hold the silk.   Price **10/6** each.

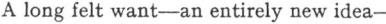

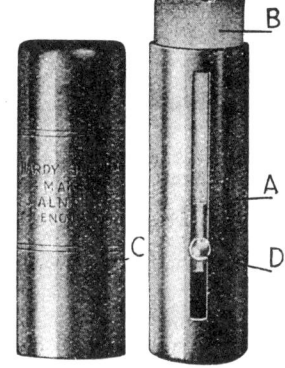

Hardy's Joint Lubricator and Container

Illus. actual size.

A long felt want—an entirely new idea—

The container A carries our special rod joint lubricant. B is exposed for use by drawing off cap C and pushing up stud D.

When the surface of the male joint has been rubbed with lubricant it should be smeared smooth, then the joint (partially assembled) turned round a few times, taken apart and wiped. This cleans it and generally leaves enough lubricant.   Price **1/-** each.

IMPROVED SALMON FLY HOOK.

HARDY'S PATENT OVAL WIRE.

THE ROUND
AND
OVAL SECTIONS
ARE OF
EQUAL AREA.

THE "OVAL"
IS 30 PER CENT.
STRONGER IN
LINE OF PULL.

ROUND SECTION.

From D to C represents depth of cut in making Barb.

From C to E shows thickness of metal left after cutting up Barb.

OVAL SECTION.

AREA A represents increase over the round in line of stress.

D to C represents depth of cut in making Barb.

C to E metal left after cutting up Barb.

B to C represents increased thickness of metal, amounting to 30 per cent. left after cutting up Barb.

These Hooks are made sizes 6/0 to No. 9, both Single and Double, and with Tapered or Hardy's Improved Eyed Shanks.

HARDY BROS.,
Manufactory, ALNWICK.

DEPÔTS

LONDON—61, Pall Mall, S.W.
EDINBURGH—5 & 50, South St. David St.
MANCHESTER—14, Moult Street.

HARDY'S NEW PATENT "PERFECT" REEL.

No. 412.

All striking is done from the reel, and the exact stiffness of ratchet required is regulated at will by the small screw **A**
See Fig. 4.

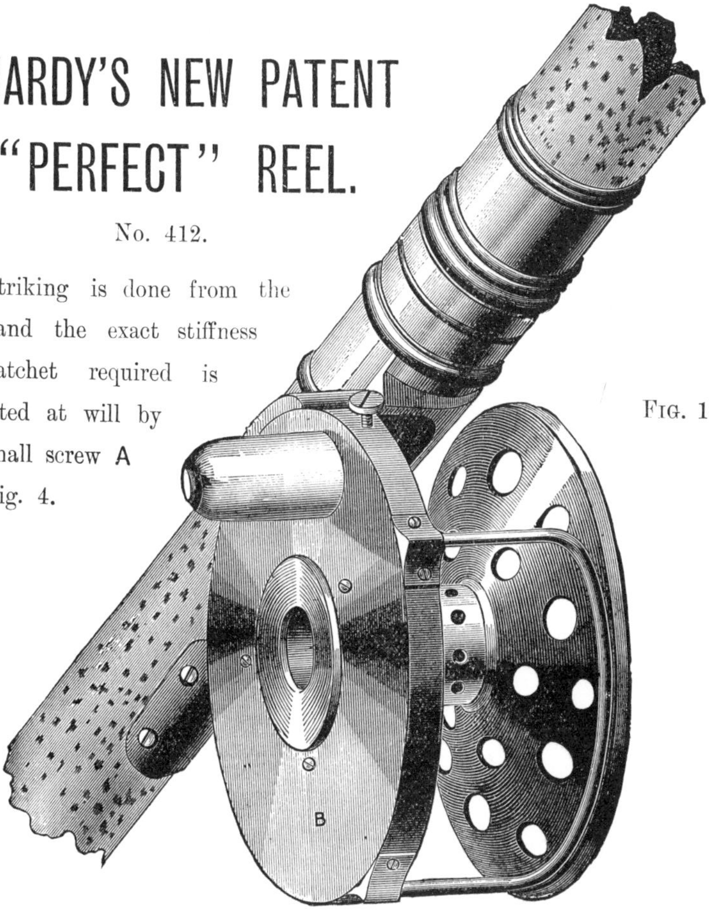

FIG. 1.

We have pleasure in introducing the new "Perfect" Reel. It has been made the subject-matter for two patents, and has taken some three years to bring to perfection. Messrs. HARDY made and practically tested something like twelve varieties of construction before they arrived at the above illustration, which they fearlessly claim to be the *best reel made anywhere*, and this they do with a full knowledge of all reels manufactured on either side of the Atlantic.

	£	s.	d.			£	s.	d.
No. 413—2¼ in. ...	1	5	0	No. 420—4 in. ...		2	0	0
„ 414—2½ in. ...	1	5	0	„ 421—4¼ in. ...		2	5	0
„ 415—2¾ in. ...	1	7	6	„ 422—4½ in. ...		2	10	0
„ 416—3 in. ...	1	10	0	„ 423—4¾ in. ...		2	15	0
„ 417—3¼ in. ...	1	12	6	„ 424—5 in. ...		3	0	0
„ 418—3½ in. ...	1	15	0	„ 425—5¼ in. ...		3	10	0
„ 419—3¾ in. ...	1	17	6					

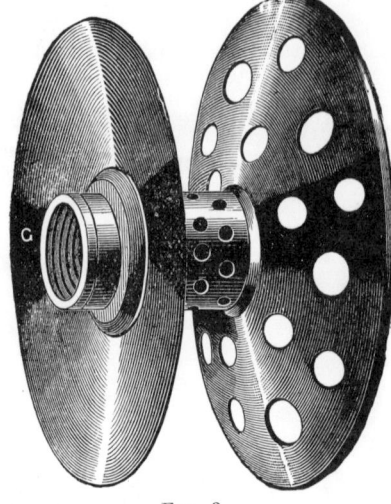

Fig. 2.   Fig. 3.

It is lighter and has a greater line-carrying capacity than any other pattern.   It is perfectly ventilating, and, so far as possible, assists in drying the line.   It has a regulating check and running on ball bearings, is almost frictionless.   It can be taken to pieces to clean instantly without any

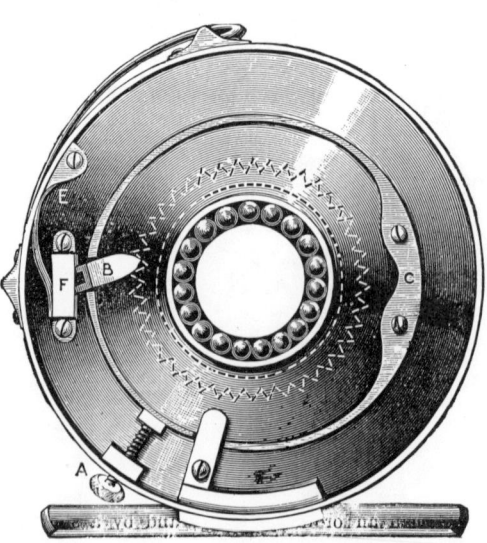

Fig. 4.

mechanical knowledge or tools.   The workmanship is of a higher class than has ever before been introduced into reels, everything being most carefully attended to ; all springs, tongues, bridges, &c., properly finished, hardened, and tempered, so that they will wear for years.   It will be plain to all that such a reel cannot be produced at a competitive price with ordinary cheap reels, yet, with a view of making it popular, the price has been kept very low for the quality.   Fig. 1, page 54, is the "Perfect" Reel complete. Figs. 2, 3, and 4, page 55, are the three main parts composing the reel.   To arrange these parts it is only necessary to pass bearing G on Fig. 3 through bearing on Fig. 4 from the opposite side and screw nozzle on Fig. 2 B into G. To take the reel to pieces, the handle on Plate B is screwed the reverse way while holding G.   On Fig. 4, which shows working parts, A is the regulator and C the spring, B the tongue, F the bridge, and E the cushion spring.   In the reverse motion of a reel, that is when the line is drawn off, it is an enormous advantage to be able to regulate the resistance so as to prevent any possible breakage of tackle by too hard striking or holding a fish, and with this reel this can be done to the most minute degree by regulating the reel and striking from it.   A trout reel may be regulated that, strike however hard, you cannot break gossamer gut, nor tear out a 000 midge hook, but by turning down A the same reel can be made strong enough to strike No. 7 Limericks into sea trout, or even stronger for spinning a minnow.   This regulating is effected perfectly and simply.   It will be noticed that the tongue B is not fixed by a screw in the usual manner as in other reels, but has an improved arrangement.   The tongue being slotted works on a pivot on the underside of bridge F and against a cushion spring E, which regulates exactly the pressure on ratchet wheel, and takes up all wear and tear by pressing the tongue a little more forward to the work.

BRITISH SPORTSMAN.

"It is the lightest, simplest, and most perfect reel ever introduced.   It has the greatest line-carrying capacity.   The strength of the spring for winding-in or letting out line can be regulated externally ; and the spindle, running, as it does, on ball-bearings, reduces the friction to a minimum.   This winch can be taken to pieces and put together again in a few moments without the aid of any tool."

FIELD, April 11th, 1891.

"It carries more line than an ordinary reel.   The check is regulated by means of a screw on the outer edge, causing it to run quickly and easily from light to stiff as the different kinds of fishing may demand.   This reel may be taken asunder without the aid of any tools.   The revolving plate is readily taken off, and each part exposed for cleaning."

ROD AND GUN, April 11th, 1891.

"An admirable implement—works with marvellous ease.   The line on the reel cannot kink.   It never gets into the hopeless tangle over which every man using an ordinary reel—the reel with bars—has had to weep when the trout were in their most taking mood."

LAND AND WATER, April 11th, 1891.

"Holds more line than an ordinary winch, and by a simple arrangement the pressure of the check can be regulated to a nicety."

ALUMINIUM REELS.—It is the opinion of Messrs. HARDY, formed from experiment, that this metal in its present state is too soft for reels—the bearings wear out directly.

MILITARY EQUIPMENT STORES AND TORTOISE TENTS CO., LD.,

"Alumin" Fishing Reels.

The metal called "Alumin," of which most of our best Reels are now partly made, is an alloy consisting of a proportion of other substances with Aluminium, to impart to the latter metal rigidity and strength. The combination of qualities thus produced is absolutely unique; as no other metal suitable for Reels has yet been introduced, which combines hard wearing qualities with strength. To put the matter plainly, "Alumin" taken bulk for bulk is equal in strength to the best wrought iron, and *only one third the weight.* The superiority in Reels made of our "Alumin" is not solely due to the quality of the metal used in their manufacture, but is in part attributable to the improved method of construction, which admits of special treatment in manufacture that cannot be applied in the case of other metals. It consequently makes the strongest and lightest Reels hitherto produced.

Comparative Table of the Mechanical Properties of Aluminium and "Alumin."

Name of Metal.	Specific Gravity.	Resistance per square m/m in kilos.	Resistance per Square inch in tons.	Elongation per cent.
Pure Aluminium (Cast)	2·56	8·2	5·27	3
Hardy's "Alumin" (Cast) ..	2·75	36·7	23·76	5

Alloys of Aluminium are *Not* anti-friction metals, and therefore all wearing surfaces and bearings in our Reels are made of hard Gun Metal or Bronze.

It is worthy of note that our charges for Reels of "Alumin" metal are no higher than for our usual gun metal mixtures.

"Hercules" Metal—The improvement in the tensile strength of metals by the introduction of from three to twelve per cent. of aluminium, has been of the greatest practical service, as we can now reduce the weight and, at the same time improve the wearing qualities. It would not be wise to say what particular mixture of metal we have (after a long series of expensive experiments), decided to use, as this would not benefit the purchaser, and only expose to the multitude of copyists the material which we prefer they should find out for themselves. Suffice it to say that this metal is as hard as steel, and will even make most excellent springs, so that we are now in a position to say, we have a metal in use which is a vast improvement on anything hitherto employed for this purpose, which we call "Hercules." This metal of course is more than twice the weight of "Alumin."

Hardy's "Field" Reel.—(Pages 103—104).—In answer to a request from correspondents, and with the assistance of the angling editor of the "*Field*" (by whom it was named,) we introduced this reel, to meet a request for a plain light fly reel, so arranged that it was possible to brake a fish by pressure of the fingers on the rim of the revolving plate. This we succeeded in doing after some trouble, and those which have since (about 12 months,) been made and tested by the editor of the "*Field*" and his angling friends, and anglers generally, have given the greatest satisfaction. For mahseer work in India a more perfect reel cannot be imagined. They are made in "Alumin," and so are very light and strong.

☞ FOR GOLD MEDAL CANE-BUILT ROD, SEE PAGE 150.

No. 1.
Black & Blea.

No. 2.
March Brown.
(Male.)

No. 5.
Greenwell's Glory.

No. 4.
March Brown.
(Spider.)

Sizes
3 Sneck

No 7.
Woodcock & Hare's Ear.

No. 9.
Blue Upright.

No. 15.
Blue Dun.

No. 19.
Dark Snipe and
Orange.

2 Sneck.

No. 20.
Red Spinner.

No. 29.
Whirling Dun.

No. 41.
Olive Dun.

No. 32.
Dark Partridge.

1 Sneck.

No. 45.
Hofland's Fancy.

No. 47.
Black Gnat.

No. 54.
Red Quill Gnat.

No. 51.
Red Hackle.

0 Sneck.

No. 58.
Red Ant.

No. 65.
Iron Dun.

No. 67.
July Dun.

No. 59.
Dotterell and
Yellow.

1 Sneck.

No. 68.
August Dun.

No. 71.
Hardy's Favourite.

No. 74.
Prince Charlie.

No. 70.
Black Spider.

2 Sneck.

No. 26.
Sand Fly.

No. 49.
Coachman.

No. 62.
Yellow Sally.

No. 33.
Light Partridge.

4 Sneck.

PRIZE MEDAL TROUT FLIES.

No. 1.
Green May Fly.
(Male.)

No. 2.
Green May Fly.
(Female.)

No. 3.
Brown May Fly.
(Male.)

4.

No. 4.
Brown May Fly.
(Female.)

No. 5.
Spent Gnat.
(Male.)

No. 6.
Spent Gnat
(Female.)

3.

No. 1m.
Summer Duck.
Detached Body.

No. 3m.
Summer Duck.

No. 4m.
Egyptian Goose.

4.

No. 5m.
Dyed Drake.

No. 7m.
Champion.

No. 8m.
Green Midget.

3.

No. 9m.
Spent Gnat.

No. 10m.
Hackle May.

No. 12m.
Lough Erne
May.

2.

MAY FLIES ON LONG MAY HOOKS, SIZES AS IN MARGIN.

Nos. 1 to 6 Mr Halford's New Patterns, see page 74.   Nos. 1m to 12m, see page 76.

No. 7. Black Ranger.

No. 0. Sherbrook.

No. 1. Blackdose.

No. 2. Red Drummond.

No. 3. Wilkinson.

No. 6. Murdoch.

No. 5. Red Sandy.

No. 4. Bull Dog.

THE "AARO" PATENT COMBINED FLY AND SPINNER.

These flies are arranged in actual sizes and colorings for assistance in ordering.

Silver Wilkinson.

Thunder and Lightning.

Silver Doctor.

Childers.

Greenwell

Gordon Ranger.

Dusty Miller.

Popham.

Black Doctor.

Durham Ranger.

Jock Scott.

Butcher.

Hardy's Patent "Perfect" Reels (pages 99 to 101), we have still further improved in construction. The great advantage of the regulating check; the greater line-carrying capacity; the extreme simplicity of construction, and the ease with which they can be dismounted, render them the leading and most perfect reels for fly-fishing ma nufactured. We have selected the 2¾ of this pattern as the "Houghton" reel, and we believe it to be among the best for dry fly work. (See also special contracted forms, page 102.)

Hardy's New Patent "Silex" Reel (page 107) promises to revolutionize all spinning reels of the "Nottingham" and other types, used for Spinning and Prawning for Salmon, Pike, Trout, etc. It is on the centre pin principle, but without the serious drawbacks peculiar to these reels. The whole system and arrangement for casting is reve s d. The check is automatic, and is always in work, unless the little lever projection is pressed, when the barrel at once becomes free. In making a cast the finger is pressed on the lever, which allows the barrel to run free until about half the distance the bait is intended to travel is accomplished; when it is rel-ased and the silent check immediately resumes its control over the barrel, and allows only so much line to be drawn off as the bait requires. This prevents over-running and entanglement of the line, and there is no check to adjust when preparing to wind up, or on hooking a fish, as the check is always at work except when the lever is pressed for casting. See description of mode of working, page 38.

Hardy's New Patent Combined Fly and Spinning Reel (page 106.) has been a great success. In place of a centre pin, the spindle ends of our new patent reel bears on the plates at both sides, and no amount of pulling can injure it any more than would happen with a plain salmon reel. We particularly desire our clients who spin for pike, trout, or salmon, and who require a reel which may be used either for fly or spinning, to give these a trial and we are sure they will be pleased. They are much liked for Mahseer.

Hardy's Special Hard Metal Reels.—(Page 105)—In these a new style of fitting the check has been introduced which places them far beyond all others of this class. Another development is the production of them in "Alumin" as well as in "Hercules" metal at same price. which is so done that none of the wearing qualities are lost, while the reels are considerably lightened.

Gunmetal Bronzed Revolving Plate Reels.—(Page 108.)—These remain the same, with the exception that we have lightened and improved them in some minor details; and, although noted in our list as second quality, they are really (in consequence of the high standard of our work,) better than those Brumagem productions sold by nearly all retailers as "best."

Crank Handle Reels.—(Page 109.)—The cheaper crank handle reels we need hardly mention. They are capital for boys, or anyone wanting a low priced reel. Those listed being our own manufacture and guaranteed sound.

Sea Reels.—(Pages 254, 255.)—In these, besides the "Ocean" reel, which has been largely used, we have introduced another form called the "Farne," made of "Alumin," which is a vast improvement on all sea reels. It is a very comfortable, easy, and durable tool to work with.

☞ IN ORDERING FROM THIS LIST PLEASE QUOTE LETTER **G.**

Hardy's Patent "PERFECT" REEL.

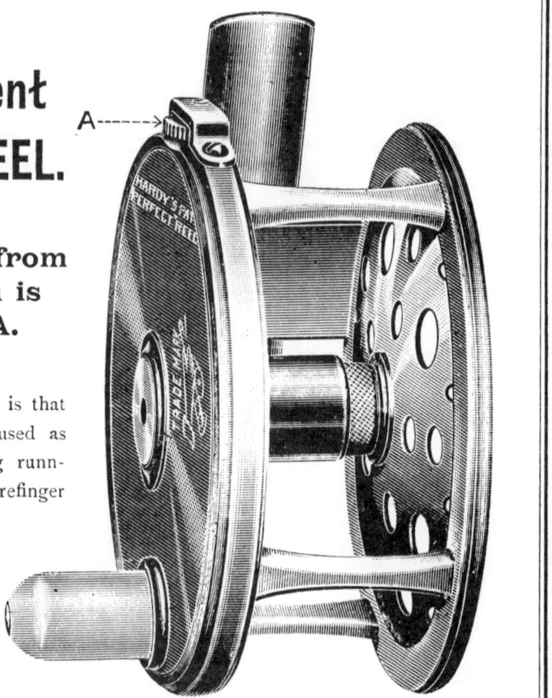

A----->

All striking done from the Reel, which is regulated at A.

A most important feature is that the perforated plate can be used as an extra check against strong running fish by pressing the forefinger against it.

The line carrying capacity is equal to others of a ¼-in. larger diameter.

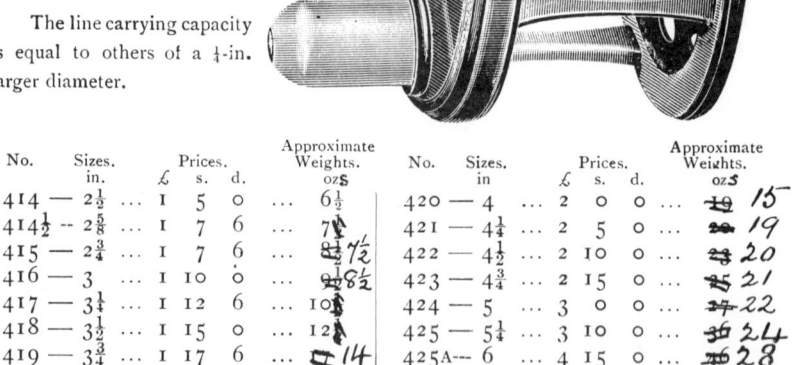

No.	Sizes. in.	Prices. £ s. d.	Approximate Weights. ozs	No.	Sizes. in	Prices. £ s. d.	Approximate Weights. ozs
414 —	2½	1 5 0	6½	420 —	4	2 0 0	~~19~~ *15*
414½ --	2⅝	1 7 6	7	421 —	4¼	2 5 0	~~20~~ *19*
415 —	2¾	1 7 6	~~8½~~ *7½*	422 —	4½	2 10 0	~~23~~ *20*
416 —	3	1 10 0	~~9~~ *8½*	423 —	4¾	2 15 0	~~25~~ *21*
417 —	3¼	1 12 6	10½	424 —	5	3 0 0	~~27~~ *22*
418 —	3½	1 15 0	12½	425 —	5¼	3 10 0	~~30~~ *24*
419 —	3¾	1 17 6	*14*	425A---	6	4 15 0	~~7~~ *28*

Instructions for Cleaning and Oiling the "Perfect" Reel.

To dismount the Reel—Remove with a coin, the small **left handed** screw in centre of plate. Hold the line drum, Fig. 3, with the left hand, while with the right unscrew the revolving plate, Fig. 2, by turning handle to the left; when the plate is unscrewed the drum may be taken out. All should then be wiped clean, and the parts oiled. To put Reel together, replace the drum taking care that the end of line is clear of guard, and screw down revolving plate; replace small left hand screw.

AUCKLAND, October, 1894.

Having fished once with one of your "Perfect" reels I should not care to use any other. They are *the* reels for the varied N.Z. fishing.   C. E. S. GILLIES.

Fig 2.   Fig 3.

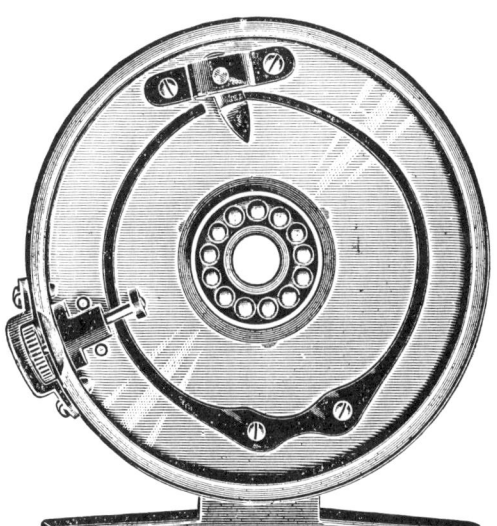

FIG. 4.

☞ FOR FLY MAKERS' MATERIALS AND TOOLS, SEE PAGE 93.

"PERFECT" SALMON REEL,

with Patent Revolving Line Guard, and Improved System of Check Work

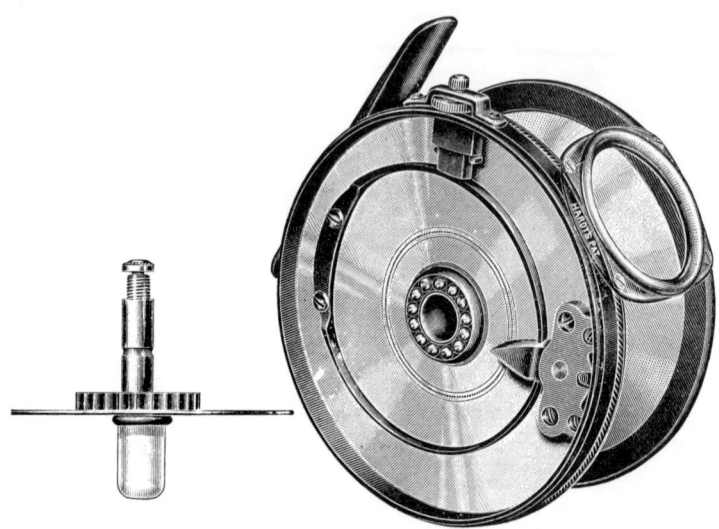

The "Perfect" Reel has gained a world-wide reputation as the very best fly reel ever invented, either for trout or salmon fishing. Its simplicity and great strength of construction are at once apparent — the ease with which it can be regulated to give any reasonable brake pressure. The fact that its brake pressure is adjustable only as to *drawing out* line, so that it does not interfere with the normal pressure used while winding in, marks it as the only reel in which alteration of the brake action is wisely applied.

The salmon sizes—$3\frac{3}{4}$ in. to 5 in. inclusive—have all been further improved by the addition of a *patent revolving line guard*, while an improved system of check work of a new and very strong character has been applied. Referring to the former, all anglers are aware of the trouble caused by the line getting behind the reel—particularly if shooting line. Many line guards, both metal and leather, have been designed to obviate this, but the employment of this ring renders any form of guard quite unnecessary, as the line does not find its way round the back.

FIG. 3.	FIG. 1.	FIG. 2.

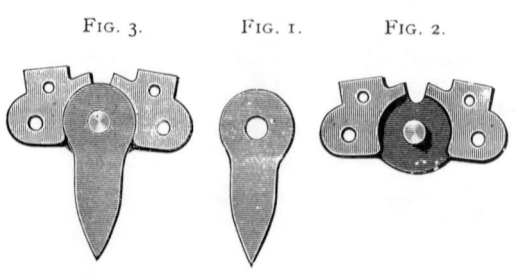

The second improvement will be seen on reference to the illustration.

Fig. 1 is the ratchet with enlarged circular back end which is received into the bridge piece, Fig. 2. Fig. 3 shows the arrangement when fastened in position. This new form of ratchet was developed from a suggestion made to us by Frazer Sandeman, Esq., author of "By Hook and by Crook" and "Angling Travels in Norway," for whom we made the first reel with this form of tongue. Fig. 3 shows ratchet and bridge piece turned upside down—this has been done to show the enormous strength of the arrangement. Should the steel peg carrying the ratchet at any time break the circular end of the ratchet will continue to work in the recess which receives it, so that a breakdown from this cause is almost impossible.

All the working parts of this reel are made of the highest class of steel procurable, finely hardened and tempered.

Regulating Check.

We wish it to be distinctly understood that this reel is totally different in principle and construction from any other so-called regulating check reel. We mention this as there are one or two so-called regulating check reels which have a screw or other device to create a resistance between the revolving plates, in order to retard the action and which makes the reel equally stiff, whether winding in or paying out the line. The best one can say of such an arrangement is that it is very crude indeed, for the reason that it is not desirable to increase the friction in winding up. In fact, the resistance in this direction should be as light as possible, and arranged so as not to be alterable. The portion of the check, which it is necessary to alter, is that which is brought into operation by the drawing out of the line, and it is in this respect only that the "Perfect" reel can be altered. The value of this arrangement over any other existing plan is very apparent.

A not inconsiderable advantage of this reel is that you can add additional brake power by slightly pressing the fingers against the exposed plate of the drum in the position indicated in the illustrations

BRAKING A FISH WITH THE "PERFECT" REEL. RINGS UP.

BRAKING A FISH WITH THE "PERFECT" REEL. RINGS DOWN

HARDY'S PATENT "PERFECT" REEL

Made of "Alumin."

Without doubt the lightest and most perfect Fly Reel the world has ever seen—Ball Bearings and Regulating Check.

NOTE.—Illustration shows the patent revolving line guard as applied to salmon reels; for trout reels with this guard see page 129.

No.	Sizes. in.	Prices. £	s.	d.	Approximate Weights. ozs.	No.	Sizes. in.	Prices. £	s.	d.	Approximate Weights. ozs.
414 —	2½	1	6	6	4¾	420 —	4	2	6	0	14¾
414½—	2⅝	1	7	6	5	421 —	4¼	2	12	6	17
415 —	2¾	1	8	6	6	422 —	4½	2	15	6	19¾
416 —	3	1	10	c	7¾	423 —	4¾	3	0	0	21
417 —	3¼	1	12	6	8½	424 —	5	3	5	0	22
418 —	3½	1	15	0	10¾	425 —	5¼	3	15	0	24
419 —	3¾	2	2	6	14	425A—	6	5	0	0	28

Patent Revolving Line Guard to Salmon Reels, 3¾ ins. and upwards, 7s. 6d. extra.
"Special" Reel Oil in Nickelled Oiler with Spout and Screw Cap, 1/- each.

Instructions for Cleaning and Oiling the "Perfect" Reel.

To dismount the Reel—With a coin remove the small (**left-handed**) screw in centre of plate. Hold the line drum, Fig. 3, page 124, with the left hand, while with the right unscrew the revolving plate, Fig. 2, by turning handle to the left; when the plate is unscrewed the drum may be taken out. All parts should then be wiped clean, and oiled with our "Special" Oil which does not oxidize. To put Reel together, replace the drum (taking care that the end of line is clear of guard), and screw down revolving plate; replace small left hand screw.

☞ SEE TO KEEP REELS CLEAN AND IN GOOD ORDER, PAGE 125.

HARDY'S PAT. "PERFECT" REEL,

Special contracted form for Dry Fly, &c., suggested by Capt. H. MANN.

With Ball Bearings and Regulating Check.

WINCHESTER, January, 1897, season and I shall use them WM. COOKE DANIELS.

The contracted reels worked perfectly last altogether in 1897.

A new form of our "Perfect" Reel—designed for dry fly and general trout and sea trout fishing. The reel is much contracted, with large barrel for quick winding of the line, and practically serves the purpose of a multiplier without the complication of cog-wheels. It is made in our new "Alumin," all wearing parts being steel or bronze. By this arrangement a reel of larger diameter than usual may be employed.

NOTE.—This is the same reel as on page 110, only the barrel is larger in diameter and narrower. Illustration is the full size of a 3⅝ in. reel.

This contracted form is only made in these sizes, For regular form, see page 110.

Diameter.	Price.	Width between plates.	Line carrying capacity.	Weight.	Suitable for rods.
3⅛	30/-	1 1/16	30 to 35 yds.	8½ ozs.	9 to 10ft.
3¼	32/6	1 1/16	35 to 40 yds.	9⅝ ozs.	10 to 10ft. 6in.
3½	35/-	1 1/16	40 to 45 yds.	11 9 ozs.	10ft. 6in to 12ft.
3⅝	37/6	1 2/16	40 to 50 yds.	13 10 ozs.	12 to 14ft.

The "Perfect" Reel combines the advantages of being able to disconnect in one minute (the only tool required being a coin,) with the power of regulating the check, and braking a fish, by pressure of the fingers on the exposed plate of the revolving drum.

See also our Special "Field" Reel, page 115 arranged on the same system.

Hardy's Patent "Perfect Reel."

(CONTRACTED).

With Ball Bearings and Regulating Check.

The contracted reels worked perfectly last season and I shall use them altogether.
WM. COOKE DANIELS.

Illustration is the size of a $3\frac{1}{8}$ in. reel.

A form of our "Perfect" Reel—designed for dry fly and general trout and sea trout fishing. The reel is much contracted, with large barrel for quick winding, and practically serves the purpose of a multiplier without the complication of cog-wheels. It is made in our new "Alumin," all wearing parts being steel or bronze. By this arrangement a reel of larger diameter than usual may be employed.

NOTE.—This is the same reel as on page 122, only the barrel is larger in diameter and narrower.

Diameter.	Price.	Width between plates.	Line carrying capacity.	Weight.	Suitable for rods.
$3\frac{1}{8}$	30/-	$\frac{11}{16}$	30 to 35 yds.	$5\frac{3}{4}$ ozs.	9 to 10ft.
$3\frac{3}{8}$	32/6	$\frac{11}{16}$	35 to 40 yds.	$7\frac{1}{4}$ ozs.	10 to 10ft. 6in.
$3\frac{5}{8}$	35/-	$\frac{11}{16}$	40 to 45 yds.	8 ozs.	10ft. 6in. to 12ft.
$3\frac{7}{8}$	37/6	$\frac{12}{16}$	40 to 50 yds.	$8\frac{3}{4}$ ozs.	12 to 14ft.

Spare Barrels, $3\frac{1}{8}$in. and $3\frac{3}{8}$in., 7/6 each; $3\frac{5}{8}$in. and $3\frac{7}{8}$in., 8/6 each.

The "Perfect" Reel combines the advantages of being able to disconnect quickly, the only tool required being a coin, with the power of regulating the check, and braking a fish, by pressure of the fingers on the exposed plate of the revolving drum.

HARDY'S
Patent " Silent Check " Fly Reel.

Suitable for
Dry Fly or
any kind of
Trout
Fishing.

Silent
Check, with
Regulator
and Ball
Bearings.

Holds 50 to
60 yards of
line.

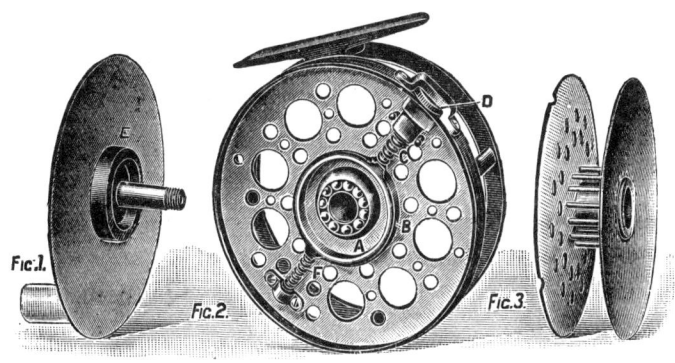

FIG.1.   FIG.2.   FIG.3.

This is a new design of a silent check reel. As may be seen from Fig. 2, the clutch B is actuated by spring C at F and bears on hub E (see Fig. 1) which fits into space A on Fig. 2, the pressure being regulated by milled nut D on the rim, which may be increased by turning screw to the left or decreased by turning to the right, as may be desired.   The arrangement is practically the same as in our Patent " Perfect " reel. This is the only Silent Check reel which has a smooth easy action and may be regulated to any required stiffness.

The reel is fitted with ball bearings and may be taken apart in the same manner as that described on page 122.   The diameter is $3\frac{5}{8}$ in., width between plates $\frac{3}{4}$ in. It carries 40 yds. of heavy double tapered trout line with 20 yds. of backing, while the weight is only $6\frac{1}{2}$ ozs. It is an ideal reel for those who dislike the noise of a check, and while mainly intended for trout fishing, may, from its large line carrying capacity, be used for loch, sea trout and even grilse. Price 40/-, if fitted with agate guide ring as on page 129, 7/6 extra.

SPECIAL "PERFECT" REEL.

A new type of reel specially designed to meet the wants of those who require a trout reel very light and yet capable of carrying 35 yards of I.C.I. "CORONA SUPERBA" or "TOURNAMENT" Line and 60 yards of No. 2 Silk Backing Line, making in all 95 yards. As a "dry" fly or general reel it is preferable, in our opinion, to any other, as the very large barrel enables one to recover line very quickly. It is made on the lines of our Patent 'Perfect" Reel, with ball-bearing and regulating check.

Size - 3¼ ins.
Weight 6 ozs.
Price - **42/-**

HARDY'S "BOUGLÈ" REEL (Patent).

A form of our "Perfect" Reel, made of Alumin, designed by Mons. Bouglè, as a light creel with great line capacity, suitable for using with 4 to 8 oz. rods. Solid frame and drum with ball bearings, regulating check and revolving centre bar.

Size. Weight. Price.

3 ins. 4½ ozs. **42/-**
3¼ ins. 5½ ozs. **47/6**

Hardy's New Patent Compensating Check.

Most anglers have experienced annoyance, by the check work of a reel sticking at some time or other. This has hitherto been due to the absence of **elasticity** in the arrangement, the tongue being a fixture. The possibility of sticking, is now happily overcome, by our new method, which is perfectly elastic, and allows the tongue to move freely in any direction.

The above diagram shows the tongue, or pawl, held under a strong steel bridge, on the under side of which is a steel peg, on which the check works. The pawl is slotted as shown by the interior dotted lines. The outer dotted lines show the path of the check, while working in the direction of E or D. It will be clearly seen, that the slot allows the check to move at any angle from C to B, while at the same time it can rise or fall, under pressure of spring F, and so take up wear and tear; or may rise away from the wheel in case of any irregularity, and so **prevent any possibility of locking.** The spring F keeps the pawl to its work, but allows it to rise should any excessive pressure be applied. The form of the spring gives a pleasant light and fine check when winding in. When the drum is turned in the direction of the arrow D (as when a fish takes line), the check can be regulated to almost any stiffness, by turning the screw of the regulator H, which forces arm G to compress spring F, and give the required pressure.

This important improvement calls for no comment, as the immense advantage is at once apparent, and must appeal to all.

The illustration shown is the exact size of the interior of our 4¼ in. " Perfect " salmon reels. Clients will be glad to know that we have decided to fit all our fly reels, down to and including the " Uniqua " quality (which latter, however, has not the regulator), with this improved check work, from the date of the issue of this catalogue, **without any increase in prices.**

Great Improvement in Reels

(Pat. Nos. 24245 ; 145904 ; 9261 ; and U.S.A. 369867).

A Notable

Improvement

Standardized

Reels

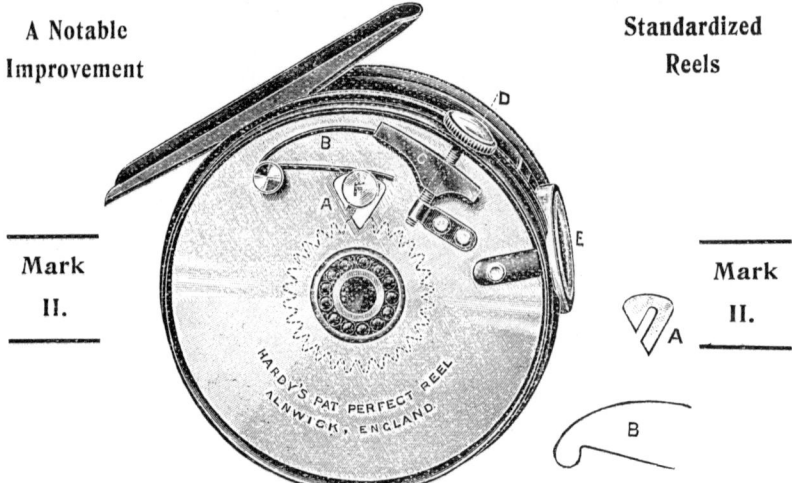

Mark

II.

Mark

II.

All our " Perfect," " St. George " and " Uniqua " trout reels have been much improved, by the *standardization of all parts.* This is a new era in the manufacture of fishing reels, and is the first occasion on which reels have been standardized by any firm in the world.

All parts in these reels bearing the Marks I. and II. are now interchangeable with any others, of a given size, Mark and description. A valuable feature is, that either ratchet or spring may be removed and replaced without the aid of any tools, other than the end of an ordinary writing pencil, to push back the end of the spring.

The value of the above facts can hardly be over-estimated. We consider it the most important development in reels for many years. As is well known to every engineer, standardization is a work requiring a large number of accurate machines and gauges, and is only possible in large and perfectly fitted works. The only parts ever likely to require replacement are tongues and springs. If extra parts are required, they may be had at the small cost of 1/3 each. It seems hardly necessary to say, that those who contemplate going far for their sport, will appreciate the confidence an extra spring or tongue will give them.

The new drum sent for my 3½ in. "Perfect" reel is very satisfactory and a most accurate fit, due no doubt to your perfect standardisation. This is a great advantage to your clients abroad. On my last fishing trip I took spare parts for my reels and the confidence given me that, if necessary I could do my own repairs in the wilds was great. One only needs to have a breakdown in the hills to appreciate this confidence. Happily during this trip I did not require to do any repairs.

NEW YORK.   J. F. G.

BRAKING A SALMON REEL.—In reference to the note in the *Field* of Jan. 6, 1917 (" Passing Comments "), " Checking a Salmon," I may say that Messrs. Hardy Brothers have a reel with which you can put on a very heavy check ; you press your fingers and thumb on the side of the reel opposite the handle. I have used this reel for some years now in Norway and Scotland and with the Tyee salmon in British Columbia, and have been able to put on almost any amount of check.—SALMON REEL. (This reference is made to our celebrated " Perfect " reel).

Further Improvements in Reels
(Patent Nos. 24245 ; 145904 ; 9261 ; and U.S.A. 369867).

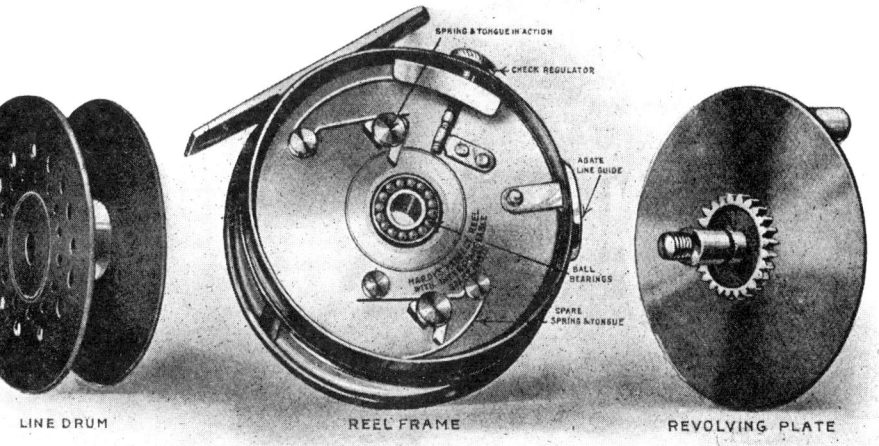

LINE DRUM   REEL FRAME   REVOLVING PLATE

HARDY'S "PERFECT" CONTRACTED REEL DISMOUNTED.

Hardy's Patent Agate Line Guard

Silent Check "Perfect" Fly Reels

Patent No. 196736.

REEL FRAME

LINE DRUM REVOLVING PLATE

Some anglers prefer a reel with a silent brake instead of the usual noisy ratchet check action sometimes called " The music of the reel."

The illustration shows the patented action of the reel. The hide-faced brake arm **A** bears on the polished hub **B** on the revolving plate. The strength of the spring **C** which controls the brake arm can be regulated by screwing the milled head **D** which moves the block **E**. As the reel will require to be taken apart occasionally for cleaning and oiling, it should be remembered that before assembling, the regulating block **E** should be screwed as far as it will go towards the milled head **D**, this enables the spiral spring **F** to pull the brake arm **A** out of the way of the hub **B** and allow the revolving plate to be replaced.

The brake action is so arranged that the "wind in" is always lighter than the "pull off."

In sizes				$3\frac{1}{8}$ in.	$3\frac{3}{8}$ in.	$3\frac{5}{8}$ in.	$3\frac{7}{8}$ in.
Price—Trout, seatrout, etc.				44/-	46/-	48/6	52/6

Agate Guide Rings - 9/6 extra.

				$3\frac{3}{4}$ in.	4 in.	$4\frac{1}{4}$ in.	$4\frac{1}{2}$ in.
Price—Salmon -	-	-		61/-	67/-	74/6	81/6

Agate Guide Ring - - 9/6 extra.

HALF EBONITE REELS.

Brass Bronzed Reel, one side Ebonite, German Silver Bound, the Revolving Plate coming out to the edge of the binding. These are very light, and of best quality.

391	—2¼ in.	...	6 ozs.	...	14s. 6d.	394½—3¾ in.	...	17 ozs.	...	26s. 0d.
392	—2½ ,,	...	7 ,,	...	16s. 6d.	395 —4 ,,	...	21 ,,	...	28s. 0d.
392½—2¾ ,,	...	8½ ,,	...	18s. 6d.	395½—4¼ ,,	...	22 ,,	...	30s. 0d.
393 —3 ,,	...	10 ,,	...	20s. 0d.	396 —4½ ,,	...	23 ,,	...	32s. 0d.
393½—3¼ ,,	...	13½ ,,	...	22s. 0d.	396½—4¾ ,,	...	27 ,,	...	34s. 0d.
394 —3½ ,,	...	15 ,,	...	24s. 0d.	397 —5 ,,	...	31 ,,	...	36s. 0d.

SPECIAL PATTERN HARD METAL REELS.

The object aimed at in introducing these reels was lightness combined with strength. The plates are made of fine metal, hammered very hard. The reel is much contracted, and thus gives great winding power. Ratchet and bearings are of the best possible description. The reel is fully one-third lighter than the ordinary brass and other reels.

Fishermen know how they suffer from having to carry heavy reels, and will, we believe, fully appreciate the great advantages these offer.

Special Pattern
"Hercules" Metal Reels.

HANDSOME.

LIGHT.

STRONG.

EFFECTIVE.

DURABLE.

RECOMMENDED.

The object aimed at in introducing these reels was lightness combined with strength.   The plates are made of fine "Hercules" metal, hammered very hard.   The drum is much contracted, and thus gives great winding power.   Ratchet and bearings are of the best possible description, the tongue working under a bridge.   The reel is fully one-third lighter than the ordinary brass or other reels.

NOTE.—At the moment of going to press, we are making improvements in this reel so that those we send out may not be quite the same.

Made in "Hercules" Metal.

Ins.		Ozs.		Bronzed.	Ins.		Ozs.		Bronzed.
399	—$2\frac{1}{2}$	...	5	...	18s. 6d.	$400\frac{3}{4}$—$3\frac{3}{4}$	...	16	...	28s. 0d.
$399\frac{1}{4}$	—$2\frac{5}{8}$	...	$5\frac{1}{2}$	...	19s. 6d.	401 —4	...	18	...	30s. 0d.
$399\frac{1}{2}$	—$2\frac{3}{4}$	...	6	...	20s. 0d.	$401\frac{1}{4}$—$4\frac{1}{4}$	...	20	...	34s. 0d.
400	—3	...	8	...	22s. 0d.	$401\frac{1}{2}$—$4\frac{1}{2}$	...	22	...	38s. 0d.
$400\frac{1}{4}$	—$3\frac{1}{4}$	...	10	..	24s. 0d.	$401\frac{3}{4}$—$4\frac{3}{4}$	..	24	...	42s. 0d.
$400\frac{1}{2}$	—$3\frac{1}{2}$	...	13	...	26s. 6d.	$401\frac{7}{8}$—5	...	26	...	46s. 0d.

BADMINTON LIBRARY —"To those who desire light reels made entirely of metal, Hardy's revolving plate will commend itself."

Made in Special "Alumin."

399 A. $2\frac{1}{2}$ ins. ...	... 21s. 0d.	$399\frac{1}{2}$ A. $2\frac{3}{4}$ ins.	...	... 25s. 0d.
$399\frac{1}{4}$ A. $2\frac{5}{8}$,,	... ... 23s. 6d.	400 A. 3 ,,	...	... 27s. 6d.

See page 97.

☛ SEE "HOUGHTON" CREEL, PAGE 244.

HARDY'S PATENT
COMBINED FLY & SPINNING REEL
with Compensating Steel Pivot Bearing,
for Salmon, Mahseer, Trout, Pike, &c.

No. 395.

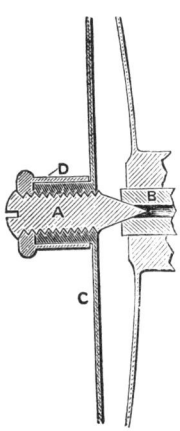

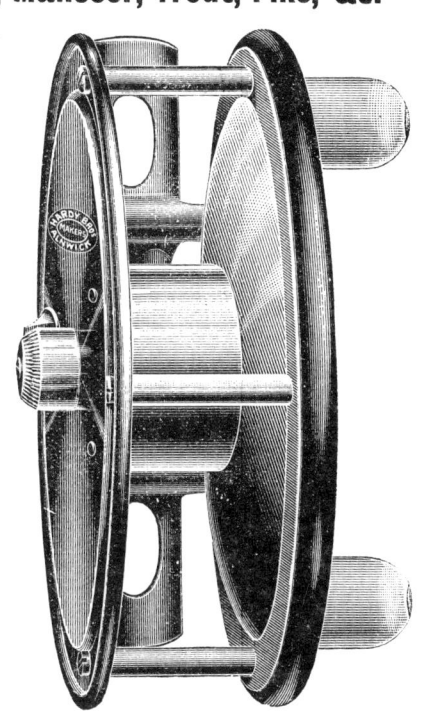

Section
of adjustable
Compensating
Steel Pivot
and Bearing.

The plates and drum are made of our special aluminium alloy. The spindle is hardened steel, working on a centre-point at one end, and a parallel bearing on the other, with an adjustable screw, and screw cover cap. The ratchet and wheel are hardened steel, and adjustable at will with slide thumb-piece. All work is of the very highest description. As will be seen from the section, **A** is the adjustable steel pivot, **B** the steel bearing in drum, **D** is cap protecting oil hole and acts as a lock nut to **A**, bearing against **C** side plate of reel.

The only perfect centre-pin spinning reel. Combines all the qualities of the class without their inherent weakness, and is equally good for fly-fishing, and very light. See page 98.

Sizes	2¾ in.	3 in.	3½ in.	4 in.	4½ in.	5 in.
Prices	25/-	27/6	32/6	37/6	42/6	50/-
Weight	6 ozs.	7 ozs.	10 ozs.	12½ ozs.	14½ ozs.	18 ozs.

" Equally well adapted for fly fishing and for spinning "—*Rod and Gun.*

☞ IN ORDERING FROM THIS LIST PLEASE QUOTE LETTER **G.**

Nottingham Wood Reels.

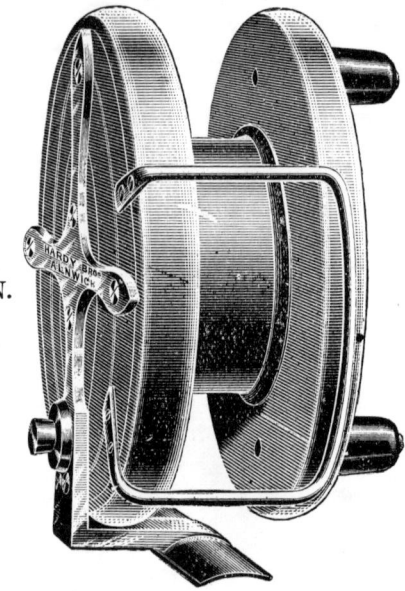

No. 409 N.

This quality of Reel may now be had fitted with our . .

Patent "Silex" Action,

as well as the ordinary.

PRICES BELOW.

STAR BACKS, BRASS HANDLE BEARINGS, ADJUSTABLE CHECKS, AND BICKERDYKE LINE GUARDS.

Sizes	3-in.	3½-in.	4-in.	4½-in.	5-in.
Ordinary Checks	8/-	8/6	9/6	10/6	11/6
Patent "Silex" Action Checks	9/6	10/6	11/6	12/6	15/-
Without Checks or Line Guards	3/6	4/-	4/6	5/6	6/6

Gunmetal   Bronzed

CRANK   HANDLE.

410	...	2-in.	...	4/6	411½	...	3¼-in.	... 9/6
410¼	...	2¼-in.	...	5/-	412	...	3½-in.	... 11/-
410½	...	2-½in.	...	6/-	412¼	...	3¾-in.	... 12/6
411	...	2¾-in.	...	7/-	412½	...	4-in.	... 14/-
411¼	...	3-in.	...	8/-	412¾	...	4½-in.	... 15/6

A good sound check Reel, with crank handle.
The screws and tongue are steel, and although low in price, it is very sound and serviceable.

Hardy's "Field" Reel.

(Usual Pattern.)

(PATENT.)

Made partly in our "Alumin," wearing parts of Aluminium Bronze or Steel.

Diameter.	Price.	Width between Plates.	Line carrying capacity.	Weights.	Suitable for Rods.
2⅝	21/-	$\frac{13}{16}$	30 to 40 yds	6 ozs.	9 to 10 ft.
2⅞	23/6	$\frac{14}{16}$	30 ,, 40 yds.	6½ ozs.	10 ,, 10½ ft.
3⅛	26/6	1$\frac{1}{16}$	35 ,, 50 yds.	7 ozs.	10½ ,, 12 ft.
3⅜	30/-	1$\frac{2}{16}$	40 ,, 50 yds.	9 ozs.	12 ,, 13 ft.
3⅝	32 6	1$\frac{3}{16}$	50 ,, 60 yds.	11 ozs.	13 ,, 14 ft.
3⅞	35/-	1$\frac{4}{16}$	60 ,, 80 yds.	13 ozs.	14 ,, 15 ft.
4⅛	37/6	1$\frac{6}{16}$	80 ,, 100 yds.	15 ozs.	15 ,, 16 ft.
4⅜	40/-	1$\frac{8}{16}$	80 ,, 100 yds.	17 ozs.	16 ,, 17 ft.
4⅝	45/-	1$\frac{9}{16}$	100 ,, 120 yds.	20 ozs.	17 ,, 18 ft.
4⅞	50/-	1$\frac{10}{16}$	120 ,, 140 yds.	22 ozs.	18 ,, 19 ft.
5⅛	55/-	1$\frac{10}{16}$	120 ,, 150 yds.	24 ozs.	19 ,, 20 ft.

☞ FOR GUT CASTS, SEE PAGE 86 TO 88.

Hardy's "Field" Reel.

(Special contracted pattern for dry fly, &c.)

(PATENT.)

This contracted form is only made in the sizes given below.
For regular sizes see page 95.

A new form of our popular "Field" Reel, specially designed for dry fly, and general trout and sea trout fishing. The Reel is much contracted for quick winding of the line, and practically serves the purpose of a multiplier without the complication of cogwheels. Made partly in our new "Alumin," with wearing parts of aluminium bronze and steel. By this arrangement a reel of larger diameter than usual may be employed.

Diameter.	Price.	Width between Plates.	Line carrying capacity.	Weights.	Suitable for Rods.
$3\frac{1}{8}$	26/6	$1\frac{3}{16}$	30 to 35 yds.	7 ozs.	9 to 10 ft.
$3\frac{3}{8}$	30/-	$1\frac{3}{16}$	35 ,, 40 yds.	9 ozs.	10ft. to 10ft. 6in.
$3\frac{5}{8}$	32/6	$1\frac{3}{16}$	40 ,, 45 yds.	11 ozs.	10ft. 6in. to 12ft.
$3\frac{7}{8}$	35/-	$1\frac{3}{16}$	40 ,, 50 yds.	12 ozs.	12 to 14 ft.

☞ See also our "Perfect" Reel, page 99, arranged on the same system.

IN ORDERING FROM THIS LIST PLEASE QUOTE LETTER **G**

Hardy's "Uniqua" Reel (Patent).

For Trout.

A style of Reel, similar in shape to our contracted "Perfect." The frame and body are solid. It is very light, quick winding and strong.

By unseating spring holder on spindle end, the drum can be removed in an instant without the aid of any tools.

Illustration is the 3⅛ size.

Dia. in inches.	Price.	Weight in ozs.
2⅝	15/6	3¼
2⅞	16/6	3½
3⅛	17/6	4
3⅜	18/6	4½
3⅝	21/-	5¼

For Salmon.

As the "Uniqua" trout reel has proved such a great success, we have added the following sizes in order that it may be used for Salmon fishing. In these sizes it is the same width and proportions as our "Perfect" Salmon Reel. They are made in our patent Alumin, very light and strong. In two parts only. By slackening the large screw on washer at end of spindle, the drum can be instantly removed.

Dia. in ins.	Price.	Weight in ozs.
3½	22/6	9
3¾	25/-	11
4	27/6	12½
4¼	30/-	14½
4½	33/-	16

A better reel than is listed as best by other makers. It is second only to the "Perfect."

The "Saint George" Fly Reel.
MODEL 1911.
(PATENT APPLIED FOR)

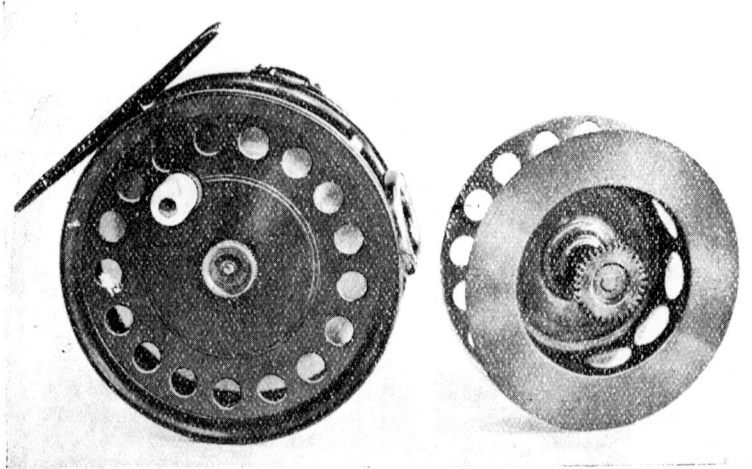

FIG. 1.   FIG. 2.

An entirely new design in trout fly reels, which promises to be a great favourite. The size ($3\frac{3}{4}$ in.) means of course, great line carrying capacity, and very quick recovery of the line in winding. The drum, as may be seen from diagram 2, is of unique design, cast in one solid piece and cut out. The spindle is of finest tool steel; the bridge, tongue, ratchet wheel and all working parts are of cast steel, properly hardened.

To remove the drum for cleaning, the circular nut on end of spindle, should be turned to the right to unscrew, (as the screw is left-handed), when the drum may be taken out. We had a few made up last season for private trial, and used them on both river and loch, with much satisfaction. The arrangement of the check work, is of an entirely new and improved design, whereby wear and tear is reduced to a minimum.

At present we are only making this reel in the $3\frac{3}{4}$ in size. The frame is fitted with agate line guard, and regulating check work, similar to that in the " Perfect."

Size, $3\frac{3}{4}$ in.   Weight, $6\frac{1}{2}$ ozs.   Price, 45/-.

Line carrying capacity 80 to 90 yards, according to thickness.

The agate line guard you fitted to my reel is a beautiful piece of work-manship. It saves the line considerably, and prevents grooves wearing in the sides of the reel. It entirely prevents the line catching up behind the reel.
LONDON.   J. N. H.

☞ IN ORDERING FROM THIS LIST PLEASE QUOTE LETTER U.

The "Saint George" Fly Reels

For Trout, Sea Trout, etc.

(Patent Nos. 24245 ; 9261 ; and U.S.A. 369867).

| Fig. 1. | Fig. 2. |

Fig. 1 shows the original check reel assembled, and Fig. 2 the mechanism of the new Silent Brake Pattern, the line drum being removed.

A beautiful and practical design in trout and sea-trout fly reels. The large contracted drum means, of course, great line carrying capacity, and very quick recovery of the line in winding. The drum is of unique design, cast in one solid piece and cut out. The spindle is of the finest tool steel ; the tongue, ratchet wheel and all working parts are of cast steel, properly hardened.

To remove the drum for cleaning, the trigger of the latch catch on end of spindle (see Fig. 1) is pulled over with the forefinger, when the drum may be taken out.

The frame is fitted with agate line guard similar to that in the contracted "Perfect" (see page 131).

No. 1. Fitted with Patent Compensating Check Action as in the "Perfect" reels (see page 131).

No. 2. Fitted with Regulating Silent Brake as Fig. 2 above.

The brake action in the No. 2 pattern (Fig. 2) is silent and can be adjusted to any desired tension by the regulator C, which actuates through spring B on to lever A. Spring D holds lever A in place when the drum is removed and so permits easy replacement.

Size.	Approx. Weight.	Line Carrying Capacity.	Price.
3 in.	$4\frac{1}{2}$ ozs.	50 to 60 yards.	72/6.
$3\frac{3}{8}$ in.	$5\frac{1}{2}$ ozs.	60 to 70 yards.	75/6
$3\frac{3}{4}$ in.	$6\frac{1}{2}$ ozs.	70 to 90 yards.	80/-

I know no better trout fly reels than your "Saint George" pattern, they are light and most serviceable.

Johannesburg.   J. H. D.

FOR SOLID LEATHER REEL CASES, SEE PAGE 137.

The "Saint George" Salmon Fly Reel.

(1920 Model.)

FITTED WITH COMPENSATING BRAKE CHECK and "SILENT WIND-
IN" ACTION.   Pat. Nos. 24245; 9261; and U.S.A. 369867.

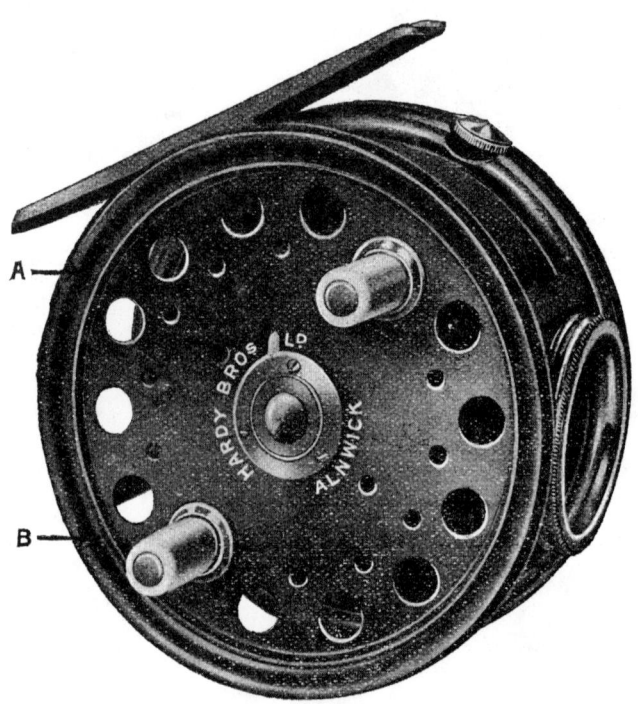

A form of the "St. George" reel designed to meet the requirements of salmon anglers who prefer a light reel with large line-
carrying capacity.

In design it is similar to the "St. George" trout reels, page 132,
and is fitted with patent regulating compensating check (as in the
"Perfect," page 127) with the addition that the winding-in action is
silent.   The frame, which is fitted with two handles and metal line
guard, may be had with a section cut away from *A* to *B* exposing
the flange of the line drum, so that extra breaking power may be
applied with the thumb or forefinger when desired.

A beautiful and practical salmon fly-reel, **size 4¼ ins., weight approx.
14½ oz.** line-carrying capacity, 100 yards.   **Price 110/-.**

The " St. George " Junior Fly Reel

Pat. Nos. 24245, 9261 and U.S.A. 369867.

← Agate Line Guards

This little reel $2\frac{9}{16}''$ diameter and weighing only $3\frac{1}{2}$ ozs., is the counterpart of the St. George reel which has been so great a favourite for many years. It has been specially designed to correctly balance with our various patterns of light weight Fly Rods. The illustration above is the handle of a $7\frac{1}{2}$ ft. Marvel (page 262) and "St. George Junior."

Line carrying capacity 35 yds., I.E.I. and 20 yds. No. 2 Solidae Silk Backing "Corona Superba," Price **53/6.** Spare Drums, **24/-** each.

The "Saint George" Multiplying Fly Reel

Pat. Nos. 24245, 9261 and U.S.A. 369867.

Designed to give quick recovery of line in dry fly fishing when so often the line is pulled in with the left hand in fishing out a cast and allowed to fall on the ground from where it cannot be rapidly recovered with a single action reel when a fish is hooked. When changing from one place to another it is of great assistance in getting the line and fly off the water before they become "drowned" and also an advantage when a fish runs towards the angler.

Gear ratio, 2 to 1.

The $3\frac{3}{4}$ size is designed specially for dry fly fishing for salmon using a light single-handed rod.

Size.	Line Carrying Capacity	Price.	Size.	Line Carrying Capacity.	Price.
$3\frac{3}{8}''$	60-70 yds.	**77/6**	$3\frac{3}{4}''$	110-115 yds.	**84/-**

Spare Drums, **24/6** and **26/-** each.

FOR " L.R.H. " DRY FLY ROD, SEE PAGE 248.

1930

81

Hardy's "Saint John" Fly Reel

(1923 Model). Patent No. 9261.

The original reel Mr. John James Hardy had made for his own use, when trout fishing, using a light weight rod. The special features are, lightness in weight, and large contracted line drum, which means quick recovery of the line and command of a fish. The No. 1 reel carries 35 yds. of double tapered line and is specially suitable for use with light rods as the "Fairy," etc. The No. 2 with special line drum, carries 35 yds. of double tapered line and 80 yds. No. 2 silk backing. It is designed for dry fly fishing for Salmon, etc., when using a light single-handed rod, see pages 34 and 260.

Made of special alumin alloy, in two parts only. Fitted with regulating "Compensating" check, with duplicate spring and pawl (see page 129).

To dismount reel, pull over the lever of latch with the forefinger.

Diameter, $3\frac{7}{8}$ ins. ; width between plates of line drum, $\frac{15}{16}$ in. ; approximate weight, $6\frac{1}{4}$ ozs.

Line Carrying Capacity, 40 yds. Price, Pattern No. 1 and No. 2, **52/-** each.

PARIS, 14/3/22.

I want to tell you how satisfied I am with the "Filip" line. I always used your "Corona," and it was the first trial I had of the "Filip." I find casting much easier, and with less effort than with the ordinary double tapered lines, and especially when you have a long line out, it gives very much less strain to the rod, thus increasing the quickness of the action. L. DE L. CHOMEL.

Hardy's New "U.S.A." Fly Reels

WITH " RADIO " SILENT VARIABLE BRAKE.   (Pat. No. 9788.)

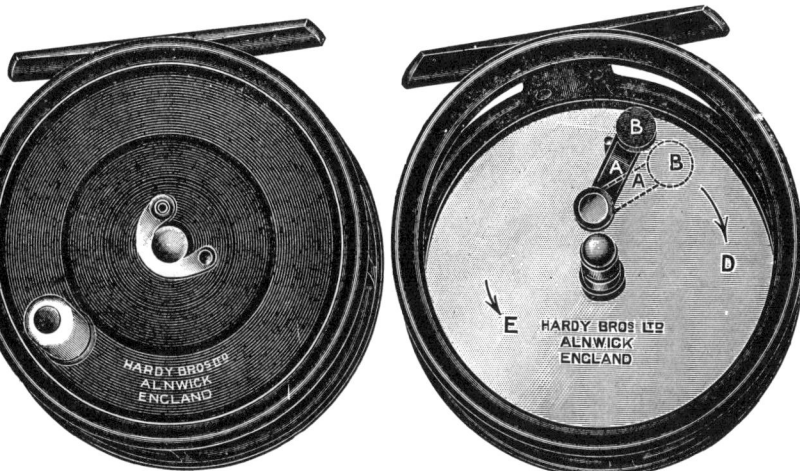

FIG. 1.   FIG. 2.

Similar in design to the " Uniqua," made in two solid parts of special " Alumin." To take out the drum, unseat spring on spindle end with the finger-nail.

This patent " Radio " action is an entirely new departure in silent brake mechanism. It embodies the important feature of an automatic variable pressure brake. The " wind in " is easy and pleasant, while the reverse action, as on a fish taking off line, is automatically and gradually increased.

Illustration (Fig. 1) shows the interior of the reel. The spring arm A carries the friction pad B, which is in contact with the inner face of the line drum, and is free to move in either direction D or E. The face of the line drum is designed so that with the inner face of the frame it forms a wedge-shaped space gradually increasing from the periphery to the centre of the reel.

On rotating the line drum in the direction of D, as in winding line, the arm A, with pad B, is moved to the position shown by the dotted lines, that is, towards the base of the wedge. In this position the tension is light and gives a pleasant wind in. On reversing the action, in the direction of E, as when a fish is running, the arm A is instantly carried towards the periphery of the reel, into the narrower part of the wedge, when the pressure is automatically increased.

Sizes	$2\frac{5}{8}$ in.	$2\frac{7}{8}$ in.	$3\frac{1}{8}$ in.	$3\frac{3}{8}$ in.	4 in.	$4\frac{1}{4}$ in.
Prices	**23/-**	**26/-**	**27/6**	**30/-**	**43/6**	**47/6**

F

The "SUNBEAM" Fly Reel
For Trout, etc.

Made of "Alumin," in two parts and fitted with line guard, the check work is our "Compensating" design, and spares may be had guaranteed to fit. Price **1/-** per tongue or spring.

Dia. in ins.	Approx. weight.	Price.
$2\frac{3}{4}$	4 ozs.	**14/6**
3	4 ozs. 10 drms.	**15/6**
$3\frac{1}{4}$	4 ozs. 12 drms.	**16/6**

IMPROVED REEL GRIP
Patent No. 272409

The illustration shows a patent Screw Grip Reel Fitting with the palm of a reel in position on a rod butt. The outer face of the reel palm is screwed as **C** to the same pitch as the locking sleeve **D** and the slide **B** in the screw grip fitting. The sleeve **D** securely locks the reel palm, slide and rod handle together. All our reels are now made with the screw grip palm.

The " Cascapedia " Reel

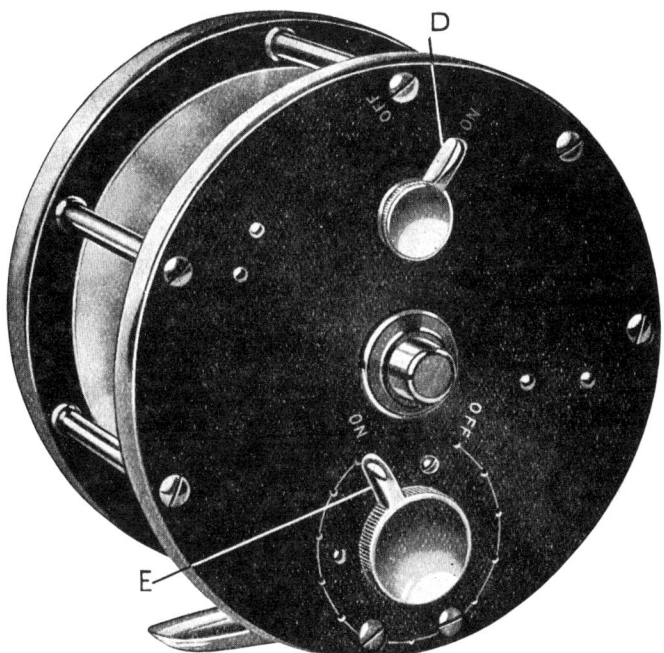

There are two revolving pillars, to suit either for " rings down " or " rings up " style of fishing.

The reels are also fitted with two segments of hardened rustless steel, which protect the line and prevent the ebonite plate wearing when the line is pulled over it. As all moving parts of the reel can be oiled from the outside, there is no need to dismount it.

A sound, practical engineering job of the very highest quality.

No.	DIA.	LINE CAPACITY.	SUITABLE FOR RODS.	PRICE.
1/0	$3\frac{1}{8}''$	35 yds. I.C.I. Corona Superba & 100 yds. No. 2 silk backing.	General Trout Rods.	**140/-**
2/0	$3\frac{3}{8}''$	35 yds. I.B.I. Corona Superba & 100 yds. No. 2 silk backing.	12' and $12\frac{1}{2}'$ and strong shorter Rods.	**145/-**
3/0	$3\frac{5}{8}''$	42 yds. No. 6 Corona Superba & 80 yds. No. 3 silk backing.	13', 14' and 14' 6".	**155/-**

We recommend the 12 ft. " Gold Medal " as a most suitable rod for use with the 2/0 reel.

The " Barton " Dry Fly Reel

THE IDEAL REEL FOR DRY FLY FISHERMEN

This reel has been designed at the suggestion of Dr. Barton, the President of the Flyfishers Club, to produce an ideal reel for Dry Fly Fishermen.

The outstanding features of this reel are :

1. The reel weighs 7¾ ozs. which at this weight helps to balance the rod in the hand.

2. The plates of the drum are parallel to each other and not domed as is usual, so that the line when being wound on cannot fall over itself and thus cause a tangle, jambing itself at a critical moment when it ought to be free to pay out to a running fish.

3. The rim is extra strong in order to resist any chance blow or fall, which by bending the rim would cause the revolving drum to seize. For the same reason a slightly larger clearance is allowed between rim and drum.

4. A comfortable handle is provided.

5. The line guard permits the line to have access to the full width of the drum, and possessing a smooth round surface it saves the line and edges of the reel.

6. The many teeth of the ratchet wheel convert a noisy clatter into a pleasant purr.

7. The check can be regulated from the lightest run out to one capable of preventing over-run even with a strong fish.

8. The saddle is made with the ends of unequal length so that when the reel is used with rods which have their reel seats at the extreme end of the butt, the reel does not project beyond the end of the rod, thus the reel is protected from any blow on the ground when the rod is grounded.

Size, 3 ins. diameter.

Weight, 7¾ ozs.

Line Carrying Capacity—35 yds. I.C.I. "Corona" with 40 yds. No. 2 "Solidae" Silk Backing.

Price   -   -   - **63/-**

The " FORTUNA " Fly Reels

Made under licence " Andreas " Patent No. 123405.

These reels are made of special " Alumin " alloy which withstands the action of salt and fresh water, and are fitted with a quickly adjustable silent brake, the invention of Mr. H. Andreas of New Zealand. This brake is applied by turning the washer A to the right. When the line is running out, as in playing a fish, the handles remain stationary, so that the pressure may be altered without fear of injury to the hand.

To dismount the reel, unscrew B and take out drum with handle bar and washer A.

The 3½ in. size is suitable for use with a stout single-handed rod for sea or large lake trout; the 4¼ in. and 5 in. are excellent salmon fly or trolling reels.

Size			3½ in.	4¼ in.	5 in.
Price	-	-	75/-	100/-	150/-

For 6 in. and 7 in. sizes for Big Game fishing see page 339.

The "Lightweight" Trout Fly Reel
WEIGHS ONLY 3¼ OZS.

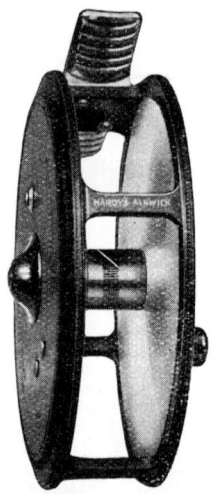

Made of our special aluminium alloy. $3\frac{3}{16}$ in. dia. Contracted drum for quick winding, holds 35 yards I.C.I. double tapered Corona line and 30 yards No. 2 silk backing. Drum easily taken out for cleaning. All parts of best material and workmanship. A very fine looking reel. Weight 3¼ ozs.   Price, **35/-**.

The "DAVY" Reel

Designed to meet the requirements of M. B. Davy, Esq., who desired a quick winding light reel to balance with the special dry fly rod we made for him—see page 256. Made of "Alumin." The drum is bushed with phosphor bronze and runs on a high grade steel spindle. Fitted with our patent compensating check and spare parts with screw regulator, two winding handles, size $3\frac{1}{2}''$ dia. $\times \frac{1\,7}{3\,2}''$ between plates.

Capacity 35 yds., I.C.I. "Corona" line, and 20 yds. No. 2 "Solidae" Silk Binding. Price **47/6**. Weight 6 ozs.

HARDY'S
PATENT "SILEX" REEL.

The new form for all kinds of Spinning, Prawning, or General Coarse Fishing.

A is the lever for
working drag on
barrel.

WEYBRIDGE, January, 1897.

I am immensely pleased with the new reel. I can throw just as far as with the ordinary loose barrel Nottingham reel, but the curse of fast reels is practically done away with by the new check arrangement. During the whole afternoon I only had one slight over-run, and that entirely my own fault, through trying too much—endeavouring to reach an impossible distance. I consider the reel invaluable, especially to beginners. I find the throw can be regulated with ease; the adjustable check put on with the finger for a moment and then released, the bait falling steadily into the water, and the final pace slackening properly. I was quite surprised to find I could do so well with it on the first trial. The silent check is excellent, no jar or scraping.

CHAS. H. WHEELEY.

The Patent "Silex" Reel is especially intended for spinning and prawning for salmon, spinning for pike, Thames trouting, &c. and as a general reel for all kinds of spinning or float fishing.

There is nothing made which approaches this reel for ease in working. It differs from all other reels used for this class of work, as in winding up after a cast there is no turning of the reel or putting on of check necessary. and it wears out spinning lines *less* quickly than any other form. For full particulars and manner of using, see pages 38 to 41.

Sizes	...	3	3½	4	4½ inches.
Prices	...	25/-	30/-	35/-	40/-
Weight	...		7½ ozs.	10½ ozs.	

FOR NEW SPINNING ROD, SEE PAGE 195.

1897

DIAGRAM

Shewing Positions in Casting a Prawn or Spinner from Hardy's
Patent " Silex " Reel, see page 107.

THIS illustratio
shews the corre
positions in castin
a prawn or spinne
with our new pater
"Silex" reel, directio
of stream indicate
by the arrows.

Position (1) Angler
face to river, with ro
as at F in fishin
feet at A.A. Positio
(2) Angler's face fror
river, holding rod a
at C, preparatory t
making a cast, feet a
at B.B.

Stand on positio
A.A., reel up you
line until not mor
than 1½ yards pro
jects from rod poin
make a right whe
until your feet are o
positions B.B , rod a
C. Swing bait gent
to and fro a few time
press your finger o
the little projectio
on reel, then with
steady, sweeping, up
ward motion, cas
your bait towards G
at same time turnin
to the left into posi
tion A.A. again. I
doing this, when yo
come to D try t
carry the rod to E a
nearly as possible a
right angles to th
river, by drawing th
elbows in as you approac
E. This will cause you
bait to go straight. Th
stroke or cast must be stopped a
or before reaching E. If thi
has been done correctly, and th
bait dropped at G, commence to reel up
holding rod as in position F, as fast a
the nature of the stream or pool may
require.

Bear in mind that at the moment o
casting, you are to press the little knob on reel, and that when your bait has travelled abou
half the intended distance, or less, remove the finger smartly from the knob, when the weigh
of the bait will draw off sufficent line. A little practice on the grass with one or two ounc
leads will help. Begin with the heavier, and gently make short casts until you can plac
your bait straight, and lengthen a few yards at a time. When you can do fairly well wit
the heavy lead, try with the lighter one.

HARDY'S PATENT
"SILEX" REEL

The new form for all kinds of Spinning, Prawning, and General Coarse Fishing.

THE "SILEX" REEL
HARDYS PAT ALNWICK

A is the lever for working drag on barrel.

The Patent "Silex" Reel is especially intended for spinning and prawning for salmon and pike, Thames trouting, &c., and as a general reel for all kinds of spinning or float fishing.

There is nothing made which approaches it for ease in working. It differs from all other reels used for this class of work, as in winding up after a cast there is no turning of the reel or putting on of check necessary, and it wears out spinning lines *less* quickly than any other form.

Sizes	...	3	3½	3¾	4	4½	inches
Prices	...	25/-	30/-	32/6	35/-	40/-	
Weight	...	5½ ozs.	7 ozs.	8 ozs.	10 ozs.	11 ozs.	

DEAR SIRS,—I have given your newest pattern "Silex" Winch a good trial, and can speak most favourably of its action.

I find no difficulty in making long throws from it with 1oz. (one ounce). The arrangement of the "brake" or check for preventing over-running is excellent and very ingenious. The only time there can be any trouble is when one throws with too much force. When the catch is released towards the end of the throw the bait does not stop dead, but falls nicely on the water.

The workmanship leaves nothing to be desired; there seems to be no possibility of sticking or straining. The winch runs easily and truly, and, in my opinion, very little, if any, difficulty will be found in its management by anglers who have hitherto neglected throwing from the winch, if they will throw gently at first.—Faithfully yours,

CHARLES H. WHEELEY, Ed. of "Coarse Fishing" n the Angler's Library, &c.

Bait Casting Extraordinary —"On Saturday, October 8th, 1898, at the Gresham Angling Society's tournament, Mr. J. T. Emery, using a 2¼ oz. bait, a "Hardy" Murdoch steel-centre built cane rod, and a "Hardy" patent "Silex" winch, succeeded in reaching the enormous distance of **87 yards 2 feet.** This is the world's greatest record for casting direct from the reel reported."—*Fishing Gazette, Rod and Gun, Sportsman,* &c.

For mode of using the "Silex" Reel see page 35.　　　Ask for Special Pamphlet.

☞ IN ORDERING FROM THIS LIST PLEASE QUOTE LETTER H.

Hardy's Patent "Silex" Reels,

With Jewelled Bearings.

Acknowledged the best for all kinds of Spinning, Prawning, and General Fishing.

Fig. 1.

K. Regulating screw.
J. Automatic presser brake lever.
F. Adjustable auxiliary check lever.   (Fig. 2.)

Fig. 2.
Reel Frame with Line Drum removed.

A. Automatic presser brake which, under pressure of spring B, bears on hub D (*see* Fig. 3 and dotted line on this illustration).   J is operating lever.   G is the tongue of adjustable auxiliary check worked by spring H.   F is the operating lever for throwing into gear with ratchet wheel E (*see* dotted line) The lever F and tongue G are shown out of gear.

The advantages of this Reel are :—

1.—**Great Strength and Stability combined with Lightness.** This is gained by rigidity of construction, and the use of a special light but strong aluminium alloy. The frame (including all pillars and ring) and the flanged line drum are cast in one *solid piece*. doing away with the usual screws and piecing up of the parts. The spindle is made of the finest tool steel available, and runs on a jewelled bearing.

2.—**Perfect control of the Line Drum.** This is effected by the action of the automatic presser brake A (*see* Fig. 2), which, on being released in making a cast, instantly takes command of and controls the drum, so that OVER-RUNNING IN CASTING IS PREVENTED.

3.—**The Adjustable Auxiliary Check** is fitted in a very superior manner. The pawl G Fig. 2 being held underneath a hardened steel bridge, and working on a leg ground solid on this bridge. The operating lever is fitted in an ingenious manner ; and the movement being on the circle works smoothly without undue friction. This check is intended to be used as soon as a fish is struck, and is instantly brought into action by a simple motion of the forefinger on lever F.

4.—**Perfect Workman= ship.** This is of a higher order than has ever before been applied to spinning reels. The reel throughout is constructed as well as engineering skill and best materials can make it, with a view to producing an article most perfectly adapted for the purpose for which it is intended, and to enable sportsmen to perform, what has always been a more or less difficult operation, easily.

The New Bait Casting Reel—
The "SILEX" No. 2 PATENT.

FIG. 1.

FIG. 2.   FIG. 3.

A.   Controlling lever.
B.   Hub of spool which is controlled by
C.   Pressure lever.
D.   Spiral spring (connecting levers A and C), which exerts an
        elastic pressure on hub B when in contact.
E.   Main spring.   G.   Ratchet.
F.   Regulator.   H.   Fig 3, Ratchet wheel.

NOTE.—Part of B and H are only shown, to illustrate the position of these parts, when drum is on spindle.

The "SILEX" No. 2 Spinning Reel

This new Casting Reel, the No. 2 "Silex," is at once the climax and perfection of all casting reels. The action is so simple, and so easy, that anyone may use it.   See page 35.

REGULATING THE REEL.

In the first place, the reel must be regulated to suit the weight of the bait, about to be used. Hold up the rod at an angle of about 20 degrees to the body, with about four feet of the line and trace projecting from its point. Press the lever in the direction of the rod and hold it firmly ; then turn the regulating screw F to the left until the reel is free, and the bait falls to the ground ; now turn the screw to the right, until the reel is just stiff enough, to lift the bait without turning the spool. **Don't forget that the lever must be gripped firmly, while the regulating is being done.**

TO MAKE A CAST.

The rod should be held as shown in diagram (page 146), the body being slightly turned to the right. The bait should then be gently swung to and fro to get a little momentum, and just as it reaches the top of the backward movement, the cast should be made up and over the place where the bait is intended to alight ; at the same instant **the lever A, must be pressed towards the rod by the left forefinger, and held firmly in that position, until the bait touches the water.** The instant the finger is removed, the ratchet returns automatically into check. In this reel, there is **no throwing on of the check after hooking a fish ;** no manipulation of the reel in any form is required. The whole thing is so absolutely simple, that if these directions are followed, one will become expert in a very short time. It should always be remembered, that in this method of casting, it is necessary, to aim at a point considerably to the right of where you want the bait to fall, but this, is only necessary in initial practice. After a short time the action becomes quite natural, so that one merely looks at the place where the bait is intended to go, and *it goes.*

In making a cast with this new type of reel, the mechanical action may be explained by reference to diagram 2, as follows :—The first movement of the lever A, frees the drum ; the second part of the movement, brings lever C against the hub of the drum B, slightly retarding it, by the elastic pressure of spring D, and eventually stopping it when desired.   The moment the lever is released, the spring E forces the check automatically into action, when the reel is under perfect control.

PRICES OF "SILEX No. 2" REELS.

Size.				Price.
3¼ in.	..	..	..	..	**35/-**
3½ in.	..	..	..	..	**37/6**
3¾ in.	..	..	..	..	**40/-**
4 in.	..	..	..	..	**45/-**
4¼ in.	..	..	..	..	**48/-**
4½ in.	..	..	..	..	**52/-**
4½ in. Special Mahseer	..	..	**60/-**

WHAT OTHERS THINK ABOUT HARDY'S PAT. No. 2 "SILEX" REEL.

Extract from "THE FIELD," October 8th, 1910.

THE NEW FORM OF "SILEX" REEL.

The merits of Messrs. Hardy Bros., Ltd., "Silex" spinning reel are well known and appreciated, as is shown by the number of anglers who use it. We have lately been giving trial to the new form of it which has lately been devised TO MAKE CASTING EASIER. OUR TRIAL SATISFIED US THAT THESE CLAIMS ARE JUSTIFIED. We used the 3¼-inch reel, and were surprised to find how light a weight it would throw. A bullet weighing a quarter of an ounce could easily be cast 25 to 30 yards, which is quite as much as one wants for ordinary trout fishing. The adjustment of brake pressure by the screw F is very sensitive and delicate, and can easily be manipulated.

The new casting reel, the "Silex" No. 2, is a most perfect little reel, and the essence of simplicity. Liability to over-run is practically eliminated; indeed, with a little practice and proper adjustment there should never be the least tendency to do so. IT WAS ENTIRELY DUE TO THIS REEL THAT I WAS ABLE TO WIN the gold medal for the ½ oz. accuracy event in Paris. As you know, I had never tried this kind of work ten days before the tournament, and the reel's smooth performance in this event, where practically every variety of reel was most capably represented, puts it clearly ahead of all others as a fishing reel, and in capable hands it will, I am sure, prove its superiority in distance casting.

REGD. D. HUGHES.

Extract from the "FISHING GAZETTE," July, 1911.

Mr. Emery, who used a No. 2 "Silex," commenced to cast, and at his third attempt he made an enormous CAST of 309 ft. 6 in. This constitutes a world's record, a truly remarkable cast.

The remarkable casting of Mr. A. Piercy with the light float tackle and 1¼ drms. of shot on the cast is worthy of some mention. Using an 8¼ ft. "Victor" rod and a 3¼ in. No. 2 "Silex" reel, he got his four casts well inside the court, every one of which was over the previous world's record.

I have thoroughly mastered the No. 2 "Silex" reel, and can cast splendidly with it. It is marvellous the distance one can cast with this reel and the "Victor" rod. The wonderful part of it is THE LINE HAS NEVER ONCE OVER-RUN. Spinning all day without a tangle is indeed a new and enjoyable experience.

ST. CATHARINE'S, ONTARIO, CANADA.   A. MOWER.

I have two of your No. 1 "Silex" reels, and thought them grand, and so they are, but THE No. 2 IS SIMPLY SPLENDID, and I am delighted with it.

HAMILTON.   J. GETTINGS JOHNSTON.

I am especially pleased with the "St. George" fly reel, which I consider one of the best pieces of angling mechanism I have ever seen. The No. 2 "Silex" bait casting reel impresses me fully as well. I have been using your reels for the past 6 years, and not one of them has ever failed to perform efficiently at all times.

AVERY ISLAND, U. S. AMERICA.   C. WILLIS WARD.

I had my first days fishing yesterday with the "Silex" No. 2. It is everything you say as regards its working. No man with any hands could have any difficulty in using it. I got into my first good fish of the season and the reel worked beautifully, and I landed him successfully.

OMAGH.   R. McCORMACK, MAJOR.

1913

THE "MR. J. J. HARDY" NEW METHOD OF USING THE "SILEX" REEL

Positions,   1.   2.   3.

Hardy's "Silex Major" and "Silex Minor" Casting Reels

Patent Nos. 2206, 21131, and 4163, Feb. 1922.

The illustration on page 138 shows the "Silex Major" reel, acknowledged the climax of all reels used for bait casting.

The "Silex" is now made in two forms, "Major" and "Minor." The "Major" embodies all latest improvements, and is virtually the "Silex de Luxe," the last word in casting reels. It is fitted with our new regulator; ratchet check; **"Silent Wind In"** action; jewelled bearing and latch fastener, in sizes $3\frac{3}{4}$ in., 4 in., $4\frac{1}{4}$ in. and $4\frac{1}{2}$ in. The sizes 3 in., $3\frac{1}{4}$ in. and $3\frac{1}{2}$ in., and the $4\frac{1}{2}$ Ex. Wide, are not fitted with 'Silent Wind In.'

The "Silex Minor" is made in sizes 3 in., $3\frac{1}{4}$ in., $3\frac{1}{2}$ in., $3\frac{3}{4}$ in. and 4 in. They are lower priced reels not having a regulator, and instead of a ratchet check have a silent variable brake. They are fitted with jewelled bearings and latch fastener, and are in all other respects identical to the "Major" in design.

Since the introduction of the "Silex" reel in 1892 we have received thousands of testimonials from clients in all parts of the world, expressing the greatest satisfaction.

1923

The Pat. "Silex Major" or "Minor"

WITH RECTANGULAR LEVER.   REGISTERED No. 557604.

FOR SINGLE-HANDED CASTING.

As shown by the diagram, reels for single-handed work have a special (registered and patented) form of lever which is cranked at a right angle, so that it comes into the best possible position for the pressure of the thumb when casting. The sizes made in this style are 3 in., $3\frac{1}{4}$ in. and $3\frac{1}{2}$ in., the latter may be had with either straight or cranked lever.

The working parts are the same as in the reel for double-handed casting previously described. It is unnecessary, therefore, to repeat the instructions, further than to say that the thumb of the right hand is used, in place of the forefinger of the left hand, as in casting with the larger reel (see pages 20 and 145).

With this form of reel, either the side-swing or overhead cast may be performed : for angling we advise the former wherever possible. We have already described the side-swing cast on page 143, and will now describe the overhead.

The regulator in the "Major" pattern is set to the weight of the bait as described on page 142.

The diagram on opposite page shows position of the hand for either side-swing or overhead casting.

The "SILEX MULTIPLIER" Casting Reels

Patent Nos. 2206, 21131 and 4163, February 1922.

These reels are specially designed for casting light baits, and are made in two sizes, $2\frac{3}{4}''$ for trout, etc., and $3\frac{1}{2}''$ for salmon, etc.

The line drum is very accurately balanced and completely encased. It runs on very fine steel bearings, and during the cast is automatically disconnected from the handle plate. The handle remaining stationary when casting, greatly assists in distance and accuracy.

The winding-in action has a ratio of two-and-a-half to one, which gives considerable relief when recovering line in fishing out the cast; while it is a great advantage when spinning in low or shallow water.

The $2\frac{3}{4}$ in. size for trout, etc., is used above the rod when casting and winding in. This reel may be used either with single or double-handed rods; in the latter case we recommend the "J. J. H." method of casting with both hands behind the reel (see Fig. I, opposite page 136).

The $3\frac{1}{2}$ in. reel is designed for use with a double-handed rod, the reel being used below the rod when casting and winding in.

1927

The "SILEX MULTIPLIER" Reels (*continued*)

Illustration shows the reverse side of the reel.

Method of Using.—The action of the operating levers is similar to the "Silex Major" as illustrated and described on page 128.

The brake indicator is set by the regulator screw F, so that the pressure of the brake suits the weight of the bait to be used; by turning F to the right increases the pressure, while to the left decreases it. At the moment of making the throw, the lever G is pressed firmly towards the rod and held so until the bait is delivered. On releasing G, the parts automatically resume their original position, with check in action and handle engaged, ready for winding in.

Cleaning and Oiling.—All working parts can be oiled without taking the reel to pieces. B and C are the oil holes. We recommend that oil be introduced on a fine needle pushed well into the hole. To dismount, take out the three screws A, and pull off the back plate. To dismount the handle-plate, undo the centre screw, take the reel in the left hand and turn handle to the left.

Size 2¾ ins., carries 60 yds., No. 0, " Solidae " line.   Price **£5 5 0**

Size 3½ ins., carries 100 yds., No. 1, " Solidae " or
80 yds. No. 1 " Alnwick " Line.   -   -   -   ,,   **7 7 0**

SCARBOROUGH, 21/3/26.

I fished with the " Silex Multiplier " for a fortnight and caught 10 salmon with it, and had the luck to land one of 40½ lbs. The reel was a perfect success.

E. H. RUDGARD.

Hardy's " AUXILIARY " Brake

For Holding Strong and Heavy Fish.

Illustration shows a 4½ in. " Silex Major " reel, as used for Mahseer etc., fitted with the extra finger brake for holding strong fish.

The frame guard is cut and the brake hinged at B, where a spring is fitted to hold it in the " off " position as shown.   The brake is fitted at A with raw hide pads.   To apply extra pressure on a strong fish, press with the palm of the hand at A, and so bring the raw hide pads in contact with the outer flange of line drum.

This brake is supplied to new " Perfect " and " Uniqua " Fly reels, and " Silex Major " Casting reels, sizes, 3½ in. to 4½ ins., **12/6** extra. Fitted to existing reels, **15/-**

The "SUPER SILEX" Casting Reel

AND

METHOD

OF

USING

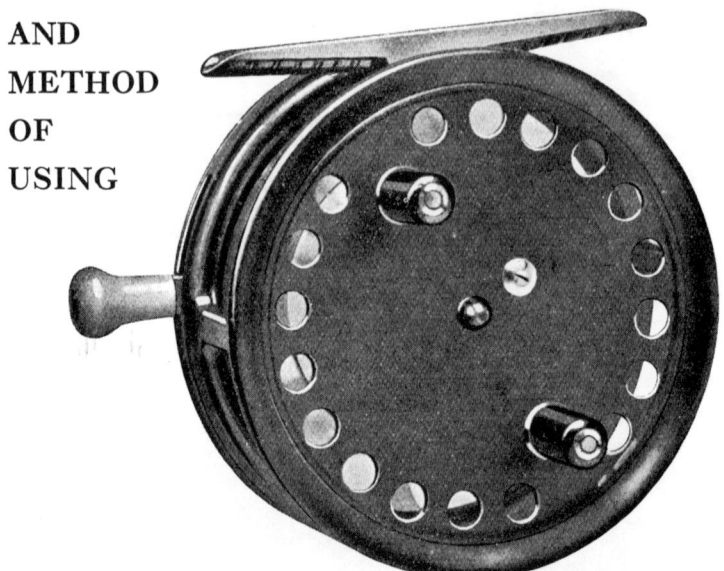

A LITTLE TALE OF THE "SILEX REEL."
IMPORTANT TO ANGLERS

Before the invention of the " Silex " method of casting a bait direct from the reel, the general method was to use what is called a " Nottingham " Reel. This in the hands of an expert was fairly good, but if attempted by the inexperienced, generally ended in disaster, from over-running and consequent entanglement. The control with the fingers was very difficult to acquire. The time had come when something more simple and effective was desirable—something any inexperienced angler could use with satisfaction—but what ? The answer was the " Silex " which with its simple external lever, could be used in a satisfactory manner by almost anyone. Naturally the demand for this reel soon became great. It, however, had one drawback, i.e. the check after casting the bait did not automatically engage at the end of the cast, ready to play a fish. After many experiments, this drawback was overcome when the reel was comparatively perfect, in which form it has been used with immense satisfaction for many years. The original " Silex " reel was then renamed the " Silex " (Major), and is perhaps the most popular casting reel in use in all parts of the world.

Some three years ago, however, Hardys developed a further improvement by which even **the most inexperienced** can make satisfactory casting, without any risk of over-running. During these last three years, experiments with this system have been made to satisfy our experts that it was a case of " ne plus ultra " before it was offered to the public (as our usual custom is). After careful consideration it was decided to retain the " Silex Major " as it is known to the public and to make another reel under the name of the " Super Silex " embodying all the features of the " Silex Major " and to add a simple action to enable the reel to be used **when casting without touching any part of it.** This is the point. Simply cast to the spot desired, and begin your " wind in." If a fish should come, strike from the winding hand, then touch the external lever, when the check gear will instantly engage.

It is all so perfect, so very simple and satisfactory, that all who have tried it are overjoyed and marvel at their success—even the " Silex " expert will be delighted.

In order that the present possessors of " Silex Major " Reels may enjoy the benefit of this new action, we will be pleased to fit it to existing reels for **10/6** each.

Regulating the " SUPER SILEX " Reel

Patent applied for for this Design of Regulator.

SHOWING INDICATORS ON BACK.

The Regulator Indicator and dial " A " are only to be used if it is desired to use this reel as the " Silex Major," described fully on page 128.

When the reel is to be used without touching it in any way with the hands set the Indicator " A " to " Heavy "—so that Indicator " C " may be used. The Indicator and Dial " C " are for use when it is desired to cast without in any way touching the reel.

Set the pointer to give the braking power required for the weight of bait you are using and the conditions under which you are fishing.   Position No. 3 in any size of reel will be found to suit most of the weights of baits within the capacity of any particular reel.

Having performed this simple job you have nothing more to do with the reel.   Simply grip the rod and cast, then wind in.

When a fish is hooked, to engage the ratchet check, simply " flick " the lever " B " upwards.

The rim of the frame is cut away to enable the fingers to be applied to the drum to assist in braking a fish or in casting.

The " Super Silex " reel can be cast with in the following methods :

1. Without touching the reel in any way.
2. As an ordinary " Silex Major " (see previous pages).
3. As an absolutely free running reel.
4. With a light brake pressure and releasing the drum from the fingers.
5. Releasing the line from the finger and thumb grip without touching the reel.
6. Releasing the line from the thumb pressing it against the cork handle of the rod (the method adopted by the late R. B. Marston, Esq.) without touching the reel.

The new Indicator and Dials are very helpful to enable users to remember what positions suit best with different baits and under varying conditions.

See the following pages.

Methods of using the " SUPER SILEX "

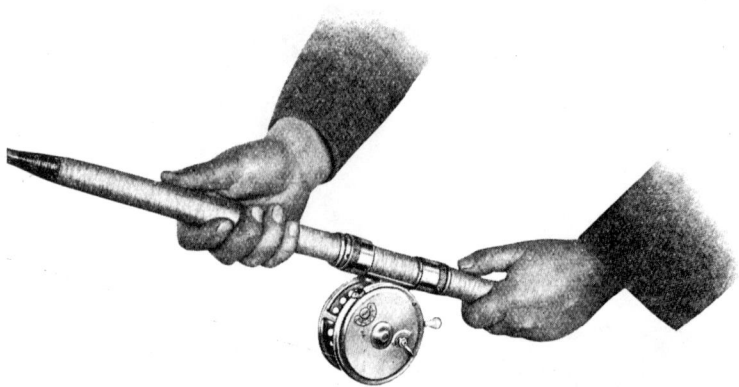

Fig. 1. Without touching the reel with the hands—notice the Indicator " A " is set at " Heavy," so that Indicator " C " may be used.   Indicator " C " is set at the required position.   Grasp the rod as shown and simply cast.   To engage the check " flick " up the main lever " B."

Fig. 2. This is a good method when light baits are used as the brake pressure may be set very light.   **To cast.**—Hold the drum with the fingers and release as the cast is made.   The drum may be controlled during the cast with the fingers. Follow the same directions as given with Fig. 1 regarding the indicators.

Methods of using the "SUPER SILEX"—*Contd.*

Fig. 3. Releasing from the line—a method favoured by many. The line is grasped between the finger and thumb of the forward hand and released as the cast is made. The line may be pressed against the cork handle with the thumb of the forward hand instead of being gripped between the finger and thumb. This method was used by the late R. B. Marston, Esq., editor of the *Fishing Gazette.*

As in Methods 1 and 2 follow the instructions regarding the indicators.

SUITABLE LINES, CARRYING CAPACITY AND PRICE.

Size of Reel.	Alnwick Spinning Line (Page 106).	Spliced to	Solidae Silk Backing (Page 108).	Cero Line (Page 107).	Price of Reel only.
	As under: Yds. No.		As under: Yds. No.	As under: Yds. No. Yds. No.	
3½"	60 1 only				
	or 60 0	,,	20 1	100 1	86/-
3¾"	60 2	,,	20 1	160 1½ or 100 2	88/-
	or 60 1	,,	40 1		
3¾" extra wide	100 1	,,	20 2		
	or 80 2	,,	30 2	160 2	93/-
4"	100 1	,,	20 2	160 2	93/-
	or 80 2	,,	30 2		
4¼"	100 2	,,	60 2		
	or 100 3	,,	40 2		99/6
4½"	100 3	,,	100 2		
	or 80 4	,,	100 2		106/-
4½" extra wide	100 4	,,	100 3		125/6

Note.—To obtain the most satisfactory Casting results **do not overcrowd the reel with line.**

The "Multiplying Super Silex" Reel

Pat. Nos. 21131, 196736, 288101.

Many Anglers find it desirable under certain conditions to recover baits more quickly than can comfortably be done with a single action reel. For instance when fishing a piece of "Dead Water," the spinner is much more life-like and attractive to the fish, when moving speedily through the water ; then sometimes the "lie" of the fish is on the far side of the stream, here it is desirable to recover the bait as quickly as possible after it has passed over the fish without the discomfort of winding very fast, on other occasions such as when fishing over shallows, etc., etc., the "multiplier" overcomes the trouble.

As the drum does not carry the handles it is lighter and better balanced, therefore it casts lighter baits than a reel the same size with handles. The rim of the drum is exposed to control the reel in casting or playing a fish. An excellent reel for light prawning and shrimping.

These Reels are made on exactly the same principles as our famous "Super Silex" Reels, and have in addition a multiplying gear, which is out of action when casting. The slogan "Do not touch the reel in casting, it will look after itself and will not over-run" applies equally to these Reels, as it does to the "Super Silex" Reels.

The " Multiplying Super Silex " Reel—*continued*

To Regulate the Reel.—By screwing the milled nut **A** more brake pressure or less is applied to the hub of the line spool. The arrow on the regulator disc **B** registers the pressure on the dial **C**. A rough-and-ready method of finding the brake pressure required is to hold the rod at about 45° to the ground with the bait trace and lead hanging from the rod's point, jerk the rod slightly and when the brake tension permits the Reel drum to make about one revolution it is about correct. Finer adjustment can be made during the first few casts. Having once set the Reel, the Angler can keep on casting without making any alteration, so long as he is using approximately the same weight of bait.

To cast.—First of all throw the gears out of engagement by pushing down the knob **D**. Do not touch the Reel. Hold the Rod as shown in Fig. 1, Page 154, and make an ordinary swing cast—without in any way touching the Reel. At the end of the cast knock up knob **D** when the gears will immediately engage ready to wind in. When the gears are engaged the ratchet check is in action. There is no separate movement to control this. This check is of our patent compensating type and is regulated by the milled button **E**.

This Reel is simplicity itself and cannot go wrong.

SIZE OF REEL.	ALNWICK SPINNING LINE (Page 125).	Spliced to	SOLIDAE SILK BACKING (Page 127).		CERO LINE (Page 126).		PRICE OF REEL ONLY.
	As under : Yds. No.		As under : Yds. No.		As under : Yds. No. Yds. No.		
3¼″	40 0		60 0		160 0 or 100 1		**100/-**
3½″	60 1 only				120 1 or		
	or 60 0	,,	20 1		100 1½		**105/-**
3½″ extra wide	60 2	,,	20 1				
	or 60 1	,,	40 1		140 1½ or 100 2		**110/-**

With Silent Wind In   -   **7/6** extra.

HINAIDI, 14/8/30.
Pleased to say I received the " Super Silex " etc. in good order on the 7th, it is everything you claim it to be ; what I like about it most, I think, is **the** rounded flange on the drum for hand control.   R. F. WEST.

I was rather nervous about it, but I am glad to say after a fortnight's fishing I am delighted with it.   JAMES A. YATES.

HOLM LEIGH STREET, SOMERSET.   Feb. 19th 1930.
Recently I sent for a couple of Artificial Pike baits to you, viz. a Gudgeon and a large sized Silver Devon Bar Spoon. Have only had the opportunity of trying the latter, but it is the best spoon I have ever used and most satisfactory to fish with.
ERNEST A. LITTEN.

1931

The 'Silex' Spinning Reel

The 'Silex Jewel'

With re-designed Automatic Brake Control

The 'Silex' reel was first designed and put on the market in 1896 when it soon became popular. With this reel J. T. Emery at the Gresham Angling Society's Tournament made the then record cast of 263 ft with a 2½-oz bait using a Hardy 'Murdoch' rod.

After this early reel followed the 'Silex' No. 2 in 1912, the 'Silex Major' in 1923, the 'Silex Multiplier' in 1924, the 'Super Silex' in 1928 and the 'Silex Rex' in 1937. All these reels were the subject of several patents. They were all very popular and were used by the best casters of their day.

In Paris in 1910, Mons. A. P. Decantelle won the open-to-the-world 2½-oz distance event with a cast of 112 yds. At the Crystal Palace in 1904, J. J. Hardy won the open ½-oz distance event with a 3½ No. 1 'Silex' and at the same tournament, L. R. Hardy won the float casting event with a small 'Silex.'

The smaller sizes have been replaced by the 'Altex,' 'Hardex,' and 'Elarex' but the larger have maintained their popularity, particularly when spinning for heavy, strong fish is practised—mahseer in India,

Tigris salmon in Mesopotamia, salmon fishing in British Columbia—and, of course, salmon and pike fishing at home in England, Scotland and Ireland. This reel is very sound in construction, easily kept clean, economical to use and a staunch companion. It gives the angler confidence when he has hooked and is playing his fish.

We have re-designed the mechanism of the 'Silex' reel to make the brake more sensitive when casting and easier to adjust.

This new pattern we call the 'Silex Jewel.' It is made in three sizes only— 3¾, 4 and 4½ ins.

Used by thousands of anglers, a great many of whom have testified to its splendid qualities—the absolute ease with which it can be used—its freedom from trouble. Over-running is impossible if the simplest of rules with regard to adjustment are observed at the beginning of the day.

Interior of the 'Silex'

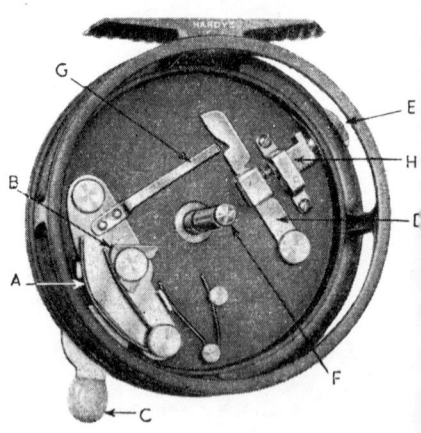

Before casting, the operating lever C is depressed. This lifts the check B (carried on check-plate A) from the ratchet wheel, and also the arm G is removed from the casting brake D, bringing the oiled felt pad against the hub F under the pressure of spring H. Spring H is controlled and set by the turn button E. At the end of the cast lift the lever C. The reel is now ready for winding.

THE NEW 'NOTTINGHAM' REEL,

with Patent Lever Action Check.

(1912 MODEL.)

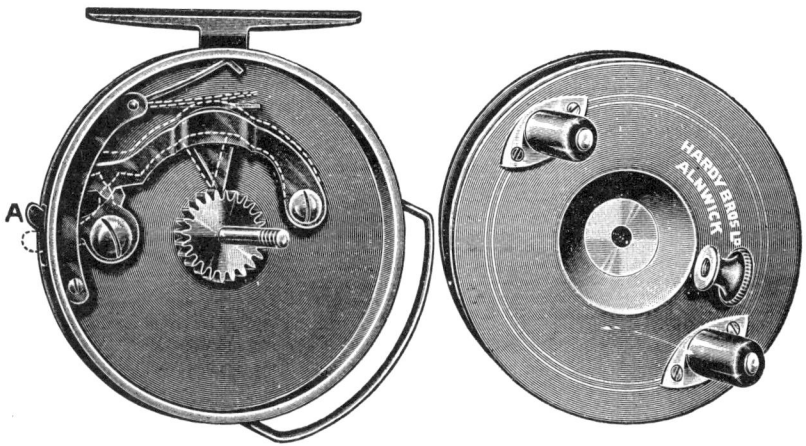

Illustration shows a new type of reel with improved check action on our patent No. 2 "Silex" principal. A is the lever end which is operated by the finger. The dotted lines show position of lever when thrown out of gear.

The reel is made of old seasoned walnut, with gun-metal star back; patent lever action check; steel ratchet and wheel with steel spindle, fitted with adjustable tension nut; Bickerdyke line guard; horn handles with brass bearings.

This reel is an immense improvement on any existing "Nottingham" reel. The check being carried on an arm which rises and falls, overcomes the possibility of the ratchet locking in the wheel, as on the least irregularity the lever rises and frees the check. The action of throwing out of or into gear is effected by the lever end A, which projects from the rim. There is no turning of the reel as is necessary in an ordinary "Nottingham." The position of the lever permits the forefinger to throw the check into or out of gear instantly, without altering the position of the hand.

Sizes from 3½ inches to 4½ inches are good for general river work. For trolling and sea fishing, either for boat work or surf casting, these are capital reels.

Sizes	3½ in.	4 in.	4½ in.	5 in.	6 in.
Price	15/-	16/-	18/-	21/-	26/6

Hardy's "EUREKA" Reel.
(1913 PATTERN).

For all kinds of Bottom Fishing; Roach, Chub, Perch,
Barbel, Grayling, &c.

This reel has been designed, after a very careful study of the
requirements necessary for the up-to-date Bottom angler, and is
pronounced by several experts who have used it, to be the most
perfect reel yet devised for the work.

It is made of our Alumin, the outside diameter being $3\frac{1}{2}''$, the
width between plates $^{13}/_{16}''$. The form is what we call "contracted."
The drum is specially designed for very quick recovery of the line.
The bearings are of phosphor bronze, the spindle being of finest tool
steel with latch fastener.   The check-work is our new and improved
patented design, similar to that of the new "Nottingham" reel on
page 146.   The ratchet is carried on a lever which rises and falls,
and so overcomes any possibility of locking in the wheel, as on the
least irregularity, the lever rises and frees it.   The action of throwing
the check out of and into gear is effected by the lever A projecting
from the rim, which can be operated by the forefinger without altering
the position of the hand in fishing.

The rim is cut away for about a quarter of the circumference,
so that the drum may be governed by the forefinger or thumb when
casting direct from the reel, or trotting a float.   The drum is excep-
tionally light and permits a small float to draw line and travel without
causing the slightest drag.

This reel is excellent for all classes of float fishing.   With it a
small float and tackle complete can easily be cast 20 to 30 yards.

All Bottom anglers who like the best gear should provide themselves with one of these, which will greatly enhance their sport.

Size $3\frac{1}{2}$ in.   Price 25/- each.

Hardy's "Triumph" Casting Reels

Pats. Nos. 24245-9261 (1923 Model).

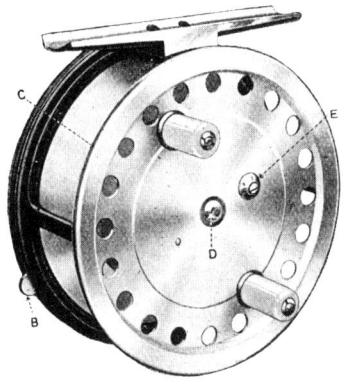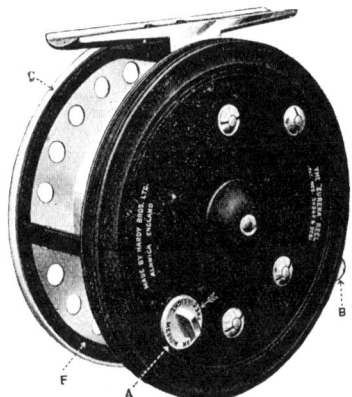

Designed for anglers who prefer an absolutely free running reel controlled by the fingers, or, when desirable, by a delicate variable braking mechanism.

The frame and line drum are made of our special Alumin in two solid parts only. When it is desired to take out the drum for cleaning and oiling, pull over latch E with the forefinger and remove.

The line drum is very light, well balanced, and provided with a smooth rounded outer flange C, accessible to either hand for control when casting or braking pressure when playing a strong fish. It is bushed with phosphor bronze, and carries a jewelled thrust bearing (D).

The frame and line guard F are in one casting.

The optional check is our patent " Compensating " design (spares may be had guaranteed to fit) : see illustration of " Longstone " reel, page 154. This mechanism is carried on an independent action plate, and operated by lever B.

The regulator is our new design as fitted to the "Silex Major" reels. It is operated by indicator A on the back of reel, and may be set to give three varying pressures or an absolutely free drum. The indicator is marked **free, light, medium** and **strong**, the pressure required being turned to face the arrow on the reel frame. The illustration shows it set at the **free** position.

This reel may be used as—(1) An entirely free drum controlled at any part of its periphery C by either hand. (2) The drum under a moderate brake, just sufficient to steady it and assist the hand control. (3) Under complete control of the brake. In the latter case the cast may be made without touching the reel in any way.

Sizes 3½ in. for light salmon or jack fishing.   Price **67/-** each.
  ,, 3¾ in. ,, salmon or pike, general work.   ,, **78/6** ,,
  ,, 4 in. ,, heavy salmon, pike, Mahseer, etc.   ,, **84/-** ,,
Extra Drums—3½ in., 30/- ; 3¾ in., 34/- ; 4 in., 36/- each.

The "TOURNAMENT" Casting Reel

A reel designed for long distance casting at Tournaments. Suitable for all weights of baits up to and including ½ oz.

In casting, the very light drum is entirely free from the winding handle, and in addition being balanced on fine adjustable pivot bearings it offers a minimum of inertia to be overcome at the commencement of the cast. During the flight of the bait when the reel is paying off line the drum is automatically controlled by governors, which prevent overrunning, but do not retard the flight of the bait.

To cast.—We recommend for tournament casting the overhead style, but this reel may be used side swing method if desired.—First (when using overhead method) wind the bait up to within about 6″ to 9″ of the point of the rod, then holding the rod and the drum with the left hand disengage the gears by unscrewing for half a turn Cap **A** which is then pushed away from the axis of the reel and locked in that position by screwing tight.—The drum is now quite free.—Grasp the rod in the right hand, the thumb resting on the bar **B** of the frame with its tip pressing on the line wound on the spool. Keeping the hand and thumb in this position the rod is brought back over the right shoulder till the bait is just clear of the ground. From this position the cast is made with a strong stroke straight forward over the right shoulder and the final effort is stopped with the rod at approx. 45° from the ground.

As the cast is made the thumb is released from the drum, and it is only required to thumb the drum again when the effort of the bait is expended and it is falling to the ground.

As fine a running line as possible should be used, but to the end to which the bait is attached a stouter piece of line should be spliced or knotted to take up the initial force of the cast ; this piece of line should extend from the bait and be coiled round the drum three or four times.

Can be supplied without governors where rules do not permit of their use.

Price, £5 5s. 0d.

The "Hardy-Decantelle" Bait Casting Reel

Patent No. 544351

The French spinning reel known to the public for some years as the "Decantelle" reel has been purchased by Messrs. A. P. Decantelle and Hardy Bros. Ltd. The sole manufacturing and selling rights are controlled by Messrs. Hardy Bros. Ltd. In future the reel will be known as the "Hardy-Decantelle" reel.

Although not possessing the refinements of our various "Silex" reels, it is nevertheless a good sound plain spinning reel and capable of standing up to any amount of hard work.

The "Hardy-Decantelle" reel is made in two main parts, the drum and the frame, of a special hard aluminium alloy. The spindle is of best cast steel and the bearings of special bronze.

The mechanism is very simple and can be understood at a mere glance.

TWICKENHAM, 27/7/31.
You have made me a beautiful rod and I am delighted with it, and particularly for the judgment you have shown in the balance of the rod which is just perfect. Many thanks to you.   H. B. C.

SURREY, 11/9/31.
The 12 ft. rod I got from you 3 or 4 years ago is as good as new and is a delight to handle.

The casts I got this year from your London house were as good as ever.
                                                          J. F.

Hardy's Stationary Drum Bait Casting Reel

THE REEL WITH THE PERFECT AUTOMATIC LINE PICK UP

(Patents Applied for)

The " ALTEX " (Regd.)

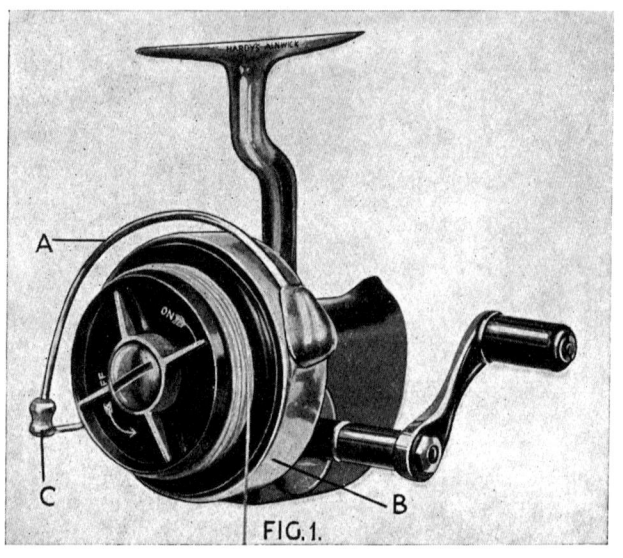

FIG. 1.

For some years we have been experimenting with various forms of " stationary drum " reels. By stationary drum, we mean a reel in which, when casting, the axis of the drum is parallel to the axis of the rod, and does not revolve when recovering the line. When casting, the line slips off the drum coil by coil, as opposed to reels of the " Silex " type where the line is taken from the revolving drum. The great advantages of a stationary drum reel are :—

1. That, as there is no inertia to overcome at the commencement of the cast (only the slight friction of the line over the polished ebonite lip of the drum) extremely light baits can be cast.

2. There is no possibility of overrunning.

From our experiments, the " Altex " has evolved, and has proved to be satisfactory in every detail. In its present form, it has stood the test of two seasons' hard fishing, and as we cannot find a fault with it, we have every confidence in offering it to the angling public as the best " stationary drum " reel that has been produced. As expert anglers, and successful fishing tackle designers of long experience, we are satisfied with it, and as it is manufactured by Hardy experts in Hardy's Reel Factory, the largest and best equipped with modern machinery in the world, we know it will give long and faithful service.

The " Altex " Reel is made on very sound engineering principles, the materials used are the very best procurable for the various functions they have to perform. The gears are of the single helical or spiral type and run sweetly and silently.

The gears and all the working parts are totally enclosed so that sand, dust, etc., cannot get into them and so cause unnecessary wear and possibly jam the reel, **nor can the fine line used become entangled with the working parts.** All moving parts can be lubricated from the outside without taking the reel apart.

The Automatic Pick Up A, Fig. 1 (Pat. applied for), is fixed to the flier, B, Fig. 1, which revolves round the drum to wind on the line. It is furnished with a highly polished hardened rustless steel guide (C, Fig. 1), over which the line runs, this greatly helps to prolong the life of the very fine lines used.

In fishing, this pick up is of the very greatest convenience and advantage, as the line cannot under any conditions be missed at the end of the cast nor at any time or through any cause can it escape from the automatic pick up. The first revolution of the winding handle automatically throws it over the face of the drum and picks up the line immediately, carrying it to the hardened rustless steel guide and so on to the drum. By this method of winding in the line, the twist which is put into it when casting is taken out, so that the " bugbear " to bait casters—a twisted line—is entirely avoided when using the " Altex " Reel.

The reel winds in very rapidly—a great asset when fishing shallow or weedy water, etc. ; the gear ratio being about 3 to 1.

As the line is wound on to the drum by the revolving flier, it is evenly distributed by the reciprocating movement of the drum. This is a very necessary feature, as only by having the line correctly distributed can long casts be achieved ; in fact with a badly distributed line casting is a practical impossibility.

HOW TO USE THE " ALTEX " REEL

Nothing could be simpler than learning to cast with the " Altex " Reel.

First see that the drum is filled up to the lip, but not beyond, with line.

If the line is dressed with "Cerolene" (see page 78 of Hardy's Anglers' Guide) it will greatly facilitate casting and add to the length of the casts.

A water logged line does not cast well : " Cerolene " keeps it waterproof and helps it to slip over the lip of the drum.

March 1st, 1932.

The new " Altex " Reel arrived this morning and it is the best thing I have ever seen. A man who was in my office went to Moult Street and ordered one. He said that it was " The Cat's Whisker " and he has been using a —— for two years.   Yours faithfully, —— ——

The "Hardex" Reel

Regd. Trade Mark.
Design Registered in Gt. Britain.
British Patent app. No. 12319/36.

A NEW STATIONARY DRUM REEL OF UNIQUE AND SIMPLE DESIGN

A good sound reel bearing Hardy's Hallmark of quality and carrying Hardy's guarantee. The "Hardex" is of a very compact design and embodies all the essential features of a modern thread line and stationary drum casting reel.

SPECIAL FEATURES OF DESIGN

Simplicity and Solidity. The saddle, standard, gear covers and bearings for flier are all cast in one solid piece. The flier, pinion and flier spindle are cast in one piece, as also is the driving gear and the handle crank.

Line Distribution. The flier revolves round the drum to wind on the line, and the drum has a reciprocating movement in the correct ratio to the flier speed to lay the line on the drum and give the least possible coil friction when casting.

Lubrication. The reel is very easily dismantled for oiling. Unscrew the retaining (left handed) nut E on the end of the handle crank spindle with a coin and lift off the driving gear when all the parts requiring lubrication are exposed.

Reciprocating Action. The pin which controls the reciprocating movement of the drum and which rides in the cam track is fitted with a hardened steel roller to lessen friction and make the reel feel more sensitive.

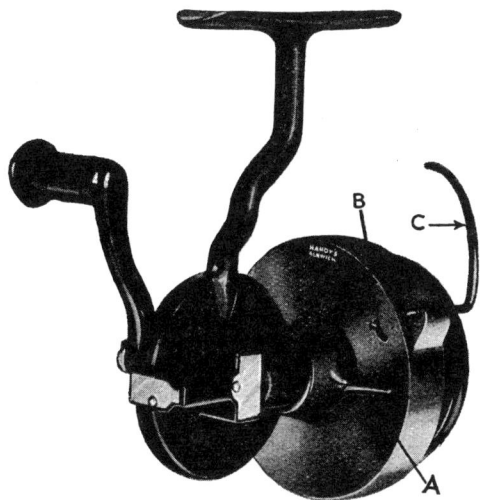

The Line Spool is made of a highly polished non-corrosive material which presents the minimum of lip friction to the line when casting.

The Slipping Clutch is very sensitive and is readily adjusted even when running a fish, by turning the tension nut D, which is an exclusive feature to the "Altex" and "Hardex" reels, and is protected by Letters Patent, and can be operated by a touch of the finger tip of either hand.

The Pick-up C is automatic. At the first revolution of the winding-in handle the trigger A releases the trip B and brings the arm C into the winding in position.

It has the same size of line spool as the No. 1 Altex.

The Finish. Chromium plated and black nickelled.

The Gears are of the bevel type with the involute teeth correctly meshed to run smoothly and silently.

Line Capacity - - - - -	140 yd.	100 yd.
Lion Gut Substitute, Breaking Strain	3 lb.	5 lb.

The reel weighs 6 ozs.

Price, **32/6** each packed in fibre box.

See page **364** of this catalogue for the Hardy Wanless rods, which are the correct rods to make a perfect combination to use with this reel.

The "Silex Rex" Spinning Reel
For Salmon, Pike, Sea Trout, and Large Trout

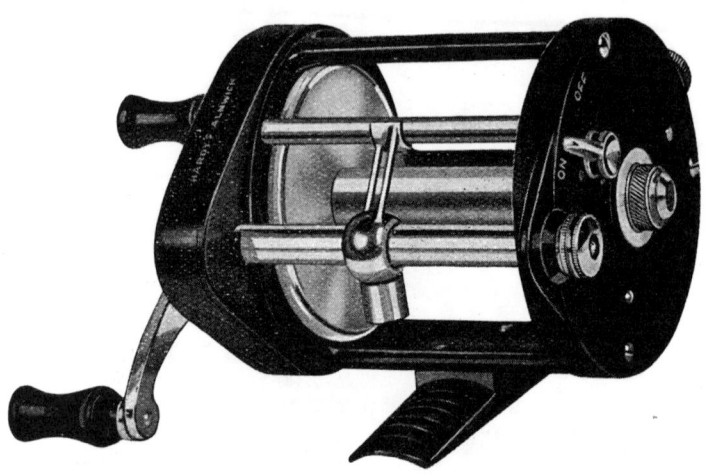

A quadruple multiplying bait casting or spinning reel with level wind line distributor, having a comfortable line capacity for 100 yards of No. 1½ of 15 lbs. breaking strain " Cero " line.

The Frame is turned from a solid casting of our special Alumin Alloy giving a strong rigid construction which keeps the spool or drum bearings in perfect alignment.

The Line Spool, or drum, is also a solid Alumin Alloy casting. It is perfectly balanced and runs on highly polished steel pivots ground into best phosphor bearings. Consequently, it has a long life and there is little inertia to overcome in casting.

The Level Wind Line Distributor, made of rustless steel, is gear driven and therefore certain in action. It is a simple well tried piece of mechanism.

Lubrication. All working parts of the reel can be lubricated without taking the reel apart.

When Casting the reel may be used in the following methods :

(*a*) In the same manner as our " Super Silex," i.e. under the absolute control of a sensitive brake which can be regulated to suit the weight of bait being used. In this type the reel is not touched in any way by hand, the drum is controlled entirely by the brake and the time of release, i.e. the moment when the reel is allowed to revolve, is automatic, and, furthermore, is **gradual,** which very largely prevents over-running. This gradual automatic release is a very important feature and a very great help to the caster.

" Hardy-Jock Scott " Reel

A————   ————— B

This is of the free-spool, multiplying rotary drum type, and embodies a number of special and exclusive features. The frame is constructed of Duralumin, a very light alloy having a tensile strength equal to that of mild steel. It is black Anodized, a finish which renders it absolutely impervious to the corrosive action of water. The fittings are chromium plated, while the drum is made of Hiduminium which, besides being impervious to corrosion, is extremely light and strong. The drum runs on pivots of steel, ground into best phosphor-bronze bushes, with the end-thrust supported by an agate-lined adjustable bearing cap.

The gears are of the involute type, correctly cut and pitched to give silent and smooth running ; the gear ratio is four to one, which permits rapid recovery of the line. As these gears are out of action while the cast is in progress they create no friction and their life is lengthened.

Prior to casting, the gears are disengaged from the drum by moving lever A, when the drum is absolutely free. At the conclusion of the cast, the gears automatically engage immediately the reel handle is turned. This is a very important feature of the design. It allows instant recovery of the line ; there is nothing to remember, and the bait cannot get out of control. The mechanism is extremely simple, and positive in action.

The reel is self-spooling, but no mechanism is employed for this purpose. The advantage here is that distance is not sacrificed as is the case when the conventional mechanism is employed. In the case of the " Hardy-Jock Scott " Reel the end-plates of the drum and the frame are so designed that the line, when being wound on to the drum, is smoothly guided back towards the centre without any tendency for the coils of line to fall over each other.

A friction clutch of special design is fitted, giving a wide range of adjustment and making the reel suitable for use with any strength of line up to a maximum of 9 lb. breaking strain. It is extremely sensitive and smooth in use, and may be instantly adjusted while a fish is taking away line. The star washer B controls the adjustment, and it should be noted that the reel handle does not revolve when casting or when a fish is taking out line. If desired, additional brake-pressure may be applied to the drum by slightly pressing thereon with the left thumb. The fish is thus always under complete control, and tension up to the maximum strength of the line can be continuously applied if desired. Indeed, one of the most remarkable features of the reel is the extremely easy and complete control which it provides, together with its ability to use tackle which, while fine enough to be unobtrusive, gives an ample margin of safety when handling large salmon, and without sacrificing length of casting.

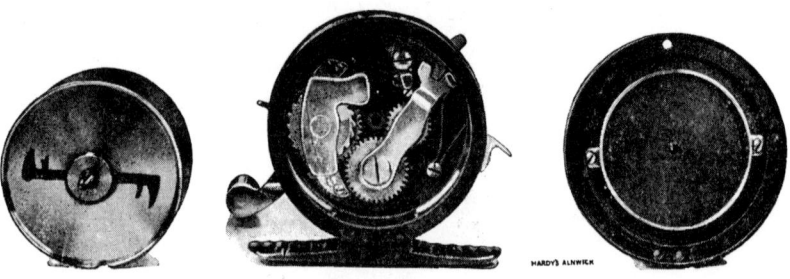

The casting brake is of special design, and operates entirely automatically, being controlled by the centrifugal force exerted by the revolving drum. It requires no adjustment whatsoever, adapting itself to any weight of bait or length of cast within the limits to which it has been designed. It should be noted that this brake gives an absolutely free drum as the cast commences, applies sufficient pressure to prevent overrunning while the bait is travelling at its maximum speed, and, of equal importance, it gradually diminishes its pressure as the bait's momentum dies away, so allowing the utmost possible freedom to bait and drum in the attainment of long casts. The astonishingly efficient functioning of this brake enables the novice to cast in a manner equal to that of the " Spinner " with many years' experience, and it is, indeed, doubtful whether human control—however expert—would provide a longer cast. This brake has been evolved as a result of our experience of casting tournaments, where distance is, of course, of supreme importance. In addition, an optional casting brake is provided, similar to that used on the " Super Silex " Reels, thus providing entirely automatic control if desired.

Lubrication is confined to three points only—clearly marked " oil "—and can be effected without dismantling the reel. An oil squirt is provided.

The complete reel weighs 5¾ oz.

An exclusive feature to the " Hardy-Jock Scott Reel " is the line drier, This drier carries two lines, as, for example, a 6 lb. and a 9 lb. Upon reaching the water, the angler may choose the line most suitable to the prevailing conditions, and instantly winds it upon his reel. Similarly, should a change of lines be needed during the day, it is a matter of a few moments to wind the line in use on the drier—where it will dry and remain until required—and to wind off the spare line on to the reel.

Price of Reel with Cork Arbor and Oil Bottle, only   £13 18 6+£1 1 9 P.T.

Price of Double Line Drier only -   -   -   -   £1 9 0+6/5 P.T.

HARDY BROTHERS Ltd. ALNWICK.

3 ins.

4 ins.

4½ ins.

IMPROVED "SWALLOWTAIL" BAITS.

2¼ ins.

2½ ins.

2 ins.

PLATE 19.

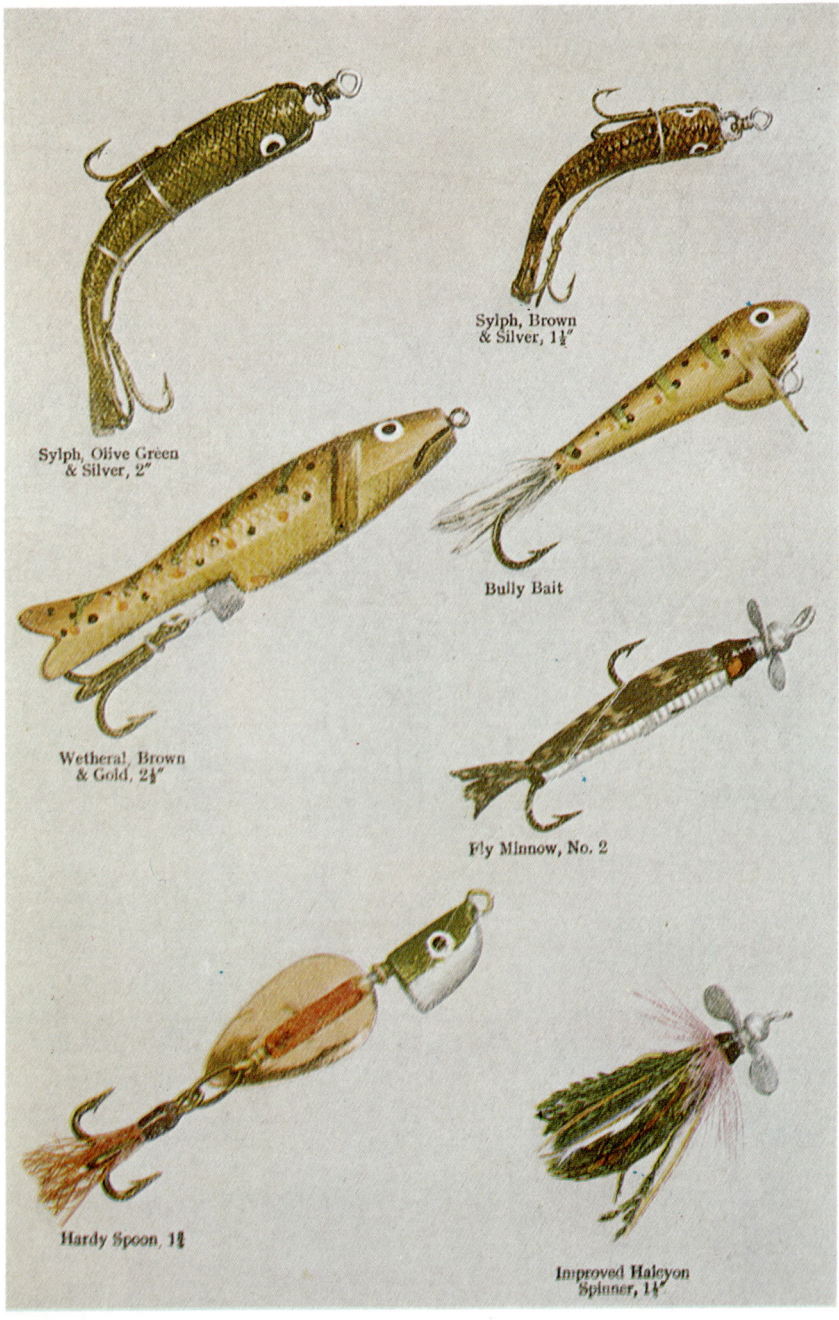

Sylph, Brown
& Silver, 1½"

Sylph, Olive Green
& Silver, 2"

Bully Bait

Wetheral, Brown
& Gold, 2½"

Fly Minnow, No. 2

Hardy Spoon, 1¾

Improved Halcyon
Spinner, 1¼"

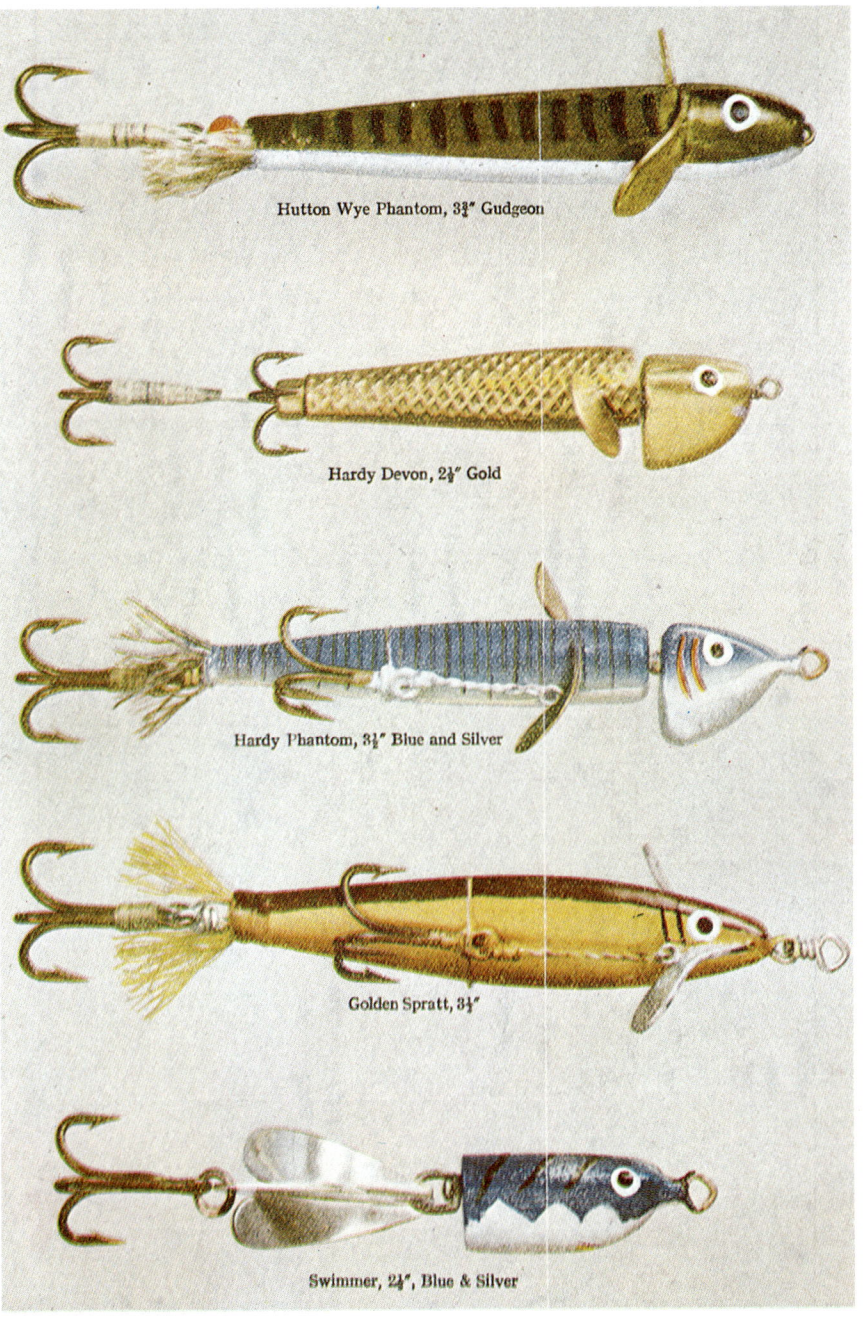

Hutton Wye Phantom, 3⅜″ Gudgeon

Hardy Devon, 2¼″ Gold

Hardy Phantom, 3¼″ Blue and Silver

Golden Spratt, 3¼″

Swimmer, 2¼″, Blue & Silver

The " Elarex "

A QUADRUPLE MULTIPLYING CASTING REEL

**Fig. 1.—Showing checkered platform or thumb rest
and hole for fastening line.**

This reel is the most completely successful of its kind ever devised.

It is the result of exhaustive experiments which Mr. L. R. Hardy, the Managing Director of Hardy Bros. (Alnwick) Ltd., has been personally making over a number of years.

The finished reel now being produced is as near perfection as human brains and skill can make it.

DESIGN AND CONSTRUCTION

THE FRAME AND REEL SEAT

This important item is a solid, sound, one piece " lantern " moulding, shock resisting and perfectly rigid. There are neither screws nor joints to loosen and throw bearings out of alignment.

The frame is made to withstand any amount of hard usage, and to protect properly the essential and delicately accurate working parts which cause the reel to function perfectly.

Three special features in the frame casting are :

1. A pair of accurately located housings on the endplates. These carry the self-aligning bearings on which the spool runs.

2. A thumb rest or platform with a checkered surface to facilitate ease of control when casting, or breaking a fish.

3. A sunk panel stating the line capacity ; the amount of line, in various sizes, the reel will hold: 150 yds. 12 lb.; 120 yds. 15 lb.; 100 yds. 18 lbs.

THE LINE DRUM

This member is of non-corrosive, High Duty Aluminium alloy, runs on accurately located, miniature, self-aligning bearings.

The arbor is provided with a hole through which the line is passed and secured.

THE GEARING

The gearing has a multiplying ratio of 4 to 1, giving the drum a relatively high speed when winding in, and also reducing the inertia of the rotating handles when casting.

The gears themselves are of the helical type, sweetly smooth and silent running ; made of the best material for their purpose, and guaranteed to give long and efficient service.

THE LINE DISTRIBUTOR OR LEVEL WIND

The distributor shaft, or spindle, runs in a protecting housing and is heavily chromium-plated to give it a hard wearing, non-rusting surface.

The " Pawl ", which engages in the path machined in the spindle and moves to and fro across the face of the spool, is of cast steel, hardened and correctly tempered.

Spare pawls will be provided at   each.

The pawl can be quickly changed by unscrewing the confining screw at the end of the pawl chamber.

The eye of the distributor engages and runs in a slotted track to ensure steady running. *Continued overleaf.*

Fig. 2.—Showing pawl chamber screw and slot in which the distributor eye runs, also knurled set brake-bottom and index

The L.R.H. Grayling and Trotting Float

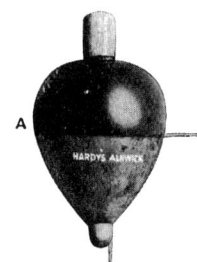

A float designed to overcome the tendency of lying on its side without being over leaded.

When Grayling fishing we experienced trouble with all the floats we tried. They had a tendency to lie on their sides. There were two reasons for this :

1. Floats with a long under shank did so because the shank is buoyant.

2. They are made top heavy by the gut being fixed to a point considerably above the water.

Even floats without the underhook lay over because of the second reason.

The L.R.H. float has no under shank and the gut is led away from the float at the water line, preventing any top-heaviness. It is extremely sensitive. Always keep cocked with a minimum of lead (a very desirable feature—as more lead requires a larger float) as the cast is readily adjusted for depth, and the top being painted red with white peg is always easily seen. To fit on cast, thread gut through hole A.B. from the slotted side, pull it down the slot to the peg hole and push in peg.

Page 183. Fig. 3. **Flexible Sprat** is also stocked in Gold with Silver belly with cross stripes in red.

Sizes	-	3 in.	3½ in.	4 in.
Prices	-	3/-	3/3	3/6

Page 189. **The " Hardy " Natural Bait Spinners** are supplied with Celluloid Transparent Spinners in the same sizes and prices.

Sand Eel Wobbler

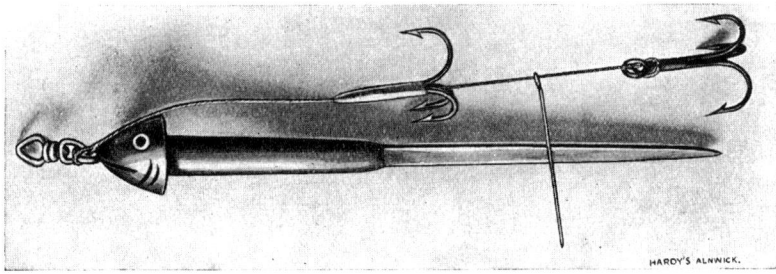

This improved form of Wobbler has been substituted for those shown on page 189.

The lead cap protects the cut end of the eel tail and gives a better finished appearance to the bait.

PRICE.

No. 1 to carry bait 4½ in. to 4¾ in., -	-	-	-	2/9 each.
No. 2 to carry bait 3½ in. to 4 in., -	-	-	-	2/3 ,,
No. 3 to carry bait 3 in. to 3½ in., -	-	-	-	2/- ,,

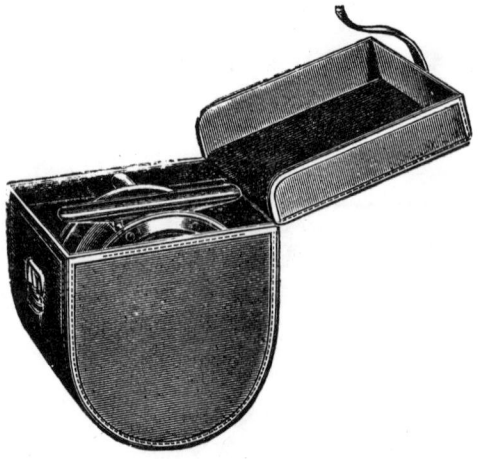

Reel Cases
SOLID LEATHER
(Velvet lined)

For Reels—	Price
3″ to 3¼″ -	- **14/-**
3⅜″ ,, 3⅝″ -	- **16/6**
3¾″ ,, 4″ -	- **18/-**
4¼″ ,, 4¾″ -	- **21/6**
5″ - - -	- **25/-**

Cases for Spare Drums, half the price of reel **case.**

"Selvyt" Reel Bags

When a case is not used these are indispensable.

For Reels	Price	For Reels	Price
2½″ to 3⅜″	3/-	5″ to 7″	5/6
3½″ to 4″	3/6	8″ to 9″	7/6
4″ to 4½″	4/-		

Extra when fitted with lightning fastener.

2½″ to 3⅜″	**1/-**	4″ to 7″	**2/-**
3½″ to 3¾″	**1/6**	8″ to 9″	**2/6**

The "Hold-All" Tackle Case

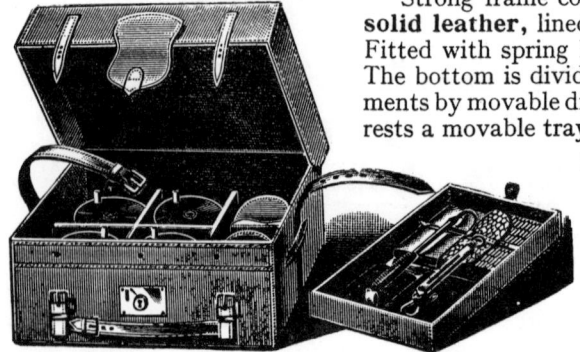

Strong frame covered **with best solid leather,** lined with red baize. Fitted with spring lock and handle. The bottom is divided into compartments by movable divisions ; on these rests a movable tray.

Size 20 × 13 × 9 deep (inside measurement)
£9 2 6
Size 15¼×10¾×8¼ deep (four compartments)
£5 7 6

472 # THE SILK PHANTOM.

(Best quality only).   **Assorted Colours.**

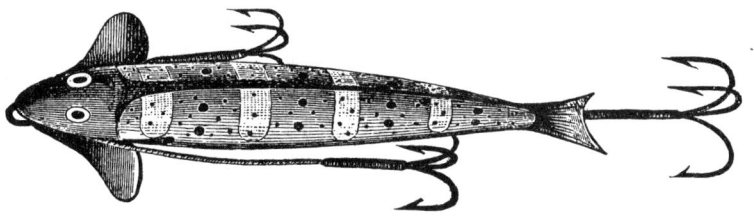

Inches,		$1\frac{3}{4}$	2	$2\frac{1}{4}$	$2\frac{3}{4}$	$3\frac{1}{4}$	$3\frac{3}{4}$	$4\frac{1}{4}$	$4\frac{3}{4}$
No.	0	1	2	3	4	5	6	7	8
Silk,	2s.	2s.	2s.	2s.	2s.	2s.	2s. 6d.	3s.	3s.

The New Zealand bait " Inanga " and " Whitebait " Phantoms, same prices as above.

SOLESKIN PHANTOMS.

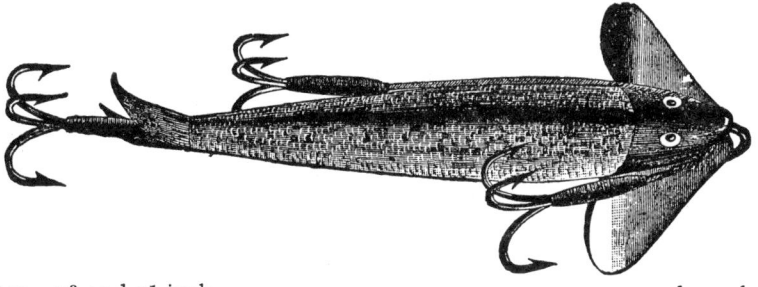

473—$1\frac{3}{4}$ and $2\frac{1}{4}$ inch	...	...	...	...	... 2s. od. each.
474—$2\frac{1}{2}$ and 3 inch	...	...	...	...	... 2s. 6d. ,,
475—$3\frac{1}{2}$ inch	...	...	...	...	... 3s. od. ,,
476—4 inch	...	...	..	...	... 3s. 6d. ,,
477—$4\frac{1}{2}$ inch	...	...	...	...	... 4s. od. ,,

HARDY'S EXCELSIOR SPINNER.

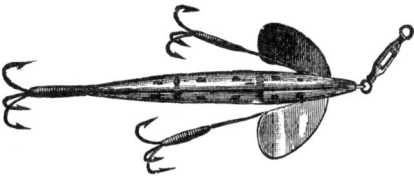

471—

This beautiful little Spinner is similar to the Quill, but made of metal.   Kills well.   It is made in Trout size only.   2s. each.

☞   FLIGHT CASES, SEE PAGE 187.

The "M.C. PATENT PHANTOM MINNOW"

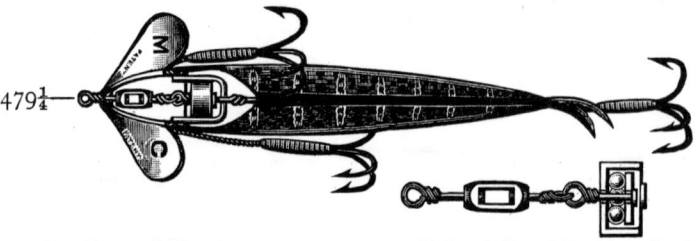

479¼—

Section of Head.   **Patent Combination Swivel.**

spins beautifully without any Swivel Trace. The Patent Combination Swivel is on the **Ball Bearings** principle, so that there is almost no friction.

These baits are made of transparent Soleskin with silvered leads inside. They are very lifelike, and kill well anywhere. We have supplied them largely to New Zealand, as they are a good imitation of the natural baits found there, and kill well.

Inches	1¾	2	2¼	2¾	3¼	3¾	4¼	4¾
Prices	3/3	3/3	3/6	3/6	3/6	3/9	4/-	4/6

479¾

THE SPIRAL MINNOW.
Best Quality—Stamped.   **(Geen's Patent.)**

Sizes—	1½	1¾	2	2¼	2½	3	3½
	1/9	1/9	2/3	2/3	2/9	3/-	3/6

480

Spoon Baits.—Ordinary.

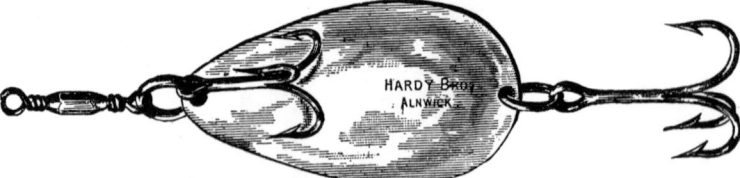

Sizes—	3 in.	2½ in.	2¼ in.	2 in.	1¾ in	1½ in.	1¼ in.	1 in.
	2s.	1s. 9d.	1s. 6d.	1s. 3d.	1s.	10d.	9d.	9d.

The foregoing are all Best Quality, and really excellent baits. From Nos. 5 to 8 Phantom, and 2 to 9 inch Devon for Lochs; Nos. 1 to 5 Phantom, and 1 to 2 inch Devon for Rivers with a fair current. They will take Salmon, Pike, Trout, or Perch.

☞ IN ORDERING FROM THIS LIST PLEASE QUOTE LETTER **D.**

Hardy's Special New Feathered Spoons and Spinners, for Mahseer, Pike, Salmon, Trout, &c.

Thickly plated solid rings and swivels.   Hooks all silver-plated.

Regd.

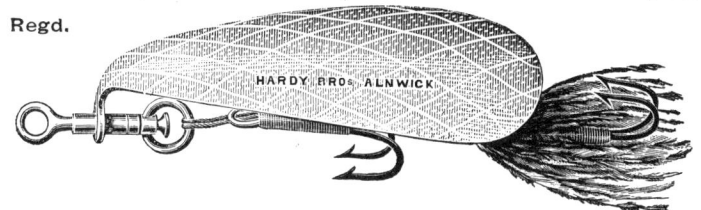

480. F. **Hog-back Flying Bar Spoon** (silver outside, gold inside).

Sizes (length of spoon only)   ¾   1   1½   2   inches.
Prices 1/9   2/-   2/3   2/6

Regd.

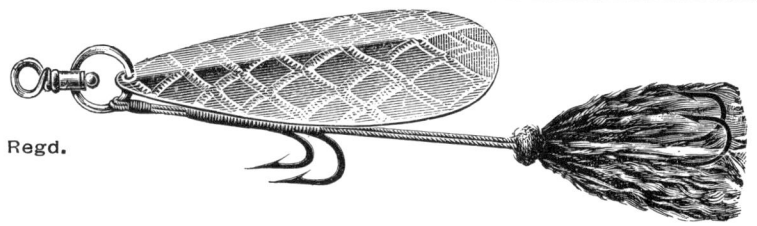

480. R. **Hog-back Revolving Spoon** (silver outside, gold inside).

Sizes (length of spoon only)   ¾   1   1½   2 inches.
Price 1/6   1/9   2/-   2/6

Regd.

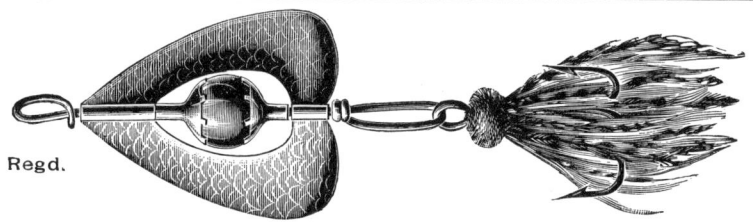

480. A.   **The Alnwick Spinner** (blue and silver).

Sizes (length of spinner only)   ¾   1   1½   2 inches.
Prices 1/6   1/9   2/-   2/6

The above spoons and spinner are especially suitable for Mahseer, the hooks being double are not so easily broken as trebles.   They may safely be relied on for all kinds of predatory fish.   The mounts for large size are "Hercules" gimp and strong hooks; all being of best and stoutest material.

BAITS MADE TO ORDER.

We will be pleased to make any special bait to order for any part of the world, but not less than 1 doz. of a size.

☞ IN ORDERING FROM THIS LIST PLEASE QUOTE LETTER **G.**

1894

The "Hardy" Phantoms.

Pat. No. 22,000.

FIG. 1.

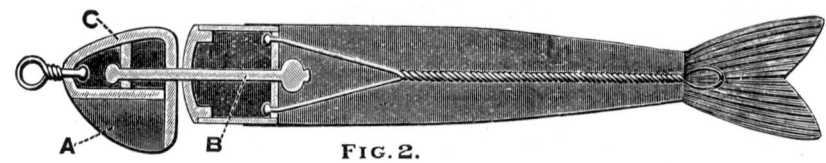

FIG. 2.

As far back as we can remember, anglers have exercised their minds in the difficult task of how to prevent *kink* and *twist* in spinning lines, due to the revolution of the bait.

Swivelled traces are not all they seem, as a very light tension, produced by a heavy bait, or one with large flanges in a quick stream, soon stops the swivels.

"Anti-kink" leads have been devised, and although they are excellent, they only tackle the trouble after it has been produced. "Preventon is better than cure," and our method in this new bait, is to *prevent the creation of* this twist, and is most effectual.

The head of the bait, is not an integral part of it, but is only attached to it by the strong swivel pin B, as may be seen in Fig. 2, which is a section of the arrangement. B, the pin above referred to, holds the head to the body. C is the metal frame work of head. A is the lower lead part of the head, virtually the KEEL. When the bait is drawn through the water, this keel A comes into position as shown on illustration and remains there.

KINK, the "Bete Noir" of the spinner, does not exist, while the appearance of the bait is very natural.

The construction of the body is the same as the "Ideal" phantom, page 195, *i.e.*, with lead centre and cork and silk covering.

We are only able to produce these Phantoms in the following sizes :—

Sizes in inches,	2½,	3,	3½.
Price,	**3/6**	**3/6**	**4/6**.

COLOURS.—Blue and Silver, Brown and Gold and Gudgeon Colour.

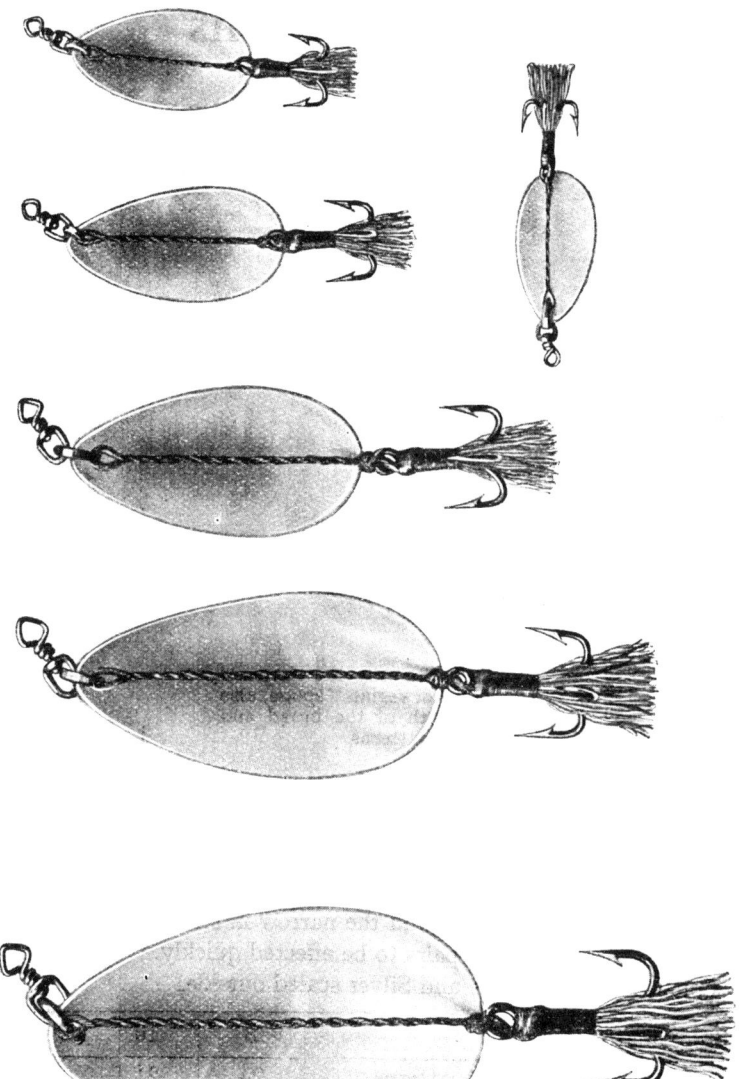

Pearl Spoons
MADE OF MOTHER-OF-PEARL

Sizes - - -	1 in.	1¼ in.	1½ in.	2 in.	2½ in.	3 in.
Prices, each -	1/6	1/9	2/-	2/6	3/-	3/6

HARDY'S PATENT "CROCODILE" SPINNING TACKLE.

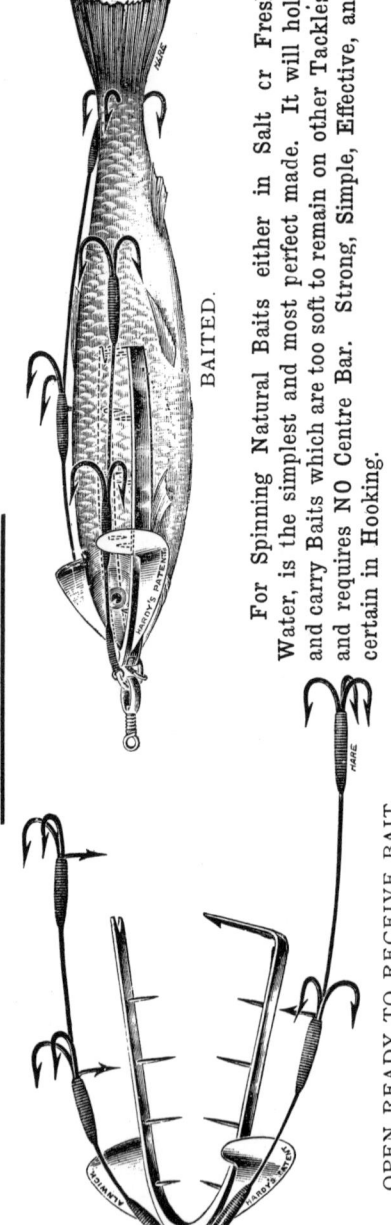

BAITED.

OPEN READY TO RECEIVE BAIT.

ACTUAL TROUT SIZE.

For Spinning Natural Baits either in Salt or Fresh Water, is the simplest and most perfect made. It will hold and carry Baits which are too soft to remain on other Tackles, and requires NO Centre Bar. Strong, Simple, Effective, and certain in Hooking.

TO BAIT.—Open the Tackle as shown in illustration, place the nose of the Bait close to the hinge and press it upon the spikes until they are close, the end one coming quite through the body. Then bring down the other side in like manner, pressing it close, when the clips at end will engage. Press the double barbed spike on hooks into Bait, and all is ready.

If baits are scarce, a piece from the belly of a Mackerel or a strip of Bacon Skin will do. We have even taken Jack spinning the tackle without Bait.

TO REMOVE BAIT.—Press back the spike which goes through the body when tackle will open.

Fishing with a friend for a few hours we took 28 Jack *using only a few baits.*

No. 1.	PIKE Size Large	for 4½in.	to 6½in.	BAITS	2/3	each.
" 1¾.	PIKE Size Medium	" 4in.	" 5in.	do.	2/3	"
" 2.	SMALL PIKE or SALMON,	" 3in.	" 4½in.	do.	2/3	"
" 3.	SMALL SALMON or LAKE TROUT,	" 2½in.	" 3½in.	do.	2/-	"
" 4.	TROUT,	" 2in.	" 2¾in.	do.	1/6	"

HARDY'S PATENT "CROCODILE" TACKLE,
ADAPTED FOR PRAWNING.

See Sandeman Tackle, page 117.

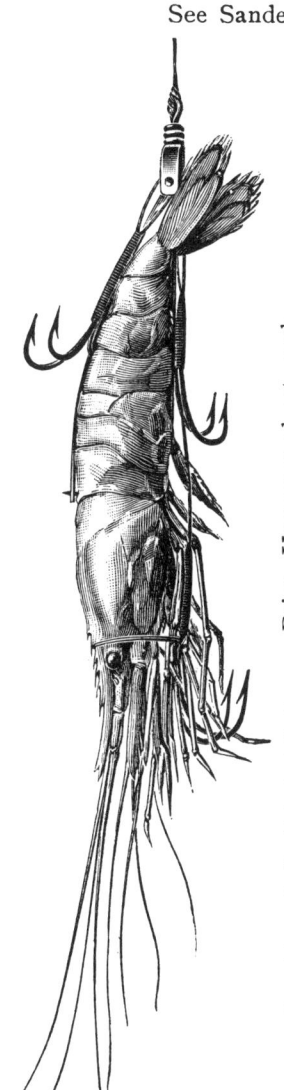

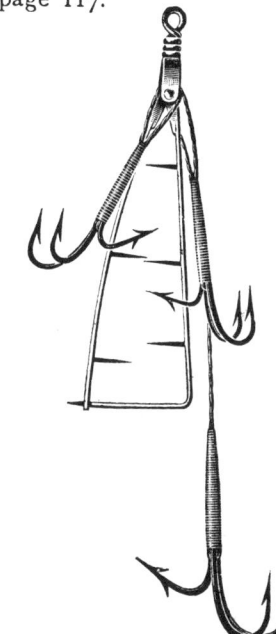

Price, Unmounted, 2/- each.

" Mounted on 1½yds. of treble gut, 2 swivels, and leaded, 3/8.

" Mounted on 1½yds. of strong single salmon, 2 swivels, and leaded, 5/8.

As this tackle has only been invented a short time, it has not had a sufficiently extended trial to say much about it, but we see no reason why it should not do well. We will willingly encourage any practical idea that aims at getting rid of the objectionable needle, which on hooking a fish is generally broken. The method of baiting is to open the tackle, select a prawn and gently straighten it with the fingers, then measure the exact length so that the fork of the tail comes over the joint at end of tackle, push the leg through the prawn from the underside taking care to arrange the short legs over, not under, the spikes on tackle; then press down the other arm until the clips at end engage. Stick in the hooks, as shown in sketch, and all is ready. A little thread may be put over the head and end hook to keep it in its place.

We made some of these in the first instance for clients in Scotland, and we hear they answered very well.

☞ FOR TRACES, SEE PAGE 89; LEADS, PAGE 127.

HARDYS' PATENT
Two Speed "Crocodile Spinner"
WITH REVERSIBLE FINS AND DETACHABLE LEAD.

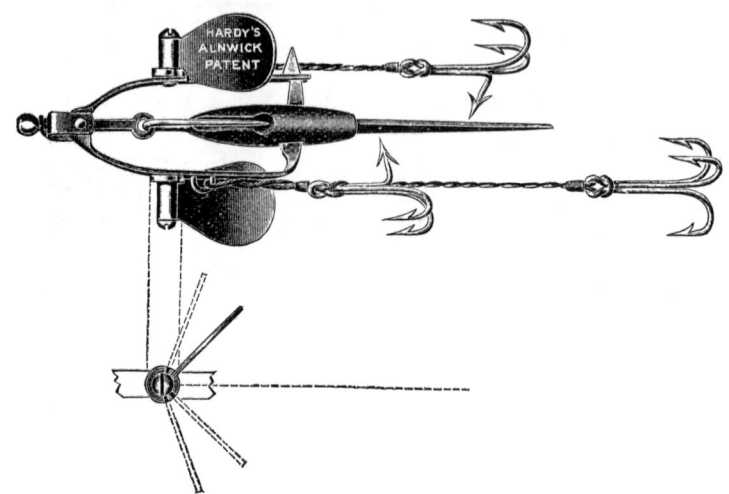

There has always been inquiry for a spinner in which the direction of the spin could be altered quickly, in order to remove the twist generated in one direction, by reversing the fins.

This development is an attempt to meet this request, and we hope successfully ; at the same time we feel bound to say, that as far as our personal experience goes, we have not found any such difficulty when using our "Silex" No. 2 reel and "Anti-kink" leads.

The illustration shows our patent Reversible Fin "Crocodile" Spinner. When it is desired to alter the direction of the spin, the fins can be lifted out of the slots and turned to the right or left. The movement should be made by turning the fin over the front of the spinner, when it will automatically lock.

The plan shows the four positions in which the fins may be fixed. It will be seen that each fin can be placed in two positions when spinning to the right or left, so that a quick or slow spin may be obtained. The method of fixing the lead is handy ; when not required it can be instantly removed.

						Leaded each.
No. 1.	—Pike size (large), will carry from 4½ in. to 5½ in. bait	-	-	**4/-**
,, 1½.—	,, (medium), ,, ,, 4 in. to 4½ in. ,,	-	-	**4/-**
,, 1¾.—	Large Salmon or small Pike ,, 3½ in. to 4 in. ,,	-	-	**4/-**
,, 2. —	Small Pike or Salmon ,, 3 in. to 3¾ in. ,,	-	-	**4/-**
,, 3. —	Small Salmon or Lake Trout ,, 2½ in. to 3 in. ,,	-	-	**3/9**
,, 4. —	Trout or Perch ,, 1¾ in. to 2 in. ,,	-	-	**3/-**

Geen's "CORKSCREW" Sand-Eel Spinners

With "Emery" Fasteners. Pat. Nos. 221545 and 223078.

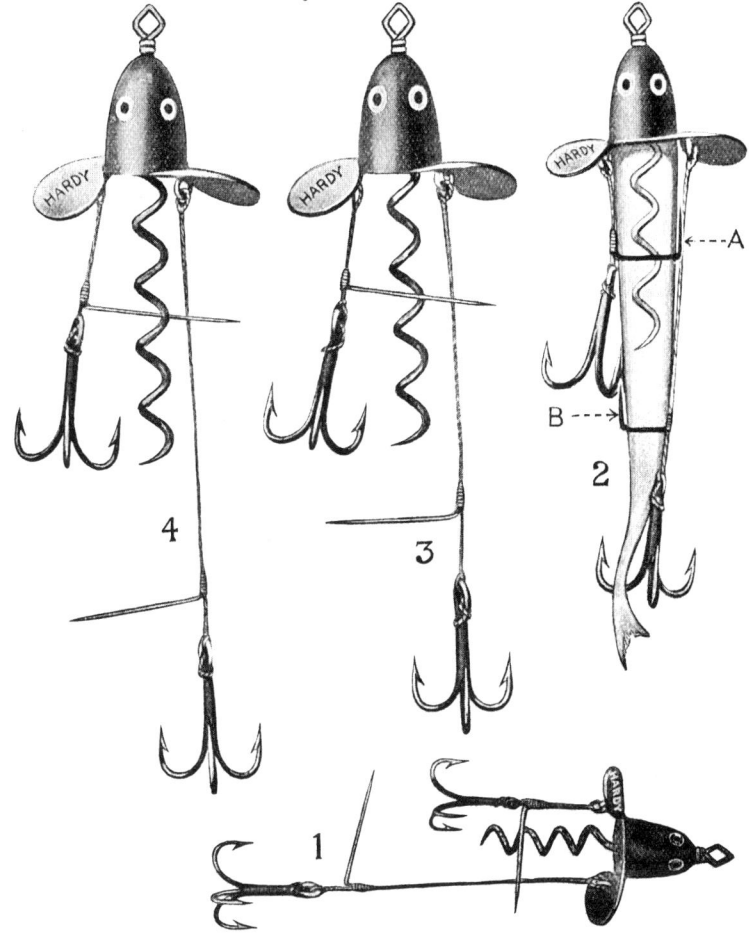

These spinners were the invention of the late Mr. Philip Geen. After cutting the sand-eel to the required length, turn it on the screw until it comes up against the head with back up, the head being leaded to assist in casting. The "Emery" fasteners hold the hooks securely. To fix, push the wire through bait and bend over the ends, see A and B in illustration No. 2 size.

To fix the hooks, push the wire through bait and bend over the ends, see A and B in illustration No. 2 size.

Prices, No. 1, **2/9**. No. 2, **3/-**. No. 3, **3/3**. No. 4, **3/6**.

FOR " COMPACTUM " ARTIFICIAL BAIT CARRIER, SEE PAGE 189.

Special Tackle for British Columbia.

Spoons, Leads, and Traces for Tighee & Cohoe Salmon in Campbell & Fraser Rivers.

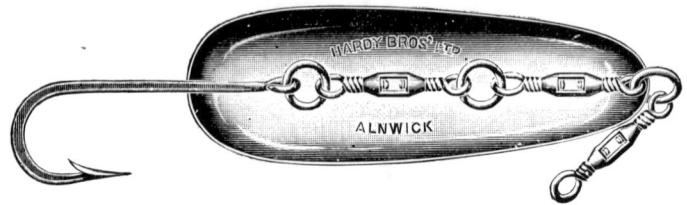

" Indian Spoon," 5 in. long, for Tighee Salmon   -   4/3 each.
Do.   do.   2½ do.   for Cohoe   do.   -   3/3   ,,

May be had Gold, Silver, or Lead colour. The practise is to use silver for a bright day, gold for a dull day, and lead for a dark day.

" Anti-Kink B.C." Lead, 5 in. long, for use with Indian Spoons, 1/- ea.

Special trace for Indian spoons, 2 yards long, made of 9-ply Punjab twisted Amalgam wire, with one link spring swivel, one centre and one end swivel, 3/- each.

The spoons, leads, and traces are also useful in many other parts of the world for large rivers and sea fishing.

For Special Ebona Reel for British Columbia, see page 331.

MARSKE HALL, RICHMOND, YORKS.

DEAR SIRS,—In reply to your letter, I found that the 5 in. spoons take all sizes of salmon in the Campbell River, but the Cohoe more readily took one of 2½ in. long fished near the surface. We were, naturally, after the big fellows, fishing deep, and when on the move they were not particular as to the size of bait. The spoons and hooks as fitted are exactly as those used by the Indians, who live by their fishing, and I consider the arrangement of swivels and strength of hook is perfectly adapted for fishing in those waters, as my bag of 307 salmon, weighing 3,673 lbs., in 28 days proved. 61 of these fish averaged over 34 lbs. each.
                                                    J. T. D'ARCY HUTTON.

BUDLEIGH, DEVON, 13TH Nov, 1905.

DEAR SIRS,—I enclose photos of some salmon caught last August with the steel centre "Murdoch" rod I got from you last April. I caught 24 Tyhee salmon 1,004½ lbs.—6 fish of 50 lbs. and over, best fish 56 lbs. ; also 43 Cohoe salmon, 297 lbs.

That foul hooked 50 lbs.—see spoon hanging on his side. I dragged that fish for half-a-mile through the rough water, and then on shore. The rod was under water most of the time, up to the lower joint—not at all fair on it. It is a thing of joy.   Yours truly,   LEOPOLD LAYARD.

WORMS (PINKTAILS) in Bags, Scoured & Packed in Moss.

One Gross, 1/9; 2 Gross, 3/-; Carriage Paid

One day's notice is required if ordered from Alnwick, London, or Manchester, as these are procured from our Edinburgh House. They may be had by return if ordered direct from our Edinburgh House, 5, South St. David Street.

These sprats are procured abroad, where they are fatter and better than those procured in this country. They are preserved in a special manner, and will keep bright for years in any climate.

The tins contain 9 to 12 of the large sized sprats, and from 15 to 24 as the sprats get smaller.

This manner of packing makes them more suitable for forwarding, as there is no fear of broken glass or leakage.

From our experience with trout, salmon, pike, and sea fish, we believe these sprats are one of the very best baits when mounted on suitable tackle.

Sprats for Trout—2 to 2½ ins.

No. 4 Crocodile—No. 4 Alnwick Spinner—Hardy's Spinning Flight—Ariel—Small Goodwin—No. 1 Wobbler.

Sprats for Salmon and Sea Trout—3 to 3½ ins.

No. 3 Crocodile—No. 3 Alnwick Spinner—Med. Goodwin— Med. Dee—No. 2 Wobbler.

Sprats for Salmon and Pike—4 to 4½ ins.

No. 1¾ Crocodile—No. 1½ Alnwick Spinner—No. 4 Wobbler.
The above are splendid baits for sea fishing.

NOTE.—For Crocodile tackle, see page 140; Alnwick spinner, p. 144; Goodwin, p. 148; Wobbler, p. 148; Dee tackle, Hardy's spinning tackle, and Ariel, p. 134.

MINNOWS,

GUDGEON,

SAND

PRESERVED

and

TOUGHENED.

PRAWNS,

SPRATS,

EELS, &C.,

PRESERVED

and

TOUGHENED.

Minnows—6 dozen in patent bottle	(Trout size)	...	...	4/0
,, 3 ,, ,,	(Do.)	...	...	2/0
,, 2 ,, ,,	(Salmon size)	...	...	2/6
Gudgeon—1 ,, ,,	(Do.)	...	...	2/6
Do. 1 ,, ,,	(Pike size)	..	...	2/6
Dace— 1 ,, ,,	... ...	...	...	3/0
*Sprats— 1 ,, ,,	(Pike size)	...	...	1/6
,, 1½ ,, ,,	(Salmon size)	...	..	2/0
Sand Eels 1½ ,, ,,	(about 4ins.)	...	...	2/6
,, 1½ ,, ,,	(,, 5ins.)	...	...	3/0
,, 1 ,, ,,	(,, 6ins.)	...	...	2/6

No charge for Bottles.

*Sprats may be had coloured red at 6d per bottle extra. These have been found to kill salmon in snow water when the ordinary Sprat has failed.

Live baits supplied direct from our London Branch.

PRAWNS IN GLYCERINE.

3/6 per bottle, containing about 1½ doz.

Price for these is subject to fluctuations, as they are often difficult to procure.

MINNOWS (SALTED).

Six dozen, Trout size   ...   .   3/- Post Free.

Six   ,,   Salmon ,, ...   5/-   ,,   ,,

SPECIAL NOTICE.

Baits preserved by us are quite different from the ordinary formalined baits sold by others. On being removed from the bottle they do not shrivel up, but remain plump and plastic for months. In handling there is no objectionable chemical smell, and fish take them better.

One trial will prove their excellence over all others.

Please note that between March 15th and June 15th we are forbidden by law to sell fresh water fish as bait. We can, however, sell sea water fish of all kinds, and we may mention that sand eels cut to proper length make an excellent substitute for minnows. See special tackles on pages 155 & 156.

☞ FOR WORMS AND SPRATS IN TINS SEE OVER LEAF.

The "Two-Bobbin" Wire Spool

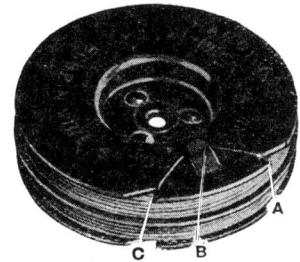

A two-bobbin spool for carrying copper wire on one spool and silver wire on the other, for mounting baits. Is also supplied with "Bait Tying" Wire on one spool and Security Wire for making Gut Substitute joints on the other.

After taking length of wire required off spool, pass it over edge A under clip B and break off over edge C.

Price with both spools fitted with wire   -   -   -   **1/-** each.

Elastic Thread

Elastic Thread for tying on spinning baits and prawns. A great improvement over wire or ordinary thread. It is easily put on, and always retains its grip without cutting into and damaging the bait.

On Bobbins, **6d.** each.

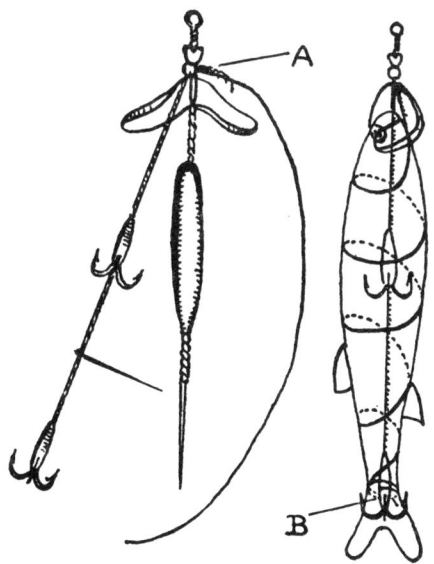

"Bait Tying" Wire

Twist the end of the wire through the eye at head of the flight at **A,** bind the bait and flight to the spinner and secure by twisting it round the hook or flight at **B.**

Supplied in two strengths for trout and salmon fishing on our Two-Bobbin Spools (see above).

When it is desired to mount a fresh bait untwist the wire from the old one and it is again ready for use.

A GOOD ROD is, without doubt, the most necessary part of the Angler's Kit, and HARDY BROTHERS have for years devoted their attention to the production of absolutely perfect rods by improved methods. So well appreciated have their efforts been that they are now by far the largest manufacturers of rods in Europe. They give the most careful personal attention to all work. The material used is of the very finest quality, thoroughly seasoned, and their appliances are not equalled anywhere. We are thus enabled to offer rods, which, for lightness, strength, casting, killing powers, and durability, are far superior to any others. This fact is amply borne out by the many high awards and testimonials from leading authorities, in all parts of the world, which they hold.

Special attention is paid to the balancing, which is in all cases medium, unless especially ordered otherwise, and will either switch or cast overhead equally well. Any balance, from the extreme stiff Scotch to Castle Connell, can be produced to order or pattern.

We are frequently asked—how is it HARDY'S rods are so much better than others? The reason is very simple. In the first place, 15-16ths of all the rods offered are either factory-made or imported, and there is not that careful detail given to construction which is so necessary, the goods being made to price without attention to quality, and naturally very different to their production. It has been no small task to bring their work to the perfection they have, and the difficulty of finding suitable canes is very great. Bamboos may be had in almost any quantity, but they have, after trying almost every district and many samples sent by the Indian Forestry Department, found that there is one particular district which produces canes of a quality superior to all others. This cane they now use exclusively, and have appointed agents on the spot who buy up all the choicest, and have them seasoned under their instructions—not burned until the fibre is destroyed as is usually the case—but properly oiled, fired, and seasoned in a special manner. This renders them exceedingly tough and springy. They are then shipped, and picked over in their works, only the very choicest being retained for their own trade, the remainder being disposed of to cane merchants.

This, then, is the secret of the great spring, toughness, and durability of these rods. But although the raw material is a very important matter, we may point out that the great care and thoroughness of the work apparent in every detail (even to the most careless observer), equally adds to the value and completeness of the rod. The method of their handling, the built-up splint-end joints, the metal lining and sealing of every part ; the perfect shape and jointing of the sections, together with the true and even distribution of power and substance, render these rods so superior to all others in point of quality and merit that they stand *alone*, and it is not to be wondered at that after years of the severest trial they elicit such encomiums as the following, which is only one of the many :—

The *Field*.—" They have left all competitors hopelessly behind, &c."

All the greenheart rods during manufacture are subjected to a special treatment which renders them much more durable than ordinary ones. They also receive all advantages equally with the cane-built rods in the matter of improved appliances, &c.

SPECIAL NOTE *re* CANE-BUILT RODS.—There are several firms advertising " English "-made Cane-built Rods (it having been proved that they are so much better than the American), and arrogating to themselves the credit for " English " rods being best. *It should be remembered that it is* HARDY'S *rods that have proved to be the best, and won the Gold Medal in* 1883 (see correspondence in *Field* and *Fishing Gazette*, pages 160 to 165, and Awards at the Great Exhibitions). As has been pointed out there are firms who are buying cheap American Rods, and offering them as English make, guaranteed to stand two years, &c., &c., and we caution unwary buyers against them. In support of this we can actually offer for sale American cane-built rods for 15/- each at a profit. Remember that HARDY'S is the only make of any value, and the name of HARDY BROTHERS is security for the quality.

THE FIELD, December 20th, 1890.
" SALMON ROD FOR THE GERMAN EMPEROR.—His Imperial Majesty the German Emperor intends to resume the sport of angling next season, and has commissioned Messrs. HARDY to build him one of their best 17ft. split-cane salmon rods. This English rod is equal to, if not superior, to the best American I have ever seen, and, at its best, there is no better in the world. The Emperor used a borrowed one in Norway last year, and was so delighted with it that he has determined to have a special one for himself."

THE CHOICE OF A ROD.

It may not be generally understood nor taken into account when ordering a certain length of rod, that it may be had in varying strengths. Although, generally speaking, rods of a given length have a corresponding weight and strength this does not in all cases hold good, except in the medium or regular strengths, regulated by the fact that rods up to 12 ft., single-hand, are generally used for trout ; 14 to 16, grilse ; and 17 to 20, salmon. Even this general line is subject to great fluctuations, as is evidenced by the fact that if one takes any three 18 ft. rods they will vary considerably in strength and balance. There are many lengths which may be almost any degree of strength, and in these notably such a length as 14 ft. This rod, for instance, we make in four different strengths. Our ordinary 14 ft., No. 548, purely a trout rod ; then the Perfection, No. 564½, a shade heavier ; then our No. 557 steel centre ; and lastly, the H. Cholmondeley-Pennell, No. 568, a grilse and salmon rod. As before stated, rods are generally made of strengths proportionate to their length and purpose for which they are intended—9 to 12 ft. single-hand, trouting ; 13 ft. to 14 ft.,

sea trout ; 15 ft. to 16 ft., grilse ; 16 ft. to 20 ft., salmon.   But it is sometimes desirable to have rods 9 to 12 ft. suitable to kill grilse, or a 14 ft.
fine enough for using with the finest XXX fine gut and midge flies.   In
both these cases the rods required are vastly different from the regular
strengths, and for this reason it is advisable we should be informed the
special purpose for which the rod is intended.   In an ordinary way where
rods are made for the trade by the piece these niceties cannot be attended
to and must be dispensed with.   HARDY BROTHERS, however, make it their
study to give the advantage of *correct* strength, which means not one atom
more or less weight than is absolutely necessary.

"I KNOW IT'S ONLY A TROUT ROD, BUT IT'S ONE OF 'HARDY'S, AND THERE'S NO FEAR OF IT BREAKING."

A very good guide is the strength of line which is most suitable to any
particular stream intended to be fished.   For instance, for trouting an
ordinary steam a No. 18 to 22 to 18 double-tapered line is most suitable ;
or, say, for salmon fishing, 24 to 30 to 24 switching line is chosen as
being most suitable and as heavy as necessary.   This being decided, the
exact strength of rod top which will carry the line without any fear of
injury is determined to the minutest degree, and this determines all the
rest of the rod, for the tops control and give the other dimensions, and are

controlled by the line. It may be a new idea to some people to work rods on this principle, but it is the one which has always to a large extent guided HARDY BROS., and where it is convenient it is very desirable to send us a piece of the line, also any other items, such as size of fish, and whether stiff, medium, or supple balance is desired.

We are often asked, " Do you recommend steel centre ? " and as a general guide we may say : For trouting for fish up to 3 lbs. if fly only is used, steel centre is not necessary ; but if it is intended to do all sorts of fishing, such as occasionally bait or spinning a minnow, perhaps do a share of loch fishing with large flies for sea trout, &c., yes. For double-handed trout rods, the same remark holds good in proportion. For salmon rods in all cases, steel centre.

"OH ! WHY DID I NOT GET ONE OF 'HARDY'S' RELIABLE RODS?"

It must be understood that all our cane-built rods with steel centre, as compared with cane-built rods which are without steel, are stronger in every detail, and are an improvement where very hard work is intended, but for ordinary fine fishing unnecessary ; that is to say, all our trout rods without steel are quite strong enough for up to 3 lb. fish. At the same time, the proportionate increase in strength in steel centres is not so great as to render them unsuitable for the same work. [P.T.O.

Re salmon rods,   For a vigorous man for all-round fishing an 18 ft. is best. At the same time, this may be in varying strengths, and where the fishing is mostly during the summer months for smaller fish with small flies the points should be lighter, as too thick and heavy tops, such as are suitable for heavy autumn fish, are apt to tear the hold away.   The 17 feet S.C. is a very fine rod, and being fully equal to an 18 ft. greenheart in power is fast taking the place of that soon to be obsolete article.   Our new rod, the " Hi Regan," 16 ft., is a clean and handy rod, up to any amount of work, and as much as any elderly man need use.   For ladies, the 15 S.C. is about the best. We cannot add any more on this subject, except to say that we are always glad to answer any questions and advise to the best of our ability when desired.

CANE SALMON RODS.

THE FIELD, August 27th, 1885.

Sir,—I should be very glad if some of your readers will give me their experiences of the new-fashioned split-cane rods that everyone now seems to talk about, and I sincerely hope they are not as disastrous as my first experience of these rods has been.   I lately, after an absence of three years, returned to my old haunts on the Conway, which, I may add, still keeps up its old reputation of being the worst salmon river in the United Kingdom.   I was fishing a favourite pool, perhaps known to many of your readers as Tyn-y-Cae, when I struck into a good fish with one of these rods, which a friend had kindly lent me—a beautiful rod to fish with, got up regardless of expense, but, as the result will show, not to be depended on.   The first run the fish took, bang went the rod, snapping like a carrot below the first ferrule in the butt.   Fortunately, a friend was looking on, who at my bidding seized the two remaining joints, which were gradually disappearing into space, or rather water ; he held them up while I stuck to the butt, and we eventually brought the fish, thanks to his being well hooked, to the gaff, when he scaled 12 lb.   It is needless to say I fished no more with this 16 ft. of split-cane, ornamented with silver plate.   I may add the makers' name on the rod in question is [we refrain from giving them]——— United States of America, and then follows the mystic word, " Best."   Pilot.

Crathie, 2nd August, 1886.

Dear Sirs,—You have so many testimonials to the excellence of your built-up cane rods that I do not suppose that further ones are of any use to you ; still, if you care to use mine you may do so in any way you please.   I am delighted with the 10 ft. rod I got from you, and it has lately been put to a test which I think few rods of its size could have stood.   While fishing on the Dee here for trout a few days ago, I saw a sea trout jump, and so took off my cast and put on one with some bright flies ; at the third cast I hooked a salmon of 8 lbs., and as I had no gaff I took my fish down the river for more than a mile till I came to a cottage where I could get one ; during the three-quarters of an hour I was fast to the fish, the rod was tried to the uttermost as I had only 34 yards of line, so I had often to bear very hard on the fish to check him ; yet, when I had got my fish I found my rod had not got the least bend in it, and was as good as before in every particular.

Yours faithfully, W. MAXWELL MAYNARD.

Norwich, November 14th.

I foolishly (being in a hurry) purchased a split-cane rod from the ———— .   This after one long steady wet day became unglued.   I sent it to them.   They sent it to their *manufacturer!* who of course replied that the rod had received unfair treatment. They refused me any redress.   I have ordered them to send it to you.   Will you report upon it ?   I think the glue is inferior, as one of your rods I have had for ten years or more was out in exactly the same weather (same boat), and was perfectly uninjured.   E. B. K. LACON (Bart).

Illustrating the enormous strength of
" PALAKONA " Regd. Bamboo

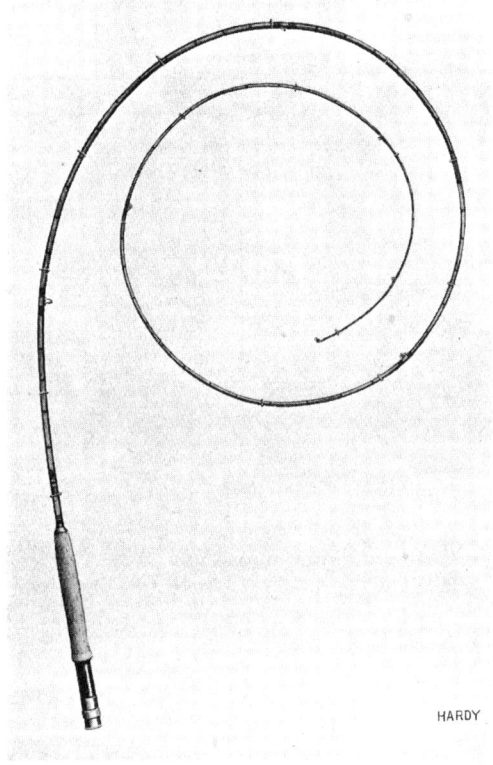

HARDY

Illustration shows a Trout Fly Rod, built of " PALAKONA " (Regd.) Split Bamboo in one perfect piece, length 9 ft. 9 in. The rod is coiled as illustrated, the spiral measuring only 19 in. × 21 in. Under this enormous strain the material does not show the slightest fracture. The original was shown by us at the British Empire Exhibition at Wembley during 1924.

The Countess of Ashburnham desires me to say that, both in appearance and action, the " Palakona " Split-bamboo Salmon rod which you built for her this Spring, is absolutely perfect. Possessing such a perfect weapon, her Ladyship says that she looks forward with confidence and delight to her trip next week on the waters of the Miramichi.

BANAVIE.

I enclose cheque for the 16 ft. Split Bamboo " Special " rod which arrived this afternoon. It is a very beautiful weapon, and I am much obliged to you for your promptness in responding to my telegram.

FIELD-MARSHAL VISCOUNT ALLENBY.

Description of "PALAKONA"

Regd. No. 246936.

SPLIT-BAMBOO SECTIONS (shown on opposite page.)

Fig. 8 is a section of "**Palakona**" bamboo.   The **V** lines show the section before cutting.   Fig. 9 is the hexagonal single building.

Fig. 10 differs materially from Fig. 9, as it is composed of twelve sections, *i.e.*, six within six.   This method is used in the butts and middles of large rods, also for heavy sea work, etc.

Split-bamboo rods are generally made hexagonal as Figs. 9 to 11, but are also occasionally built octagonal and nonagonal, as Figs. 12 and 13, single and double, and with and without steel centre.

STEEL CENTRE

Our tempered spring-steel centre rods are the most powerful produced, and practically indestructible.   When we say that the steel is tempered so that it can be coiled up, and when released will fly perfectly straight, some idea may be formed of the power obtained.

" Hardy " steel-centred rods are totally different **from any other make.**   *The steel is specially made for the work, and perfectly tempered, and runs from one end of the rod to the other.*

The question is often asked, " Do you recommend steel centre ? " As a general guide we may say : For small fish, if fly only is used, steel centre is unnecessary ;   but if the rod is intended for all kinds of fishing, such as occasional spinning, or lake fishing with large flies, then the steel centre, being the stronger rod, is preferable.   For double-handed rods the same remark holds good in proportion.   For salmon fly and spinning rods, and all rods for heavy work, steel centre is advisable.

All our split-bamboo rods with steel centre, as compared with split-bamboo rods without steel, are stronger in every detail, and better for hard work.   All our trout rods without steel are quite strong enough for regular work.   At the same time, the increase in weight by the steel centre is negligible and does not render the rod unsuitable for fine work.

COLOUR

" PALAKONA " Split-Bamboo Rods are usually finished in the natural bamboo colour.   They can, however, be finished a dull French grey, which is a good neutral colour, and the rod is less conspicuous. Any " PALAKONA " rod may be had coloured French grey to order without extra charge.

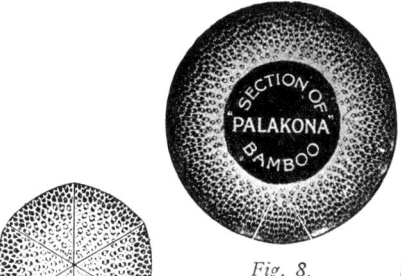

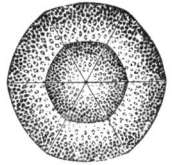

Fig. 8.
SECTION OF BAMBOO.

Fig. 9.
SINGLE BUILT.

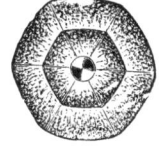

Fig. 10.
DOUBLE BUILT.

Fig. 11.
DOUBLE-BUILT STEEL CENTRE
BEFORE CEMENTING.

Fig. 11.
DOUBLE-BUILT STEEL CENTRE
AFTER CEMENTING.

Fig. 12.
SINGLE-BUILT OCTAGONAL
BEFORE CEMENTING.

Fig. 12.
SINGLE-BUILT OCTAGONAL
AFTER CEMENTING

Fig. 13.
DOUBLE-BUILT STEEL
CENTRE NONAGONAL BEFORE
CEMENTING.

Fig. 13.
DOUBLE-BUILT STEEL
CENTRE NONAGONAL AFTER
CEMENTING.

SECTIONS OF HARDY'S " **PALAKONA** " REG. NO. 246936 SPLIT-BAMBOO RODS

ROME.

I am happy to tell you that H.M. The Queen of Italy writes me, that I may let you know that the goods you have supplied to Her Majesty are excellent. You will be pleased that you have satisfied Her Majesty.

— Fishing Rods —

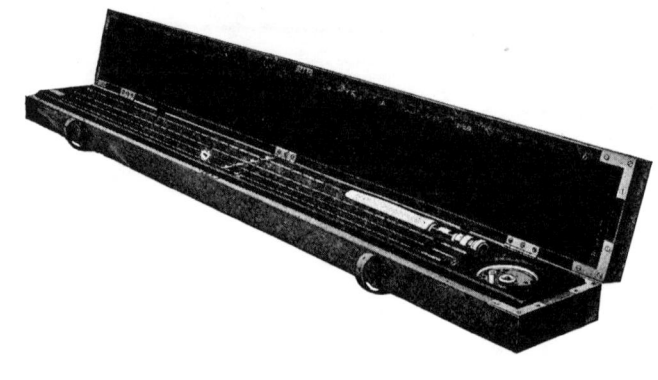

BUCKINGHAM PALACE

February 17. 1922.

To:
Messrs Hardy.

    I wish to express to you my grateful thanks for the beautiful Trout Fishing Rod with which I am delighted: I am much looking forward to having an opportunity of using it.

    I greatly appreciate your having sent me such a splendid rod as a Wedding Gift.

Mary.

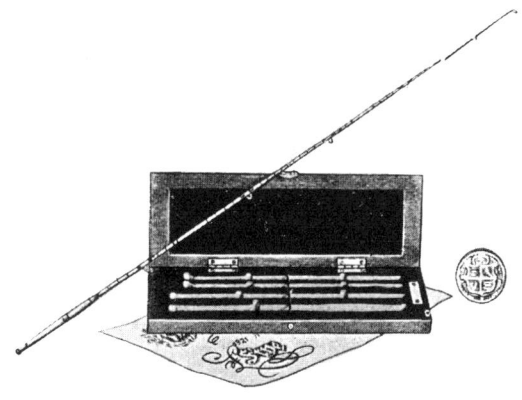

16ft Miniature "Palakona" Split Bamboo Rod in three pieces,
length when jointed 16 inches. The case measures 7 inches.
Note for comparison the £5 note and half crown.

AMBASSADORS' COURT,
S.ͭ JAMES'S PALACE,
S.W.

July 16ᵗʰ '23.

Dear Sirs

I have to thank you
very much for your delightful
contribution to the Queen's
Dolls House — The little Salmon
rod in the case is a perfect
work of art, and will be
greatly valued among the
treasures belonging to the
Miniature Palace — With
repeated thanks for your
charming gift which I assure
you is deeply appreciated

Believe me
yrs truly

To Messrs Hardy Bros.

G

Salmon-Fishing for Ladies.

From "The Gentlewoman."

First, as to outfit. A great drawback in years gone by to ladies adopting salmon fishing as a hobby was undoubtedly the heavy and cumbersome build of the rod then in vogue. This difficulty is now removed by the introduction of the cane-built rod. What is claimed for rods of this description is that they have gained lightness, reduced length, strength, and easy casting power, thus reducing the exertion of throwing the fly to a minimum. The best rods cost a good deal of money, but the best only should be purchased. No better salmon rods can be obtained than those made by the Messrs. Hardy, of Alnwick. It may be said that this firm has reduced rod-making to a science. Cheap rods, like cheap horses, have a knack of "doubling up" when called upon for any extra exertion ; and I can well imagine any lady giving up in disgust should her first salmon leave her with a broken rod in her hand. Like the rod, lines and reels should be of the very best make only.

From "The Sphere."

The Duchess of Fife not only holds the record as the most successful lady angler on the Dee, but she is unique in being somewhat original in her manner of angling and in the selection of her tackle. She uses one of Hardy Brothers' cane-built rods—as also does the Duke of York, but of a somewhat stiffish build—casts a short but straight line, and gives little law to the somewhat coloured but otherwise game beauties she finds plentifully enough in her pools at Mar Lodge in the early days of September.

Fly-Fishing for Ladies.

From "Lady's Pictorial."

In the past, one of the difficulties of women becoming anglers was on account of the weight of the rod and its accessories which it was necessary to carry. But all this has been altered. With the growing number of women anglers special attention has been paid to their wants, and the trout-rods now turned out are veritable works of art. Their great characteristic is extreme lightness combined with strength. A lady's modern rod is a thing of beauty. It is usually made of greenheart or split-cane. The rod held by the little lady in the illustration is of the latter substance, and weighs nine ounces only. These beautiful rods are made by Messrs. Hardy, of Alnwick. They will kill any trout one is likely to come across, and can be wielded as easily by a ten-year-old as by an adult ; in fact to such perfection have they been brought that they will as easily kill a freshly run salmon-trout or grilse as the smaller quarry for which they are specially designed. The rod used by H.S.H. Princess Victoria of Teck is of this type. And all the accessories of trout-fishing are light in proportion. The outfit for trout-fishing is not a large one, but everything should be of the best. This is economy, and the fact cannot be too strongly impressed.

DOUBLE BUILT STEEL-CENTRE.

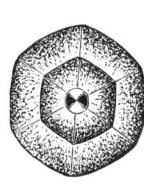

DOUBLE BUILT STEEL-CENTRE.

The "Victoria" Salmon Rods.

(The Lady's Modern Rod).

CEMENTED. BEFORE CEMENTING.

What we claim for the "Victoria" is its lightness, strength, and easy casting power, reducing the exertion of throwing to a minimum. A perfect rod for a lady's use must of necessity be an easy working one. It should not cause any strain either on the arms or back, and in balancing these rods we are especially careful in this. The rods are sufficiently strong to play heavy fish, and have a nice action in the butt, so that they will do the cast with the least possible exertion.

These beautiful rods are Hexagonal Double Cane-built with or without Steel-centre, in 3 pieces, 2 tops, Cork covered Handles, Hardy's Patent Lock-fast Joints and "Bridge" Rings, "Weeger" Universal Winch Fitting, and India Rubber Screw Button.

Number.	Length.	All Cane-Built.			All Cane-built with Steel-Centre.			Weight *about*	
568L	14ft.	£5	18	6	£7	3	6	24½ and 26	ozs.
569L	15ft.	7	3	6	8	11	0	25½ and 27	ozs.
570L	15¼ft.	8	5	6	9	13	0	31 and 33	ozs.
571L	16ft.	8	5	6	9	13	0	32 and 34	ozs.
572L	16½ft.	9	10	6	11	0	0	35 and 37	ozs.
573L	17ft.	9	10	6	11	0	0	36 and 38	ozs.

Angling as a Lady's Amusement.

"The very best for a lady is a split-cane of first quality. I have lately seen one greatly more suitable than any I had seen before and this is 'HARDY's Perfect Rod for Ladies.' They also have reels of special excellence."—*The Lady.*

IMPORTANT TESTIMONIAL.

Dear Sirs,

Some eight years ago, when fishing at Inchnadamp, as we were starting off from the place where the Boats are moored, which is in the River Loanan, the ghillie having laid my rod with the point projecting over the stern, the butt on the middle seat, with the reel downwards, a gust of wind caught the boat and sent her quickly across the narrow river, the point of my rod going into the bank, the butt being held fast by the reel against the seat. The bank was hard and the result was that the rod top was doubled backwards upon itself, into approximately the above condition. Of course I thought the rod was "done," but upon examination I found that the cane was uninjured, and even the varnish uncracked. I straightened it out as best I could and for a time it had a bit of a "kink" but this gradually disappeared, and it is quite straight now. I am still using the rod a "Palakona" Split-Bamboo of 11 ft. and I do not think you have ever had it back even for revarnishing. At the time I thought of sending you a description of the incident, but was afraid of being put down as an inventor of yarns, but "a fact is a fact for all that."

You are quite at liberty to use this as a testimonial of the undoubted quality of your "Palakona" Split-Bamboo Rods.   Pontefract, Nov. 22nd, 1912.   Yours very truly, T. B.

N.B.—ILLUSTRATION IS EXACT SIZE OF POINT OF TOP PIECE.

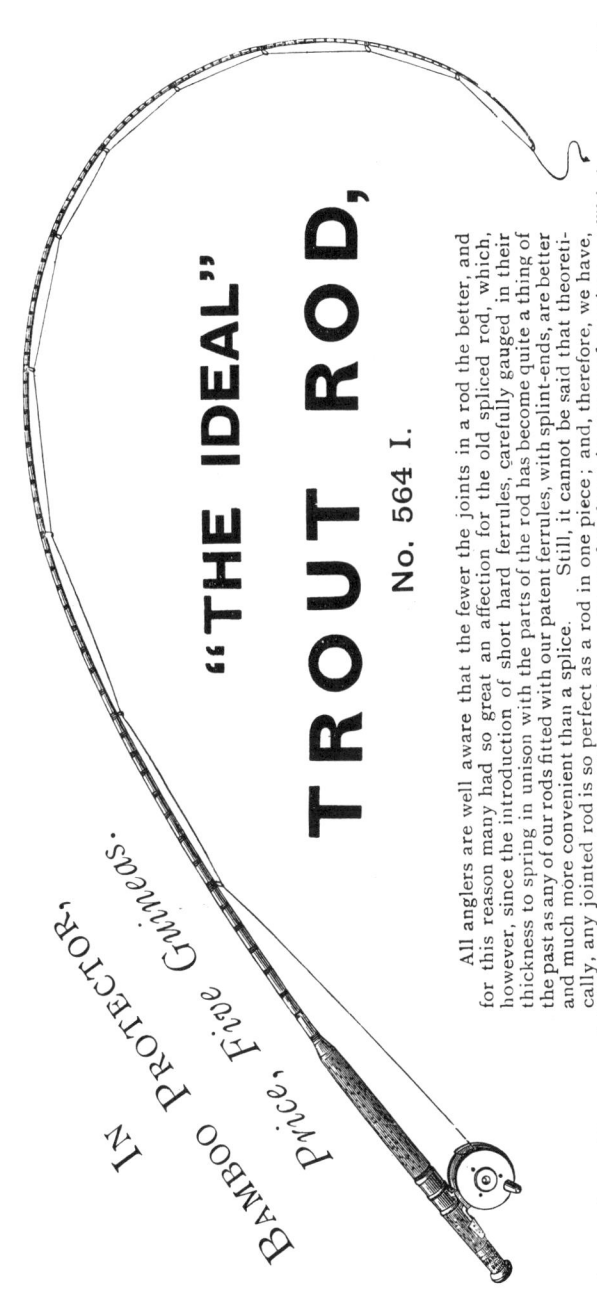

"THE IDEAL" TROUT ROD,

No. 564 I.

IN BAMBOO PROTECTOR, Price Five Guineas.

All anglers are well aware that the fewer the joints in a rod the better, and for this reason many had so great an affection for the old spliced rod, which, however, since the introduction of short hard ferrules, carefully gauged in their thickness to spring in unison with the parts of the rod has become quite a thing of the past as any of our rods fitted with our patent ferrules, with splint-ends, are better and much more convenient than a splice.   Still, it cannot be said that theoretically, any jointed rod is so perfect as a rod in one piece; and, therefore, we have, after much trouble, succeeded in producing a cane-built rod from 9 to 11 feet long, in one perfect piece. Where rods can be kept full length, a very beautiful tool to work with. Fitted with Cork Handle, Patent "Universal" Winch Fittings, and Bridge Rings, Five Guineas. If with Steel Centre, Six Guineas.

The Field.—"A specimen of superb workmanship."

The ten foot rod you built for me in one piece is absolutely perfect and very powerful. I can cast further with it than with any other rod.

P. R. NAPIER.

Catisfield House, May 3rd, 1893.

'This is a very perfect article.

The "Ideal" is simply perfect, and in over 35 years of angling and handling, and owning some 25 rods, I can safely say this one is the best. It is very light yet powerful, and is the envy of my angling friends who have seen it.

I have to thank you very much for carrying out my order so carefully and promptly.

B. C. MARSHALL.

Dulverton, March 20th, 1892.

☞ FOR "HOUGHTON" ROD, SEE PAGE 177.

The "Poole" Combination Rod and Handle-less Friction Driven Reel.

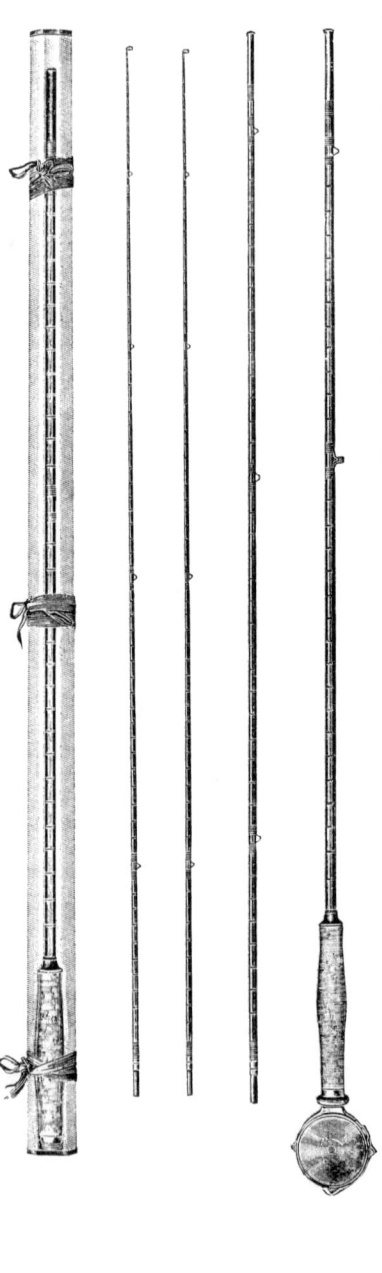

8 ft. 9 ins. "Palakona" Split-Bamboo rod in 3 pieces with 2 Tops, Cork or Cane-covered Handle, Suction Joints, Snake intermediate with Agate Butt and End Rings, and Selvyt lined, grooved wood protector to carry rod. 3 in., "Bougle" (see page 135) Handle-less Friction Driven Reel which screws to butt of rod. PRICE £8 8 0.

The combination of rod and reel is an arrangement suggested by Mr. Poole, and carried out by us for him two seasons ago. He is greatly pleased with the results, and many of his friends who have tried it also approve of it for the following reasons :—

1. The central position of the reel improves the balance, as when the rod is held in the hand.
2. Weight for weight and length for length, this system gives a longer rod and consequently more powerful, *i.e.* a rod more working material, brought down some 4 or 5 ins.
3. Greater portability and more freedom from catching up while stalking fish.¹
4. The handle-less friction drive-plate of the reel, which is operated by merely pressing the fingers against the revolving plate, and so driving it round, is simple. By removing the handle, a source of trouble is got rid of and a better balance given to the reel.

In a lecture given by Mr. Poole at the Piscatorial Society, London, on February 12th, 1912; he concludes his observations by saying "So far, I have been unable to find, in use, any disadvantages excepting the usual unaccustomedness which applies to any new tool or appliance we take in hand.

With regard to the handle-less and friction drive, in use it appears to me excellent. I don't remember anything that has given me greater satisfaction during my fly fishing experiences."

THE "N.B. PERFECTION" ROD, LANDING NET, ALPINE STOCK, AND PROTECTOR COMBINED.

564 N

Is a complete outfit as regards rod and landing net. It is a similar rod to our ordinary "Perfection," but with detachable handle, C, which with A A forms the rod. D is our folding Y net head, which screws into landing handle, B, at E. The handle, B, is hollow, and carries A A when not in use, completely protecting them. The net head and handle are carried in the bag with B, or carried in a leather protector hung on the waist belt, leaving B to be used as an Alpine stock. The arrangement of detachable handle allows the total length to be reduced, an advantage in travelling. The 10 ft. 6 in., when packed, measures 5 ft. 2 in., made in lengths 9 ft., 9½ ft., 10 ft., 10½ ft., and 11 ft.

The handle may be either cork, cedar, or pigskin. Lockjoint to handle and parts A A; all best quality.

This is a splendid rod, up to any amount of hard work, and the compactness of the arrangement may be left to commend itself. Price, complete, £4 15s.; with steel centre, £5 15s.

NOTE.—In using this rod where the landing handle is much in the water, it is advisable, on reaching home, to take out the rod and leave off the cap until it is dry.

Fishing Gazette.—"The 'N.B.' will prove a treasure to all who like to reduce their travelling *impedimenta* as much as possible, and is one of the neatest and best things we have seen."

FOR "PERFECTION" ROD, SEE PAGE 163.

The Lightest Practical Fly Fishing Rods in the World
THE " MARVEL "

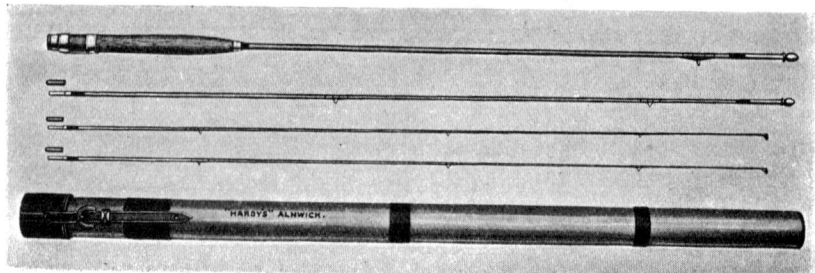

In three joints, built of specially selected **" Palakona "** split-bamboo, with two Tops, Cork Handle, " Universal " reel fittings, Hardy Suction Joints with Protectors and Lubricators, " Snake " Intermediate, with Agate Butt and End Rings. Aluminium Case to carry the complete rod.

Length, 7½ ft. ; Weight, 2¾ ozs.   Price **£8 16s. 6d.**

SHEFFIELD, 15/5/25.

    I am very pleased with the 7 ft. 6 in. " Marvel " Rod—it is just the thing for small streams. I have killed two trout of 15 ozs. and 14 ozs. on it. The length of line it will cast is wonderful.   G. R. WILSON.

The " C. C. DE FRANCE "

In two joints, " **Palakona** " split-bamboo with one Top, Cork-covered Handle, Hardy's Suction Joint, Snake Intermediate, with Agate Butt and End Rings.

7 feet, weight, 3¼ ozs. ; 8 feet, weight, 4¼ ozs. ; 9 feet, weight, 4¾ ozs. Price **£4 18s. 6d.**

To Order.—Fig 1 " Screw Grip " Reel Fitting **5/-**, " Stud Lock " joints **4/-**, " Reversible " Spear and Button, **7/-** extra.

GLOUCESTER, 13/8/25.

    I have had the opportunity of testing the " C C. de France " Fly Rod pretty thoroughly, and have nothing but praise for it. I have used it in many awkward places, necessitating an underhand cast and an avoidance of weeds, and have not yet lost a fish once hooked. I have landed fish up to 2 lbs., and have found this small rod most efficient in its work. It is a most agreeable rod to handle. Its power for such a light tool is remarkable, and I had no difficulty in casting against the wind.   N A FREEMAN.

The J. J. Hardy "Triumph" Rod

The late Mr. J. J. Hardy, Professional Champion Trout and Salmon Fly Caster, made at Norwood in 1931 the splendid cast of 27 yards with a " Hardy " " Palakona " Rod, weighing only 4½ ozs.

This wonderful rod is made under " Hardy's " New System of building " **Palakona** " (Regd.) Split Bamboo Rods, to which it owes its exceptional power and excessive lightness.

N.B.—This rod was not made as a Special Tournament Casting Rod, but an actual Dry Fly Rod of very pleasing balance. No material except " Hardy's " " **Palakona** " (Regd.) Bamboo would stand up to this extreme test.

J. J. H. Triumph Rods.

8 ft. 9 in. built of " Palakona " Split Bamboo, in three pieces, with two Tops, Cork Handle, Hardy " Suction " Joints, Universal Reel Fittings, Steel Snake Intermediate Rings, Sildur Butt Ring and Agate End Ring.

Weight 4 oz. 12 drs. Price **£6 6 0**

8 ft. 9 in. built of " Palakona " Split Bamboo, in two pieces, with one Top, Cork Handle, Hardy " Suction " Joint, Universal Reel Fittings, Steel Snake Intermediate Rings, Sildur Butt Ring and Agate End Ring. Weight 4 oz. 8 drs. Price **£4 4 0**

PRESTON, 23/11/33.

My friend wishes me to send you this Testimonial.

I was teaching a Lady Doctor fly fishing on the River Dwyfer, North Wales, when I hooked a Salmon which scaled 16 lbs. It was certainly an accomplishment for the little Rod to land the fish in 35 mins. I can assure you the Lady was indeed proud of the fish, but more so of the little Hardy Rod, which lay there afterwards with all the dignity that only a Hardy could have. R. W., Jr.

K 2

"Sir Edward Grey's" Perfection Rod.

10½ ft. in two pieces, cane-built, fitted with Cork Handle, Lockfast Joint, Universal Winch Fitting, "Bridge" Rings, Agate or Revolving Steel Gold-plated Top and Butt Rings, India Rubber Screw Button and Spear, weight 9¼ ozs.—Price, £3 3s. od.

Extract from "Fly Fishing" pages 225 and 226, by Sir Edward Grey, Bart.

. . . . "I bought my first split-cane rod, a powerful two-piece ten foot six rod, of Messrs. Hardy in 1884. The butt and joint of that rod are still as sound as ever, after landing many fish of all weights up to ten pounds, and though I have worn out one or two tops, not one has ever broken suddenly in the act of fishing, and they have stood faithfully against the most fearful shocks caused by weeds or bushes in the act of casting. It is this toughness of split-cane which, in my opinion, settles the question decisively in its favour, and though, after several seasons' hard work in all sorts of weather and in contending against down stream winds, a split-cane top may weaken, mine have always given me ample warning; never in trout fishing, since I have used split-cane, have I lost a minute's fishing by the breaking of any part of my rod. Split-cane is the most staunch of all materials; like an old and faithful servant, it is incapable of treachery or sudden change, and when it fails it does so gradually. My own original split-cane rod has become a trusted companion, used to all winds, and weathers, to burns, chalk streams and rivers of many kinds; to trout, sea trout and grilse; doing all that is asked of it, having more than once risen to the occasion of playing a salmon, and remained straight erect and fit after landing it." . .

564 P— THE "POPE" DRY FLY PERFECTION.

10 ft. in two pieces, cane-built, fitted with Cork or Pigskin Handle, all our latest improvements and patents, viz.: Lockfast Joints, "Bridge," Rings, Agate or Revolving Steel Gold-plated Top and Butt Rings, "Universal," Winch Fitting, Combined Spear and Button Ring to stick end fly into, and extra close tied. Weight 9¼ ozs. Price £3 13s.; Steel Centre £4 13s.

The above rod was specially built by us to the design and instructions of W. H. Pope, Esq., of Biggleswade. It is a splendidly powerful and easy actioned dry fly rod. A good many are in use and giving great satisfaction, so that it has become an established pattern.

Reine Britannique, Paris.—"Experiments show by evidence the superiority of the products of the House of Hardy, and notably of their cane rods with steel centres enclosed in two wrappings of cane. We have seen with great interest, at the Exhibition, the complete collection of cane-built fishing rods from the house of Hardy Brothers, of Alnwick, who are recognised as without rivals by all anglers of America and Europe."

Your "Pope" is infallible—higher praise is impossible.

W. F. BOOTH, Brighton, August, 1900.

☞ IN ORDERING FROM THIS LIST PLEASE QUOTE LETTER Q.

The " L.R.H. " Dry Fly Rod

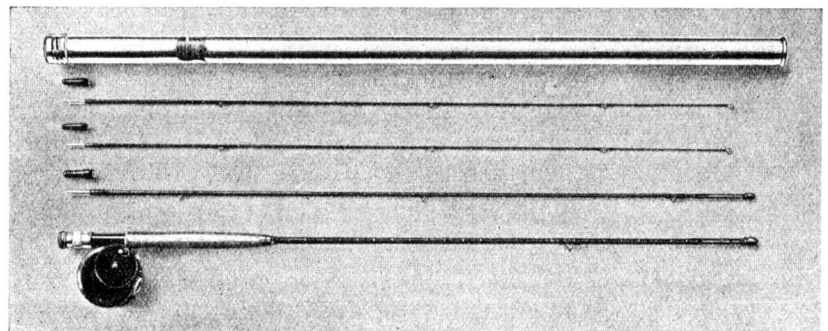

No. 1. 9 ft. 4 in. built of " **Palakona** " Split Bamboo in three pieces with two tops, cork handle, " Stud " lockjoints, with male joint protectors and lubricators, Agate rings throughout.   Fig. 2 Screw Grip Reel fitting, with " Reversible " Spear and Button.   Aluminium case to carry the whole rod.

Weight (including Spear and Button) : **7 ozs. 11 drms.**

Price, - - **£11 17s. 6d.**

Suitable reel and line, 3⅜" St. George Multiplier, page 134, with No. 1 or 2 Filip Line, page 118.

We have introduced this rod, designed by Mr. L. R. Hardy, to meet the increasing demand for a really strong, quick, light, powerful dry fly rod, to cast a long distance and to drive a line into a wind ; fitted with all our recent improvements.

No. 2. A slightly stronger rod of the same type and specification. Price as above.

(Overheard)—

A Gun-Room Dialogue (My rod box being unpacked).

> "Yon's a bonny box, Sandy."
> "Aye : there's bonnier inside it.
> Hardy, Alnwick—Ye canna beat them :
> *They're fair deils to make rods.*"

L. C. S.

47 CHURCH STREET, WEST HARTLEPOOL, 10/5/28.

I received the " L.R. Hardy " Dry Fly Rod you sent me safely and am very pleased with it. I fished a reservoir with it for six days, most of the time in a high wind, and it answered admirably.   W. T. T.

FOR DRY FLIES, SEE PAGE 58

ASSAM.

I am sending you a photo of four Mahseer taken on the Subansiri River in March. There is, of course, nothing extraordinary about the fish, but the tackle used might interest you. The three heaviest fish, 30, 25, and 22 lbs., were taken with the " Victor " Spinning Rod, using your No. 7 Spoon, 40 yards of your line, and a 3¼ in. " Silex " Reel. It was the finest fishing (in every sense) I have had this season, and my bag up to date totals 1960 lbs. I had to break the fish (using my finger on the drum of the " Silex ") to steady them in their first rush, and the little 8 foot " Victor " trembled with joy at tackling such worthy foemen. What's in a name ? a great deal with the " Victor." She put her back into the work or play and a dozen times disappointed Mahseer in his rush to the rapids, finally, ending as she began, a " Victor." I have caught roughly about 900 lbs. weight of fish on the " Victor " this season, the fish averaging 9 lbs., and she has done work which I had designed for the " Murdoch." The " Murdoch " you built me has had hard work ; two hours with a 70 lb. Mahseer ; and an hour and a half with a Goouch like a whale, in pitch darkness, my boatmen praying to their gods that the Sahib's line would break, which it did. ' The gods can't be fishermen. The " Murdoch " has landed 1100 lbs. of very big fish and has done magnificently.

WALTER LAMBERT, REVD.

The "FIELD."
A MERRY THREE HOURS WITH PIKE.

"Spending a few days at Christmas with a friend in the country, a day's jack fishing was proposed. We discovered that the only rod available was a light 10ft. 6in. "Hardy" Roach Rod, not at all fit for spinning ; but it was better than nothing, and we determined to try it. We at last succeeded in getting a pike of 9lb., which one of the boys secured by seizing him by the eye sockets. During the next quarter of an hour I landed two more, one about 8lb., the other 15lb. ; the latter I kept. Soon I had another run. It was some time before he came to the sur- face but when he did he looked about a twenty-pounder. Away went the line in another mad rush, but after a good deal of coaxing I at last got him safely into the boat ; he scaled just under 20lbs. At the second cast I hooked another, and soon knew that I had to deal with a big one. My little rod was bent nearly double, and, being alone in the boat, I had to be very careful. Out went the line, time after time, till my arm ached ; and after an exciting twenty minutes the fish was tired out, and I had him alongside. Holding my rod in my left hand, I managed to imitate the boys, and lifted him into the boat (no small trouble), and gave him his quietus with the boat hook. He measured 3ft. 8in., and scaled 25lbs. ; but, had be been in better condition, should have weighed fully 30lbs. I landed eight more, varying from 5lbs. to 15lbs., all of which I returned to the water. Altogether, I caught in under three hours over 150lb. weight of fish.—H.B.B."

Dear Sirs,—In the issue of the "Field" dated January 13th, you will see a letter headed "A merry three hours with Pike."

It may interest you to know that I was using one of your "Thames" Punt Rods, with a very light greenheart top—thanks to the good workmanship and excellent stuff it is made of, it thoroughly stood all the strain. My line was one of your fine tapered trout lines, on one of your latest patent reels.

An old fisherman told me, unless he had seen the rod he would not have believed it possible.   H.B.B.
WESTMINSTER.

Lady Sybil Grey presents her compliments to Messrs. HARDY and thinks they may be interested to know that the rod which they so generously gave to the Northumberland Stall at the National Bazaar, was raffled for as soon as she had secured 126 shilling tickets ; it was won by Lord Grey, who took 5 tickets, and given by him to Lady Sybil who was fortunate enough, while fishing in the Lakes of Killarney, to hook and land with it a small fresh run salmon, which gave her plenty of play. Lady Sybil has much pleasure in telling Messrs. HARDY that their rod has been greatly admired, and that she considers herself very lucky in being its owner.

She was also told while staying at Killarney, that a lady, 5 years ago, who was staying there, had hooked and landed after two hour's play, a beautiful salmon weighing 37 lbs. with one of Messrs. Hardy's famous rods.

The "Walpole Eyre" Crook Butt.

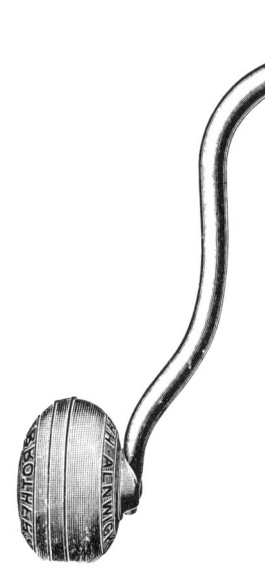

Walpole Eyre, Esq., writes:—I certainly derive much comfort from using the "Crook Butt;" it obviates that tendency to stoop over the rod, as it brings the reel and rod higher up the body, and in a more comfortable position when winding in the line. I may also add that in playing a fish, one finds the arms (with the "Crook Butt") in a very comfortable position, the right hand grasping the rubber button, the left above the reel.

We add this "Crook Butt" to our list, as it may be of comfort to those who spin, and who do not know of its existence. It entirely prevents stooping when winding in a cast.

Price, fitted to any rod, **7/6** each.

Leather Reel Line Guard.

Every angler is aware of the annoyance and danger caused by the line getting round the back part of the reel. From trials made with this article, we are satisfied that it meets the requirements in a practical way.

Trout Size, **1/4**; Salmon, **1/6**.

PNEUMATIC CUSHION FOR SALMON RODS.

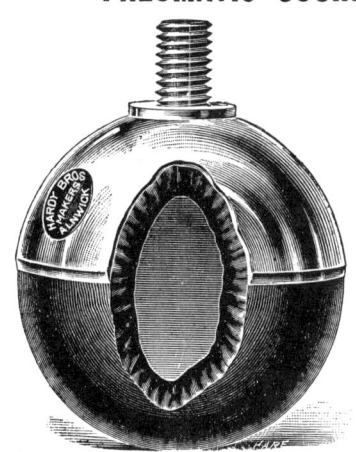

A great improvement on the ordinary India-Rubber Button, Size, $2\frac{1}{2}$ in. diameter. Price 6/6 each.

Fitted to our new Rods at an extra cost, 4/6.

I have been using your Pneumatic Balls on the end of my salmon rods, and like them very much better than anything I have seen for the same purpose before.

E. M. CROSFIELD.

☞ FOR SALMON FLIES, SEE PAGES 82 TO 99.

A New Series of Salmon Fly=Rods
THE "WYE" (1914 MODELS).

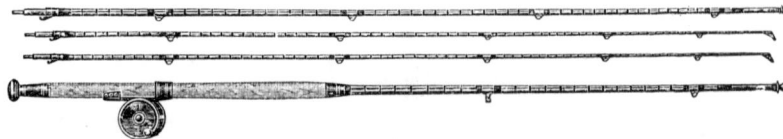

Hitherto rods of 14 ft. have generally been considered the minimum length for salmon fly fishing. Now we are adding 12½, 13½ ft. double-handed ; 10½ and 11 ft. single-handed to our list, as they are so frequently asked for. Many clients speak highly of these shorter and lighter rods for boat work, and have successfully killed large fish with them. For a lady or an elderly gentleman they are perfect. They are, of course, also excellent for heavy sea trout, rainbows in New Zealand, mahseer, etc.

The 12½ and 13½ ft. are stout double-handed, 3-piece rods with plenty of power. 10½ and 11 ft. are made both 2 and 3-piece, and are strong, single-handed rods, which can be comfortably used by men of fairly powerful physique. The handle is made extra long, so that when desired they can be used double-handed.

10½, 11, 12½, and 13 ft. "PALAKONA" split-bamboo, in three pieces, with two tops, or in 2-piece with one top, cork-covered handles and suction joint, "Bridge" intermediate, with Agate butt and end rings, patent screw grip reel fittings, india-rubber button. Made also in Greenheart with similar fittings.

3-PIECE DOUBLE HANDED.						SINGLE HANDED.				
Ft. Ins.	Split-bamboo without Steel Centre. £ s. d.	Split-bamboo with Steel Centre. £ s. d.	Lockfast Joints Extra.	Weights. Ozs.			Split-bamboo without Steel Centre. £ s. d.	Split-bamboo with Steel Centre. £ s. d.	Lockfast Joints Extra.	Weights. Ozs.
						3-piece.				
12 6	6 15 0	8 0 0	10/6	16½		10 ft. 6 in.	6 0 0	7 0 0	8/6	11¼
13 6	7 5 0	8 10 0	11/6	20		and 11 ft.	6 0 0	7 0 0	8/6	12
						2-piece.				Ozs. Drms.
						10 ft. 6 in.	4 5 0	5 5 0	3/-	11 6
						11 ,,	4 7 0	5 7 0	3/-	11¾ 0

If steel centre, weight 1 oz. heavier.

DEAR SIRS,—I have killed over 200 salmon on your one-handed rod. On looking through my diary, I find I killed 109 fish on it last season alone, weighing from 5 to 32 lbs., and also a 31 pounder the season before. It is a two jointed rod with two tops, both of which are in good order. and with fair usage may yet account for another century apiece.

Ross.　　　　　　　　　　　　　　　　　ROBERT PASHLEY.

Later he writes :

" Many thanks for the casts which are really excellent, also for your letter. Yes, sport on the Wye is splendid, and I know you will be interested to hear I killed exactly 90 fish on one of those new tops you made me six weeks ago for my rod, since Sept. 8th ; eighty of them weighing from 10 to 22 lbs., the remainder under 10 lbs. Since Sept. 7th my catch has been 108 salmon, all on the fly."

VANCOUVER, BRITISH COLUMBIA, Sept. 7th, 1916.

DEAR SIRS,—You may be interested to know that I have had the best' luck in the local streams of any angler in Vancouver, and practically all has been done with my 11 ft. "Wye" rod which arrived in March, and from then to July I had 57 steel heads, weighing from 6 to 15 lbs. My Hardy "Wye" rod is known all over the city. This is no exaggeration, as I always explained to fishermen that my good luck was more in my tools; indeed, I could demonstrate it by placing my line in any direction, and generally about 10 ft. further than others. After landing a fish with rod almost doubled for about half an hour, I would hand it to a spectator asking him to look and see if he could see a kink or any sign of the strain that had been on it, but no, it was as straight as a die.

Yours truly,　　　　　　　　　　F. J. WINLOW,

The " A. H. E. WOOD " Salmon Fly Rods

A SINGLE-HANDED ROD.

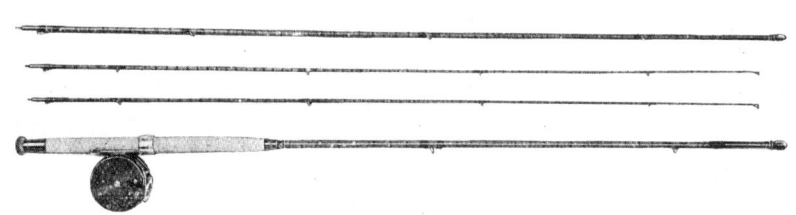

A single-handed 12 ft. rod designed with the assistance of A. H. E. Wood Esq., for his particular and successful style of Salmon fly fishing. During the last two seasons we have made many experiments to improve the balance of these rods. (Mr. Wood has again been good enough to assist us). One of the chief objects was to make a 12 ft. rod feel lighter in the hand and not be so tiring to the wrist, and yet retain all the power necessary for long casting and handling of a heavy fish. We are pleased to say that our efforts have been successful. The present 12 ft. " Wood " rods possess a particular charm. They look and are strong rods and capable of hard work, yet in the hand they do not feel as heavy as they look. Apart from Mr. Wood's style of fishing these rods are most useful in many parts of the world, particularly Canada and New Zealand.

12 ft. Built of " **Palakona** " Split Bamboo with steel centre, in three pieces with two tops, Cork covered handle, " Lockfast " joints, large " Bridge " rings with Agate butt and end rings, " Universal " reel fittings, India rubber button. Price **£9 17s. 6d.** each ; " Screw Grip " reel fitting, 6/6 extra.

No. 1. Light Rod, length 12 ft., weight 10½ ozs.

Suitable reel and line, 3⅞ in. Contracted " Perfect," page 131, with 35 yds. I.B.I. " Corona Superba " line, page 117, and 80 yds. No. 2 " Solidae " Silk Backing, page 125 ; or No. 2 " St. John," page 135, with 35 yds. I.B.I. " Corona Superba " and 100 yds. backing.

No. 2. Medium Rod, length 12 ft., weight 11¾ ozs.

Suitable reel and line, 3¾ in. " Perfect," page 130, with 42 yds. No. 5 " Corona " line, page 116, and 60 yds. No. 3 " Solidae " Silk Backing, page 125.

No. 3. Strong Rod, length 12 ft., weight 13 ozs.

Suitable reel and line, 4 in. " Perfect," page 130, with 42 yds. No. 4a " Corona " line, page 116, and 100 yds. No. 3 backing, page 125.

The " Hardy-Wanless " Rods
FOR " THREAD LINE " ANGLING

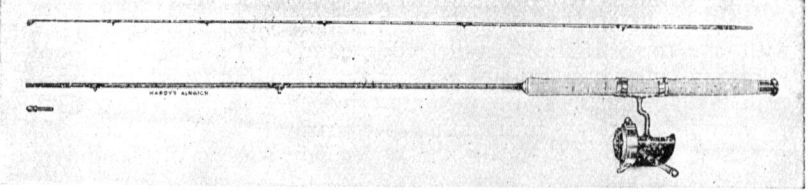

We have produced an entirely new series of rods for Thread Line Angling, developed with the assistance of Mr. Alex. Wanless (Author of " The Modern Practical Angler," " The Angler and The Thread Line " and " The Science of Spinning for Salmon and Trout.")

The special and **original** feature of these rods is that each grade is made to suit the strength of line with which it is to be used. That is to say, when a rod is under its greatest fishing stress, it will not break the line which should be used with it. Finer lines in reason can be used with any particular rod (see table showing Test Curves, etc.).

The " Test Curve " is the curve taken by a rod when under the greatest fishing stress, *i.e.* when the fish is about 15 ft. away and the rod is held at an angle of about 60 degrees from the ground (horizontal plane). The rod is bent until the angle formed by the rod and the line disappears and the line is a prolongation of the rod's point. The power required to do this denotes the test curve of the rod.

To make this clearly understood, the rods are graded and called by the breaking strains of their lines, such as the " 7 ft. 2 lb. line rod " which has a test curve of 6 ozs.

The rods are the " World's best " for this class of fishing and are a revelation of power combined with lightness. In casting the rods do the work, not the angler, because they are so perfectly balanced and attuned to the weight of line and bait that they give immediate response to a mere flick, which enables baits to be cast long distances, with great accuracy.

For example, with the 7 ft. 2 lb. rod (weighing 3¾ ozs.) and the No. 1 " Altex " reel and line of about 1½ lbs. breaking strain, a 1¼ in. Natural Minnow and leaded tackle but without any lead on the trace can be cast from 40 to 50 yds. with a mere flick of the wrist.

All the rods have, as is customary with " Hardy " products, been tested in practical angling by experts.

They are built with that perfection of construction and detail, and finished in the high class style which distinguishes a " Hardy " rod and all carry " Hardy's full guarantee."

Rods for use with Lines up to 6 lbs. breaking strain.

Specification.—7 ft. long made of Hardy's famous " Palakona " (regd. Trade Mark) split bamboo or best seasoned selected Greenheart in two pieces, with one top, " Hardy " suction joints, agate butt and end and closely spaced " Fullopen " bridge intermediate rings, long parallel cork handle for comfortable grip in casting and playing a fish, adjustable winch fittings, intermediate tyings, rubber button. Price 85/6

Rods for use with 9 and 10 lb. lines.

Single handed 7 ft. in two pieces and double handed 10 ft. in two and three pieces, specification as above.

Hardy-Wanless Worming Rod.

10 ft. built of " Palakona " (regd.) Split Bamboo, in three pieces with one top. 18 ins. parallel cork handle. Hardy's " Suction " joints, " Fullopen " bridge rings with agate butt and end rings, adjustable reel fittings, intermediate tyings. Price **120/-**

Also in two pieces to the same specification. Price **97/6**

These Worming Rods also make excellent rods for fly fishing and for light spinning.

LIST OF RODS AND PRICES

Spinning Rods

Length.	Reel to use.	B.S. of line to use.	For fish up to approx.	Test Curve.	In " Palakona " split bamboo.		In Greenheart.	
					Price.	Weight.	Price.	Weight.
		Lbs.	Lbs.			Ozs.		
7 ft.	No. 1 Altex	2	2 to 3	6 ozs.	**85/6**	3¾	**42/-**	4¾
7 ft.	No. 1 Altex	4	5 to 6	10 ozs.	**85/6**	4¼	**42/-**	5
7 ft.	No. 1 Altex or No. 2 Altex	6	General salmon fishing &c.	1 lb.	**85/6**	4¾	**42/-**	5¼
7 ft.	No. 2 Altex	9 to 10	do.	2¼ lbs.	**85/6**	5¼	**42/-**	6¾
10 ft. 2 pce.	No. 2 Altex	9 to 10	do.	2¼ lbs.	**105/-**	10¾	**52/6**	12¾
10 ft. 3 pce.	No. 2 Altex	9 to 10	do.	2¼ lbs.	**130/6**	11¼	**65/-**	13¼

Rods for Upstream Worming, Creeper and other Bait Fishing.

10 ft. 2 pce.	No. 1 Altex	1 to 2	2 to 3	6 ozs.	**97/6**	6¼	**45/-**	8¼
10 ft. 3 pce.	No. 1 Altex	1 to 2	2 to 3	6 ozs.	**120/-**	7⅛	**52/6**	8½

		Two Piece Rod.	Three Piece Rod.
Steel centre - - - - - -	extra	**15/-**	**21/-**
Agate rings throughout - - - -	,,	**17/6**	**27/6**

We do not recommend Agate rings (on account of their weight) throughout to rods for use with lines of less than 6 lbs. B.S.

While we give this table showing what we consider the best size of line to use with a particular rod, we emphatically do **NOT** say that this line must be used with this rod only. For instance, there would be no harm in an angler using a 2 lb. line with a 4 lb. rod, but reasonable care should be used and the fish played on a free or nearly free spool. We also indicate that the rods should be used for fish up to such and such a weight. This is only to give the angler an idea of the particular rod he should choose for his fishing.

Note.—All the single handed rods are made for stock in the 7 ft. length only. We find this to be the most convenient length for single handed Thread Line casting, and much less tiring than a longer rod. We will, however, be pleased to make longer rods to order at an extra charge of **10/-** each. This generally takes three weeks.

Testimonials.

WHITE LODGE, RICHMOND PARK, SURREY.

I am desired by H.R.H. the Duchess of Teck to thank you for your kind present of a fishing rod to H.S.H. Princess Victoria of Teck, and to say Her Serene Highness has much pleasure in accepting it. MARY THESIGER.

MARLBOROUGH HOUSE, PALL MALL, S.W.

Captain GREVILLE is desired by PRINCE ALBERT VICTOR to express his complete satisfaction with the Steel-Centre Cane-built Rod which was recently supplied to him by Messrs. HARDY BROTHERS.

AMBASSADE DE RUSSIE, LONDRES, 6th Oct. 1896.

The Secretary of the Imperial Russian Embassy is instructed to transmit you the thanks of His Imperial Majesty.

TORTWORTH COURT.

I have much pleasure in stating that I have fished with two of your rods of late years, under various circumstances, and find them superior to any others which I have been in the habit of using. DUCIE.

GAYTON HALL.

I have much pleasure in testifying to the excellence of your workmanship. The rods (split cane) which you have made for me, are all that I could wish them to be, and are the best casting rods that I have ever handled. ROMNEY.

RAVENSWORTH CASTLE.

I have employed the Messrs. HARDY BROTHERS for some years past, and have invariably found them most obliging and punctual in the execution of all orders, and their goods and materials of excellent quality. RAVENSWORTH.

CHIPPING NORTON.

For some years I have used your split cane trout rods, and have found them most satisfactory. I have never had a breakage, although my trout rods have been worked hard. MORETON.

CLIVEDEN, July 8th, 1893.

I have to thank you for two beautiful trout rods, the best I ever saw, which arrived safely yesterday, and for which I enclose a cheque. WESTMINSTER.

LONDON, 20th October, 1896.

I am glad to be able to tell you that I am very pleased indeed with it, being, as it is, so much lighter and equally effective as the old fashioned heavy ones. Please make me another, and forward it here, exactly the same as mine, and with a reel, WOLVERTON

LONDON, Oct. 6th, 1895.

I have fished regularly all the autumn with the rod, and cannot speak too highly of it, for it is the only rod with which I can Spey cast as well as I can throw overhead. LORD ALGERNON GORDON LENNOX.

MICHELDEVER STATION, May 7th 1896.

You are very welcome to give my name as one of those who can thoroughly recommend your trout rods. I have had two in use for many years, and they have never required any substantial repair. I caught a salmon of 8 lb. with one of them in Loch Quoich. NORTHBROOK.

☞ IN ORDERING FROM THIS LIST PLEASE QUOTE LETTER **G.**

Fishing in India

A 250 LBS, GOOUCH CAUGHT ON " MURDOCH " ROD
AND " SILEX " REEL.

Many clients have kindly given us valuable information regarding the most suitable rods, reels, and tackle for Mahseer and other Indian fishes, so that we are able to furnish the most perfect and reliable outfits for the work.

RODS FOR SMALL MAHSEER, SOWLIE, BYKRI, TROUT, etc., are from 10 to 14 feet, while for large mahseer a strong 16 ft. rod, which will stand the strain of a 3 in. spoon in heavy water, is used. The 16 ft. split-bamboo, steel centre " Hi Regan," page 267, 14 ft. " Paradox," page 263, and 14 and 16 ft. " Alnwick " Greenhearts, page 286, are excellent.

For those who prefer the usual spinning outfit as used in this country the " Murdoch " rods and " Silex " reels are recommended. See page 276 and " Silex " reels page 138.

In all our rods the ferrules are shrunk on, riveted, and splint ends tightly bound with very strong waxed silk, and well varnished. Our split-bamboo rods have metal lined and covered ferrules and tenons, completely protecting the bamboo against damp, etc.

REELS must be made of metal; wood and ebonite are useless, as they will not stand the climate. As a fly reel, the " Perfect " is preferred and praised by many, the 4½ in. to hold 140 yards of line for larger rods, and so on down to the small sizes for trout rods (see page 126). As a moderate priced article the " Uniqua " reel (page 137) is thoroughly reliable.

The " Silex " reel (page 138) is the most perfect spinning reel in the world. Thousands are now in use in India and give the utmost satisfaction. For heavy mahseer the extra large 4½ " Silex " is indispensable, as about 200 yards of line must be used.

LINES.—The " Alnwick " (page 121) is specially recommended.

TRACES.—Single and twisted gut are good, but we think our " Punjab " cable laid Amalgam steel, silver-plated, twisted wire trace, is the most reliable. A client in India writes : " I have not yet come across anything in the wire trace line that is at all as good. Nothing else was ever made like it." (See page 108.)

ARTIFICIAL BAITS.—Spoons. The " Skene Dhu " patterns (page 201), which are made of aluminium, and can be thrown with a fly rod, are excellent. Other patterns (page 201) will also be found good. These spoons are double thick, and of correct weight, mounted with eyed treble hooks and " Punjab " Amalgam steel wire.

Devons are excellent. Our " Pioneers " are mounted in a special manner, which permits broken hooks being easily replaced. The mount is made entirely of steel, and is therefore very strong. See page 194.

Phantoms with blue backs and silver bellies well leaded, Swallow Tails, and improved Halcyons, are sufficient. All baits should be mounted with " Oval " wire eyed treble hooks and " Punjab " cable laid Amalgam steel wire.

NATURAL BAITS.—" Crocodile " Spinners, and " Wobblers," are the best for spinning the chilwa or other small fish. The former has been most extensively used.

FLY CASTS.—The usual salmon and trout are suitable.

FLIES.—For Mahseer and Carnatic Carp. Blackamoor, Cock of the Walk, Smoky Dun, Alexandra, Silver Doctor, Jock Scott, Yellow Spider, Claret Fly, etc., dressed on No. 2/0 to 6 extra strong " oval " wire eyed hooks (some of which should be " Aaro's," see page 91), are known patterns and kill well. For the smaller fish, Trout, Sowlie, and Bykri, the general patterns of small lake and river flies are useful. They also take Small Spoons, Artificial Baits, and Natural Minnows on " Crocodile " Tackle, etc.

Fishing in Ceylon

By R. C. ROBINSON, CEYLON

I NOTE in your catalogue that you quote various Colonies for fishing, but omit Ceylon, at which I am surprised, as now it is becoming a favourite winter trip for people from England and the fishing is excellent.

There is very good Mahseer fishing in the Kelani Ganga River, and Mahseer are to be found in most of the rivers running from the hill districts.   The rivers around Newera Eliya, from about 4000 feet to 7000 feet, are stocked with trout, as well as the lakes in Newera Eliya.   The biggest lake at Newera Eliya is stocked with Mirror Carp which afford good sport.   This is mostly controlled by the Fishing Club, but tickets can be obtained.

There is also a fish in the Low Country artificial tanks and lagoons, which I have found give excellent sport.   The local name is Lulu, and they run to 15 lbs. or so.

In one of the estate bungalows I occupied some years ago there were three small artificial lakes, some three acres in extent, and a predecessor of mine had stocked them with Lulu.   I tried them with various bottom baits, till one morning I noticed them rising at a fly.   Thereafter I always used a dry fly, with a fine tapered cast, and a light rod, and had very excellent sport, particularly in the morning when they were basking about 18 ins. below the surface.

They will take a dry fly exactly like a trout, but have to be kept away from the weeds, or a break is certain with one of anything over a pound.

They came best at a May Fly, or an Alder with a touch of red added.

I have since caught them in Low Country tanks.

A live frog is an absolutely deadly bait for them, but bad for the frog.

I mention this as it may interest you to add them to your list of fish that can be caught with a dry fly.

Angling in Australia

By the late Mr. HOWARD JOSELAND

STOCKING of rivers is being much more vigorously undertaken now than in previous years, the result of co-operation between the Government Departments, which control the Fisheries, and various angling Societies.

The chief trout streams of New South Wales are the **Snowy** and its tributaries, among which are the Thredbo, Euecumbene and Moonbah.

The **Murrumbidgee** and its tributaries, viz. : the Tuross, Big Badja, Queanbeyan, Goodradigbee, Cooter and others (some of which run through the Federal Territory of **Canberra**).

The **Tumut** and its tributaries, the Yarrangobilly and Goodbragandra.

These are in the Monaro district, in which is situated Mount Kosciusko, the snow from which feeds the Snowy and its tributaries.

Cooma, 270 miles from Sydney, is the jumping-off place for this district.

The Fish river, Duckmaloa and Campbells rivers rise in the Blue Mountain district.

North of Sydney the New England tablelands are intersected with the head waters of the Barrington, Hastings, Clarence and others, including the Serpentine and Styx.

Victoria possesses many excellent streams, the Kiewa, Ovens and tributaries. The Delatite and others in Gippsland.   The **Latrobe** and its tributaries and the **Yarra**.   Near Ballarat are well-stocked lakes and a few streams.

The best trout waters of Australia are situated from 100 to about 350 miles from Sydney and Melbourne, in altitudes from 1,000 to 5,000 ft., and many are easily accessible by train or motor ; whilst the climate is favourable to camping. Fairly good sport can, however, be obtained within 50 miles of Melbourne.

In many Monaro streams both **Salmo Fario** and **S. Irideus** flourish together, but in some waters of Victoria and New South Wales they are kept separate Rainbows are frequently caught up to 3 lbs., and occasionally 10 lbs. and over

Brown trout seldom scale the heavier weight, but average better. A fair general average is 1 lb. The minimum lawful length is 11 in. Rainbows are the more vigorous fighters, but are capricious risers, therefore brown trout, which rise more consistently, though sluggish in comparison, are favoured by many anglers. The most successful anglers use nine to ten feet "**Palakona**" split-bamboo rods, such as the " J. J. Hardy " (page 278) or " De Luxe " (page 293), and they usually fish with dry fly, especially where there are brown trout.

The various Palmers, May flies, March Browns, etc, on No.3 to 6 hooks and small floaters, such as Ginger Quill, Black Spinner, and various duns are typical.

For wet flies, Governor, Coch-y-bondhu, Hare's Ear, Hardy's Favourite Palmers, Invicta, lake flies and small salmon flies should suffice. For lake and still water rivers such as Big Badja, Tuross and Queanbeyan, flies should be on Nos. 5 or 6 hook.

For those who have leisure and vigour to fish out-of-the-way places remarkably good fishing may be obtained. The angler who is fairly expert will meet with few blank days, and many fair baskets of good fish. The chief charm of trouting in Australia lies in the perfect conditions usually obtaining, the air is exhilarating and temperate, the rivers much less subject to spate than in the Old Country. Mosquitos are unknown on the trout streams. The majority of anglers do not wear waders, but are content with thick woollen stockings or putties.

There are Government accommodation houses, at Kosciusko, the Creel, Yarrangobilly in New South Wales and Mt. Buffalo in Victoria. No licence is required and landowners seldom object to anglers on their land ; thus the trouting is probably the best free fishing in the world, and is superior to much that is highly paid for.

The season in Victoria commences September 1st and in New South Wales November 1st, and closes in April in both states.

Another sporting fish is the perch (*percalates fluviatilis*), which takes any large fly, such as Jock Scott, Peveril of the Peak, Heckham and Red, Hornet, etc. This fish frequents the coastal streams and when hooked bolts for any shelter, so that strong trout tackle must be used. They run up to about 6 lbs., but half that weight is deemed a good fish.

Among other fresh-water indigenous fish are Murray Cod, occasionally taken up to 100 lbs., Murray golden perch, Macquarie perch and Silver perch. These are taken usually on ground bait, sometimes on spoon ; their chief merit is in their culinary properties. In Queensland a giant perch affords fine sport.

SALT WATER FISHING

The coast of Australia from Broom in Western Australia to Cairns in Queensland, the most settled portion of Australia, is too vast a seaboard to deal with, except in a sketchy way.

Along this coast are as diverse game fish as in other parts of the world such as swordfish, saw-fish, giant mackerel, devil-fish, rays, tunny, albacore, king-fish, jewfish and sharks, all waiting the angler.

Fish up to 30 or 40 lbs., and the smaller sea salmon, tailer and king fish and bonito, have been frequently caught in the harbours of Victoria, New South Wales and Queensland.

For lighter and more delicate fishing, there are flathead, bream, snapper, whiting, blackfish, drummer and jewfish, etc., which may be angled for from boat or shore, either casting off the reel or float fishing.

Australia possesses many inlets and the beaches are ideal to fish from, the sand hard, and tide rising slowly four to six feet. The best months are November to June. Visitors are referred to the various Tourist Departments ; The New South Wales Rod Fishers' Society, Sports Club, Sydney ; or the Piscatorial Association, Melbourne.

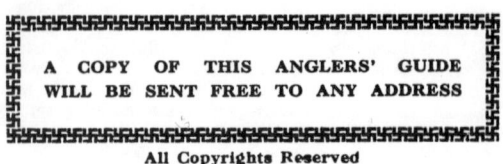

A COPY OF THIS ANGLERS' GUIDE
WILL BE SENT FREE TO ANY ADDRESS

Hardy's Patent "Royde" Net,

WITH SELF-LOCKING JOINT.

Fitted with "Baerlein" Patent
Weighing Arrangement.

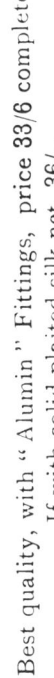

Best quality, with "Alumin" Fittings, price 33/6 complete.
If with solid plaited silk net, 36/-.

This net is the same as that figured on page 309, with the addition of Mr. Baerlein's arrangement for weighing. The butt end is fitted with a patent reversible hook on which the fish is hung, while the net is extended as in the picture. The centre of gravity is then taken on a string loop as shown, or over a bar, or held on the finger. When this is found, the lbs. and ounces marked on the scale at that point give the weight. The handle is also set off in inches, and so can be used to measure up to 20 inches.

Hardy's Patent Combined Net and Seat.

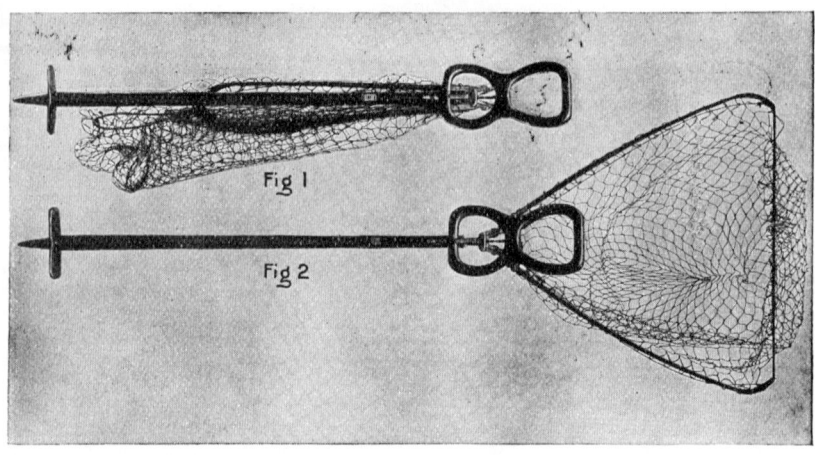

A combination of the ordinary sportsman's seat and our patent "Royde" Net, page 305. Fig. 2, Net thrown over ready for use. Fig. 1, folded for carrying.

For use as a seat the net is closed, as in Fig. 1, and the seat fixed at right angles to the shaft, where it is locked in position by a spring stud.   An excellent arrangement for the dry fly man, as it provides a dry seat or rest while waiting for a rise.   Price complete, 50/-.

The "Featherweight" Landing Net.

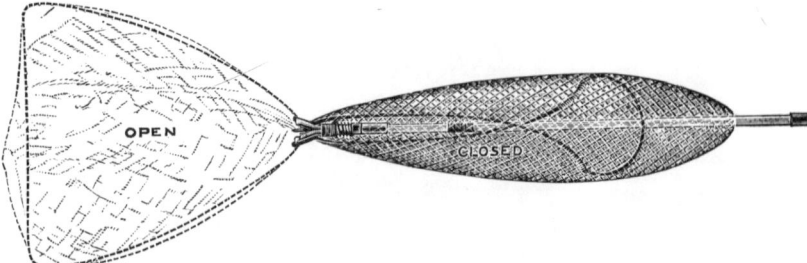

A specially light folding Net made to meet the requirements of those who favour a light kit.   The action and style are that of the Improved Self-locking "Royde," page 305.   The length folded is 2ft. 4ins., when extended 3ft. 7ins., and the total weight being only 9½ ounces.   It is a well-made strong little net of convenient type. The net is solid plaited hook proof silk.   The length of arms 15ins. Price 21/-. Carrying Sling 2/-. This net can be made with telescopic handle, as the "Eclipse," see page 306, measuring, when closed, 17 inches overall, 10s. 6d. extra.

The "SUIRVALE" Landing Net

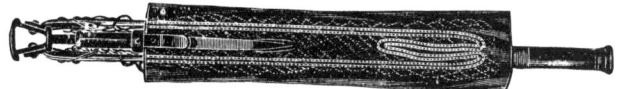

Extended in use, 62 in.   Folded as shown, 26 in.   WEIGHT 27 ozs.

The feature of this net is its protection against briars, thorn-hedges, etc. It is light, portable, easily handled, and the netting is fully protected.

The design of the net is similar to the " Eclipse," page 307. Fixed to the handle is a light waterproof cloth sheath, into which the netting is enclosed when not in use, see dotted lines.

The netting is waterproof solid plaited silk. Price, **55/-** each. The button at end of handle can be unscrewed at any time to remove sand or grit, or for oiling.

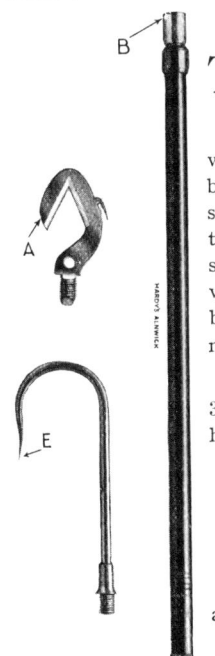

Twig Cutter for Releasing Fly

A short telescopic handle, made of light material measuring when closed 14 in. overall so that it will go into an ordinary bag or creel. To use : Screw cutter A into socket B and screw off cap C which exposes a male screw $\frac{3}{8}$ in. dia. × 19 threads (the size common with most landing nets) which is screwed into landing net enabling one to reach the twig on which the fly is caught.   This handy little instrument can be used as a telescopic handle for gaff or net. Gaff-head E made of Firth's stainless steel can be supplied.

Our " Royde " and " Featherweight " landing nets, pages 306 and 309, are made with an extension telescoping into the handle with twig cutter. Price **12/6** extra.

Price of telescopic extension with cutter and

pigskin pocket - - - - -	**16/6** each.
Price of gaff head - - - - -	**7/6** ,,

We will adapt any landing net to take in this instrument at a cost of **3/6**.

BOURNEMOUTH, June, 1929.

Will you be good enough to fill for me the small order for tackle enclosed.   I enclose amount in payment for same and am sure when they reach me they will reach the same high standard that makes all your tackle so notable and, above all, dependable. Yours faithfully,   JOHN HASLETTE VAHEY.

FOR GENERAL PATTERN TROUT FLIES, SEE PAGE 56.

1930   171

"THE DON" COMBINED LANDING NET AND WADING STAFF.

FIG. 1.

FIG. 2.

The head of this net is of the Improved Royde Style. The staff is fitted with a heavy iron shoe and has a rubber knob for use as a hand grasp when wading, Fig. 2.

FIG. 1 shows position while fishing. The staff and net hanging from the carrying strap over the shoulder leave the hands free. In this position the heavily shod end keeps the staff foot on the bed of the river.

FIG. 3.

FIG. 2. As a wading staff, the net arms being folded are out of the way.

FIG. 3. In landing a fish; the ring on the carrying strap is pushed out of the clip, when the shaft slides out to the length required. The net arms are then thrown over, when they lock and are ready for use. When a fish is in the net, the shaft is raised, and slides back through the ring into a convenient position, so that both hands may be used for unhooking and killing the fish. This avoids the necessity of wading ashore and disturbing the water.

This combination is a life-saving arrangement. A client who uses one assures us that he would certainly have been drowned but for its aid. No man who wades rough streams should be without one.

Length over all as a wading staff, 50 in.
Length over all as a landing net, 61 in.
Price complete with Carrying Sling, **60/-**

MADE TO TAKE THE TWIG CUTTER, SEE PAGE 308.

HARDY'S COMBINED GAFF AND BALANCE.

(REGISTERED.)

(Designed from an idea by Colonel S. H. N. Johnstone.)

644 G.B.

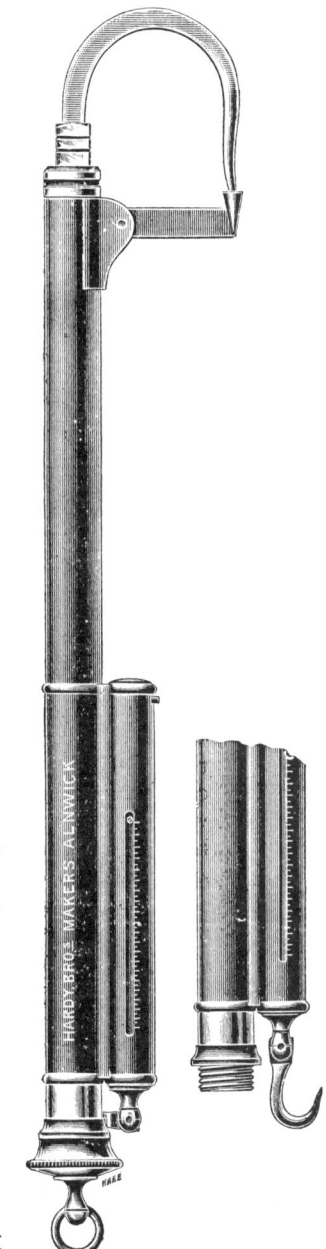

Price 30/-

A Thoroughly Useful, Strong, and well made Article, which should be in the possession of every Angler.

Length when closed is 15¾ inches.   When extended, 35 inches.

As will be seen from Illustration, the cap simply requires to be unscrewed to bring the balance (which weighs up to 40lb. by half-pounds) into operation.

☞ FOR CANE-BUILT STEEL CENTRE RODS, SEE PAGE 194.

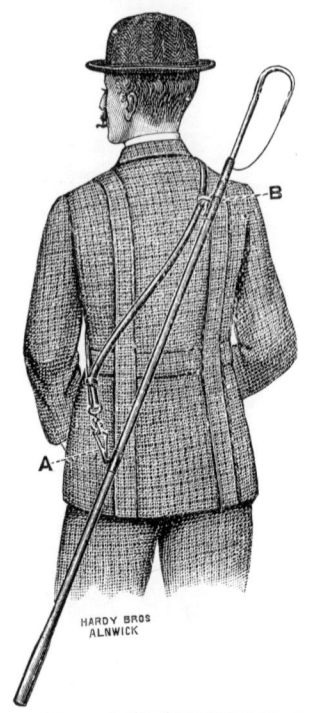

HARDY BROS
ALNWICK

Hardy's "Lash On" Gaff,

with Improved Carrying Arrangement,

Illustration shows a long handled "Lash-on" gaff with a very simple and secure method of carrying. The gaff can easily be released with one hand, and is very useful for anyone salmon or pike fishing without an attendant. To release the gaff open scissor clip A and push gaff upwards when it will release itself at clip B.

The gaff consists of a best quality steel fluted hook attached to a 4 feet hickory handle.

Price complete with carrying attachment, **15/-** each

Price without carrying attachment, **12/6** each.

"MILLER'S" AUTOGAFF. Pat. No. 17868.

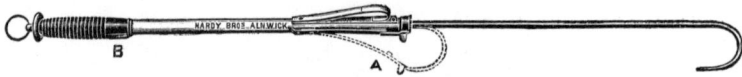

This convenient telescopic gaff which is automatic and is made from a pattern given us by Mr. Douglas Miller of Glasgow, who has used one with very satisfactory results.

The gaff is in two joints and carried either by the ring at the end or by the patent clip attachment, shown in illustration. When required for use it may be taken in either hand and the trigger B pressed by the thumb, this releases the gaff which automatically extends itself. At the same time the point protector A, which carries a stud on its inner side, locks the gaff and prevents it closing.

When it is desired to close the gaff the point protector is lifted and the gaff pressed home, where it is automatically held in position.

Price **32/6.**

If with patent carrying attachment as illustrated, **6/6** extra.

HARDY'S COMBINED GAFF & BALANCE. (Regd.)

A Thoroughly Useful, Strong, and well made Combination of a three joint Telescopic Gaff and a Sportsman's Balance (which weighs up to 40 lb. by half-pounds).

Length when closed, **15¾** inches.   When extended, **35** inches.

The "ORCHY" Wading Staff and Gaff

IMPROVED DESIGN. Reg. No. 710349.

The "Orchy" Wading Staff and Gaff combines all our latest improvements. Our original pattern, called the "Tyne" and shown on page 278, has been made by us for nearly 50 years ; and is a great favourite.

The improvements in this new design are :

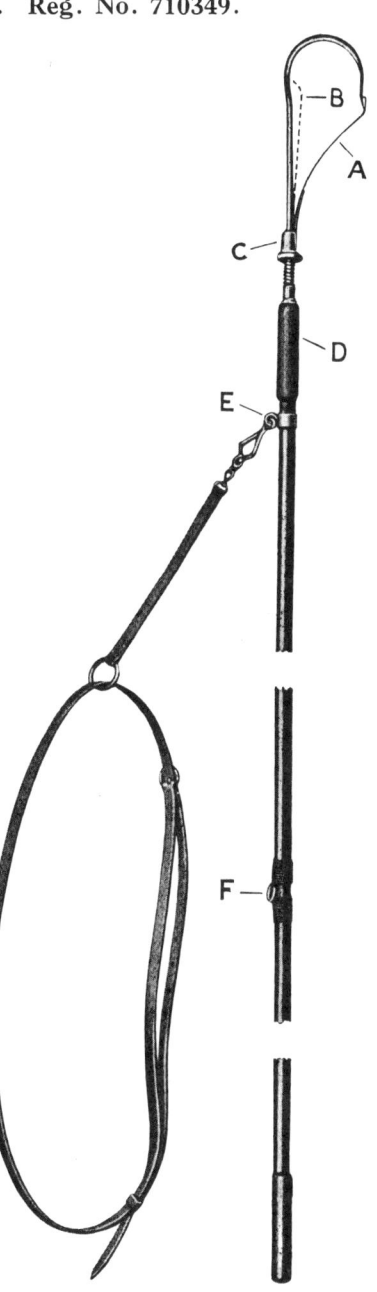

1. A perfected form of our patent point protector A.

2. A simple and handy method of releasing the protector. On pulling down the sleeve C, the protector A is released from the point and springs to position B quite out of the way when gaffing.

3. A comfortable india rubber hand grasp is fixed on the shaft at D.

The carrying sling is shown in position as for wading. The gaff is easily and quickly released at E when required. To arrange the sling for carrying over the shoulder, the end of the strap is threaded through the eye F, and the scissor clip attached at E. The gaff hook is made of rustless steel.

Length over all, 4 ft. 9 in.

Price, **47/6.**

STYLES OF CARRYING "H.B." NET AND "CARRY-ALL" CREEL.

Fig. 1.
Basket worn as a knapsack, with net carried in clip from shoulder strap.

Fig. 2.
Usual position when fishing with net carried by clip ready for use.

Fig. 3.
Basket worn suspended from the left shoulder and hips, with net trailing as

THE "PERFECT" CREEL.

Hardy's Patent.

No. 704 P.

SELECTING A FLY.

Fishing Gazette.—" A happy idea and has many advantages."

In introducing our new patent "Perfect" Creel, we claim the following important advantages:—No. 1, the lid is made to open the reverse way, *i.e.*, from the angler, and not against him. No. 2, the patent tackle book is strapped to inside of lid, and forms the most convenient tackle carrier imaginable, as it can be opened, spread out, and a fly selected while standing in the water without fear of losing any. No. 3, this book is made on a patented principle, which carries the flies and gut quite straight; if necessary it can be removed from the basket and carried as an ordinary book. (See No. 671 P, page 233.) No. 4, the creel has a top compartment for carrying lunch, &c., same as in our Carry-all Creel, page 243. No. 5 the partition for this compartment can be removed when necessary, as, for instance in carrying wading brogues. No. 6, it is also waterproof, and intended to be used as an anglers seat; when not required, it is fastened with straps to bottom of basket quite out of the way. No. 7, the addition of a net will be found most useful and convenient for carrying a light coat, wading stockings, &c., and in fishing comes in handy for dropping fish into, besides accommodating any fish too large for creel. The straps are arranged so that they can be worn either as a knapsack in travelling, or slung from the shoulder in fishing. We say, without fear of contradiction, that this is the best and most ingenious angler's creel ever made.

Sizes.

No. 1.   9 in. × 15 in., to carry 10lb. fish.   Price, complete, 35/-
No. 2.   10 in. × 16 in , to carry 15lb. fish.   Price, complete, 36/6
No. 3.   11 in. × 17 in., to carry 20lb. fish.   Price, complete, 38/-

If Baskets are required without the Book, deduct price of Book as per Page 233.   If without Net, 6s. less in each case.

"The Trout Fishers' Bag"

A strong, light, compact, practical bag made of best quality proofed flat canvas.   There is no rubber or leather used in its make-up to perish. It has one roomy compartment which is provided with a good big gusset to give easy access.   There are two inside pockets in this compartment. A roomy net, to take a fish bass (supplied) and rolled up oilskin or other kit, forms the front of the bag.   The back of the bag is fitted with a stiffener.   The opening to the compartment and net can be secured by a quick spring security fastener.   Carrying rings for net at side are fitted.

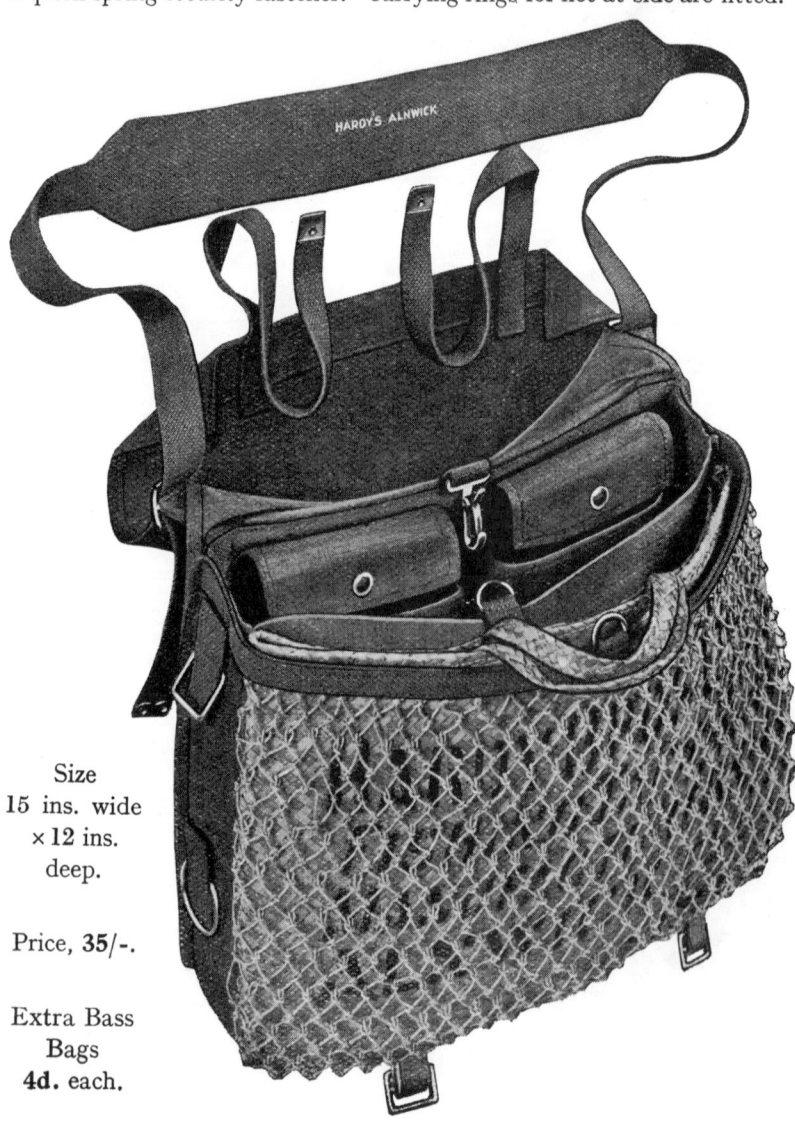

Size
15 ins. wide
× 12 ins.
deep.

Price, 35/-.

Extra Bass
Bags
4d. each.

FLY, TACKLE, & BAIT BOXES.

673   THE "H. B." EYED-FLY BOX (Registered).

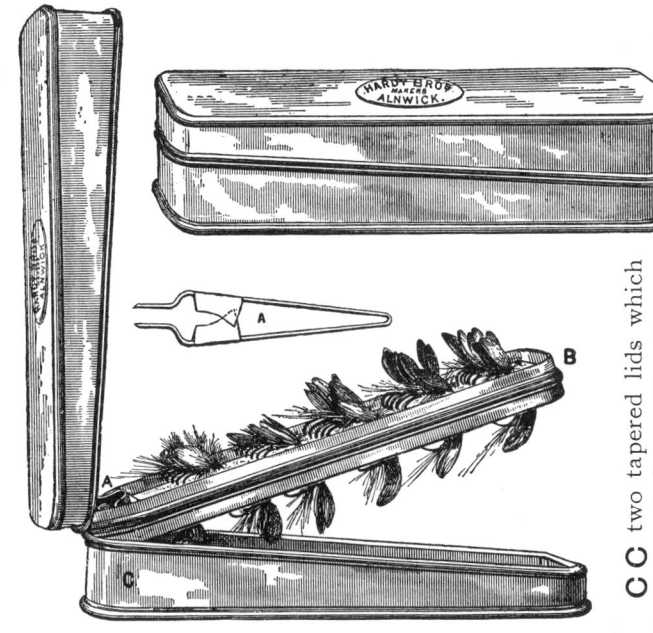

C C two tapered lids which close on corked tray **B**. **A** compartment for holding MR. PENNELL's tweezers. Size, $5\frac{1}{2} \times 3\frac{3}{4} \times 1\frac{3}{8}$ in. deep; weight, 7 ounces.

We claim for this box that it has very great capacity, holding one gross of flies easily. Having two compartments, should one be sufficient for flies, the other may be used for holding casts or tackle. From its peculiar construction it occupies very little space in proportion to its capacity, the larger flies being placed at the deep ends, and the smaller ones at the shallow. It will also do for flies on gut. Price 6s. 6d. Tweezers extra.

EYED-FLY GUT-CUTTER AND TWEEZERS.

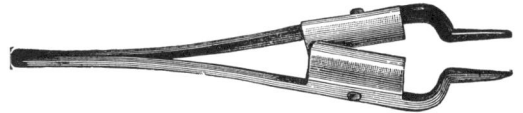

673 T.—For cutting off spare gut ends, and extracting flies from the box, &c., indispensable for comfort and efficiency in eyed-hook fly-fishing. Price 2s. 6d.

☞ IN ORDERING FROM THIS LIST PLEASE QUOTE LETTER **G.**

HARDY'S "SPECIAL" EYED FLY BOXES.

No. 673½.

THE GIRODON PRALON.—REGD.

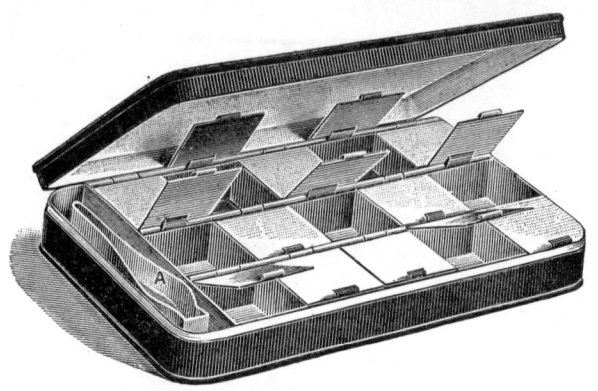

Size, 6 in. long, 3½ in. wide, ⅞ in. deep, Japanned tin, with place for tweezers, and 15 compartments for flies, so that as many different kinds can be kept separately. It is very compact and there is no danger of spoiling the flies either by damp or crushing. Price, 10s. 6d. each.

THE IMPROVED

"GIRODON PRALON" FLY BOX.

REGISTERED.

This Box has a celluloid washable tablet as an index to the compartments.

The name of the Fly is simply written against the number and reference is easy and certain.

A—place for tweezers.

Price 13/6.

☞ FOR FLOATING FLIES, SEE PAGES 62 TO 72.

THE
"Carlton" Salmon Fly & Cast Case

Regd. No. 496,582.

Fig. 2.   **Price 24/-.**   Fig. 1.

Size of leather case 8 in. × 5⅜ × 1¾, (carries **80** flies).

Fig. 1. is the fly carrier, which has two leaves. One side is deep enough to take double flies up to 3/0 ; the other is shallower, and will take single or smaller double flies. The fly holders are fixed on sheets on which the names of the flies can be written.

Fig 2. The case is made of the best grained cowhide, with flap pocket in front for casts. Provision is made inside lid for scissors and stiletto.

THE
"Roxburgh" Salmon Fly Reservoir.

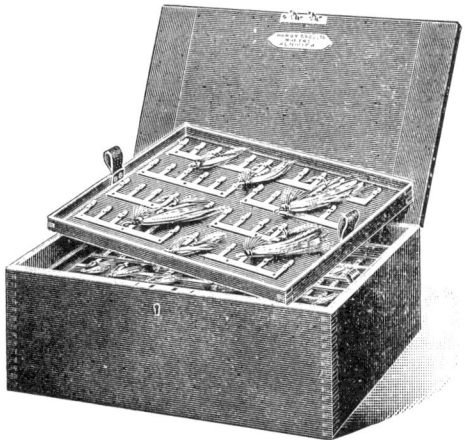

Made in polished teak, with inlaid name plate, lever lock, and leather handle. Size 10ins. × 8ins. × 3½ins., with four moveable trays fitted with german silver clips to hold flies ; one tray fitted to take Sea Trout flies. Will hold 13 dozen Salmon flies and 9 dozen Sea Trout flies.

Price £2 5s. 0d.

The "Halford 1904 Series" Dry Fly Boxes.

(1913 MODELS.)

No. 1.

MAY FLY BOX.

Size $5\frac{1}{2}$ × $3\frac{1}{2}$ ins.

× $\frac{7}{8}$ ins.

PRICE **10/6.**

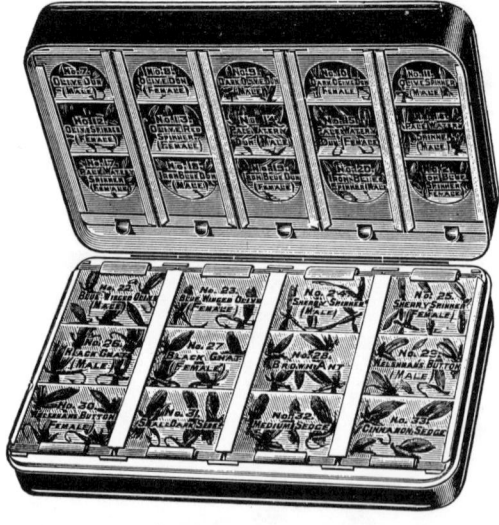

No. 2.

SMALL FLY BOX.

Size $5\frac{1}{2}$ × $3\frac{1}{2}$ ins.

× $1\frac{1}{4}$ ins.

PRICE **25/-.**

These boxes are made of Japanned Tin. The compartments are fitted with transparent Celluloid lids, so that the flies may be seen, while the name and number of each fly is printed on the lid. The No. 1 box carries the May Flies Nos. 1 to 6 (See page 74), each compartment being of sufficient depth to hold about 1 dozen flies.

The small fly box holds the flies Nos. 7 to 33, (See page 74), which complete the series. The arrangement of the lids is very handy. In the May Fly box they pull out, so that only one compartment is open at a time. The Small Fly box is also arranged as above on one side, while the other exposes three at a time.

The idea of the boxes is educational as well as general handiness; Everyone does not know his "Halford" by heart, nor can he remember the various flies. By using these boxes however, he soon becomes acquainted with the flies and their spinners by the constant reference.

The "Neroda" Drywet Fly Box

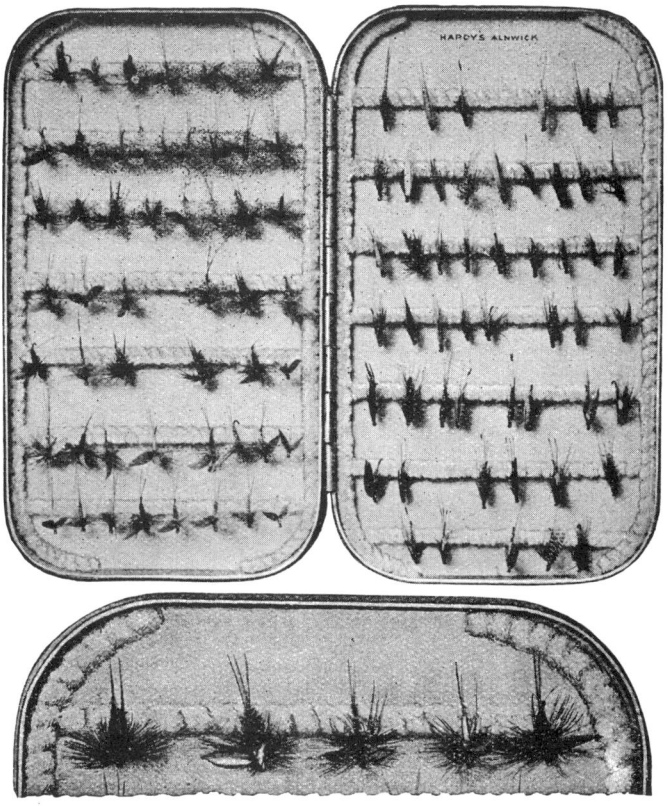

Natural Size.

An entirely new method of holding eyed flies **wet and dry.**

The flies are hooked over the Chenille-covered bars and cannot drop out or change position. A severe shaking does not disturb them. Other important advantages are that the hackles are protected and the flies are always on view. The method of holding allows a very large number of flies being carried as the flies may be in close together. The smallest trout fly to Loch flies can be carried.

Box No.	DESCRIPTION.	SIZE. in.	PRICE. "NERODA"	PRICE. ALUMINIUM
6	May Flies and Large Dry Flies.	$6\frac{1}{4} \times 3\frac{3}{4} \times 1\frac{3}{8}$	8/6	7/6
7	General Patterns—Wet or Dry Trout Flies.	$6\frac{1}{4} \times 3\frac{3}{4} \times 1\frac{13}{16}$	8/6	7/6
8	General Patterns—Wet or Dry Trout Flies	$3\frac{7}{8} \times 2\frac{1}{2} \times 1$	6/6	not stocked
9	May and Large Dry Flies in deep side and general pattern Wet Flies in shallow one	$6\frac{1}{4} \times 3\frac{3}{4} \times 1$	8/6	not stocked

BAIT KETTLES

Page 89.   Strong oval zinc kettles with inner
departments to lift out.

9 in., **9/11** ; 10 in., **11/-** ; 11 in., **12/6** each.

See The Super Bottom Fishers Tackle Catalogue
page 40.

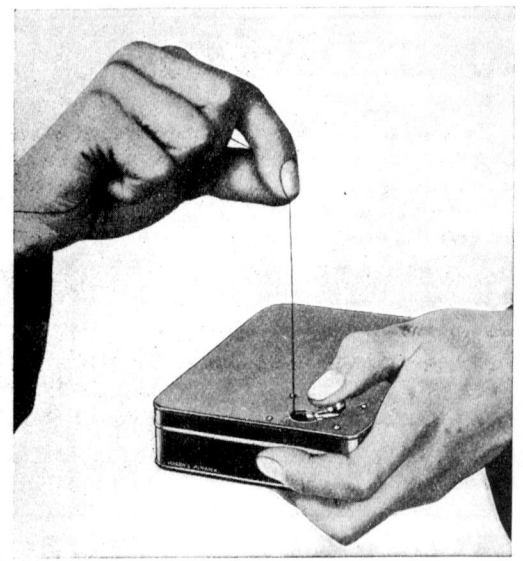

The "Attwood" Fly Box

The Illustration
shows the Guillo-
tine Lid open and
the fly in the used
compartment. On
releasing the lid
the fly is chopped
off and left.

A Japanned fly box $5\frac{3}{4}$ in. × 4 in. × $1\frac{1}{8}$ in. with 29 compartments
for flies, and a large compartment for used flies. All fitted with transparent lids.

As it is not desireable to mix the wet used flies with the dry ones,
a compartment has been specially furnished for them. This compartment is so arranged that the fly is, when attached to the gut cast,
put into it, and cut off by the Guillotine Lid.

The illustration shows a fly and point of gut cast being put into the
compartment for wet used flies, and the spring controlled Guillotine Lid
being held back with the thumb. On being released it chops off the
gut close to the fly. After the day's fishing is over all the flies used that
day can be taken out the special compartment and " Set up," the gut
ends removed, and replaced in their proper places. Price **42/-**.

Hardy's New " Multum-in-Parvo "

(Much in little)

SPINNERS BOX

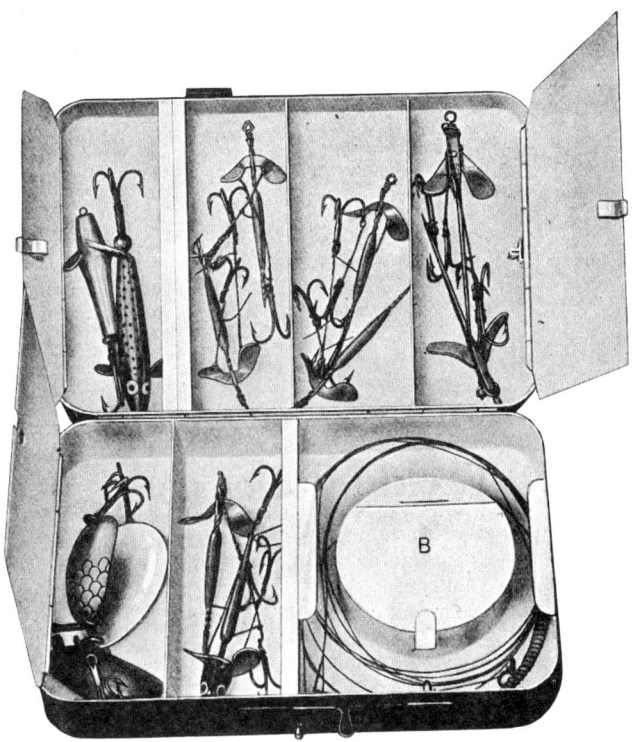

Made in Japanned tin. As the partitions are movable, the compartments may be arranged to hold a large assortment of artificial baits, natural bait tackles and traces. The circular box B holds leads, spare hooks, swivels, etc.

The lid cover is fitted with guides in which the movable partitions are carried when not in use.

The three right-hand spaces in the lid may be converted into two large horizontal compartments, and the two compartments in the bottom of box made into one large space.

A practical and useful box :—

No. 1.—Size $7\frac{1}{4}$ ins. $\times 4\frac{1}{2}$ ins. $\times 1\frac{13}{16}$ ins.   Price **22/6** each.

No. 2.— ,,   6   ,, $3\frac{3}{4}$,, $1\frac{11}{16}$,,   ,,   **19/6**   ,,

The "COMPACTUM" Case

For carrying Artificial Baits, Natural Bait Tackles, Traces, Leads, Spare Hooks, etc.

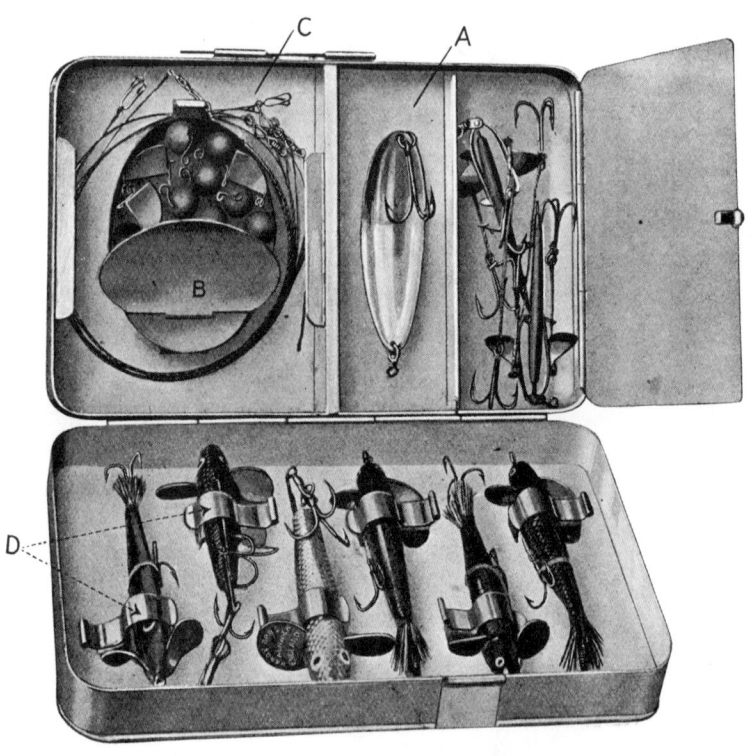

Made in Japanned Tin, and designed to carry all that is required for spinning. The method of holding the baits is novel, and permits of easy selection, while it prevents the baits being entangled and damaged.

Each size will hold 6 phantoms, devons or minnows, securely held in a spring clip, see **D.** The division **A,** which has a movable partition, holds spoons, natural bait tackles, devon mounts, etc., while **C** is for traces and **B** for leads, swivels, spare hooks, etc.

No. 1.   Size $7\frac{1}{4}$ ins. by $4\frac{1}{2}$ ins. by $1\frac{7}{16}$ ins.   Price **21/-** each.
No. 2.   Size 6 ins. by $3\frac{3}{4}$ ins. by $1\frac{1}{2}$ ins.   Price **17/6** each.

The "ALLINONE" Fly Fisher's Case

CONTAINS

FLY BOX—CAST CASE—CAST DAMPER AND SPORTSMAN'S BALANCE

The case is divided into compartments **B**, to hold an Aluminium Fly box ; **A**, a Chamois Leather and Parchment three-pocket Cast Case, and **C**, a Cast Damper with felt pads. On the Cover is a pocket to hold a Sportsman's Balance.

    No. 1. For Salmon, with the "USK" box, (see page 306), Cast Case, Damper Pouch and No. 687 Sportsman's Balance to weigh 30 lbs. × ½ lb., **37/6** each.

    No. 2. For Sea Trout and Trout, with No. 6 box, (page 307), Cast Case, Damper Pouch, and No. 684½ Balance to weigh 4 lb. × 1 oz., **32/6** each.

The 'Unique' Salmon Fly Cabinet

A very handsome and convenient Mahogany Cabinet, $9\frac{1}{2}$ ins. high, by $9\frac{3}{4}$ ins. wide, by $6\frac{3}{4}$ ins. deep, fitted with ten Salmon Fly Trays with clips to hold 266 Flies. The trays are fitted in front with washable tablets to write the names of the flies on. There is a space at the bottom with a perforated lid to hold albo carbon to keep away moths. The cabinet is made with a lid to lock in front of trays keeping all secure. Sunk brass handle and name plate. **Price £4 4s. 0d.**

We are sometimes asked to fit one or more of the Trays with smaller clips for Sea Trout Flies. This we shall be pleased to, at an extra cost of 4s. to 5s. per tray.

Cabinet in Solid Leather Case, with Handle Straps and Lock complete   ..   ..   ..} £6 6s. 0d.

Any particular fly named on the tablet in any tray can be taken out without disturbing the others, a vast improvement over the old fashioned box, with trays dropping in one over the other, and in which the particular fly wanted is often in the bottom tray, necessitating the removal of all the others to get to it.

FISHING STOCKINGS & TROUSERS.

HARDY'S "WEAR-WELL" PATENT.

THE WADERS.

These Goods are much improved. All that can be gained by a long experience of the use, and many experiments with a view to improve, has been worked into them, and we do not think a more thoroughly well-made article is produced. They are especially got up for our trade, and the following important improvements have been carried out:—By a patented process the seams and taping never become hard, but remain soft and pliable in any climate. The feet are not made in the ordinary way, but are formed on blocks and double soled, so that they fit perfectly. There are no wrinkles to annoy the wearer, and a perfectly easy fit is secured. The foot is where the most wear takes place, and here the double sole, while protecting the foot, makes them last much longer. In the trousers the buttons are fixed on in an improved manner, so that they cannot come off, being riveted through the material. These advantages, combined with the employment of only the very best materials in the manufacture, give us every confidence in offering them as unsurpassed for **DURABILITY** and **COMFORT,** while the prices will bear favourable comparison even with the ordinary common makes.

For ordinary trout fishing, stockings do very well, but for salmon fishing, where deep wading is necessary, trousers are indispensable.

☛ IN ORDERING FROM THIS LIST PLEASE QUOTE LETTER **G.**

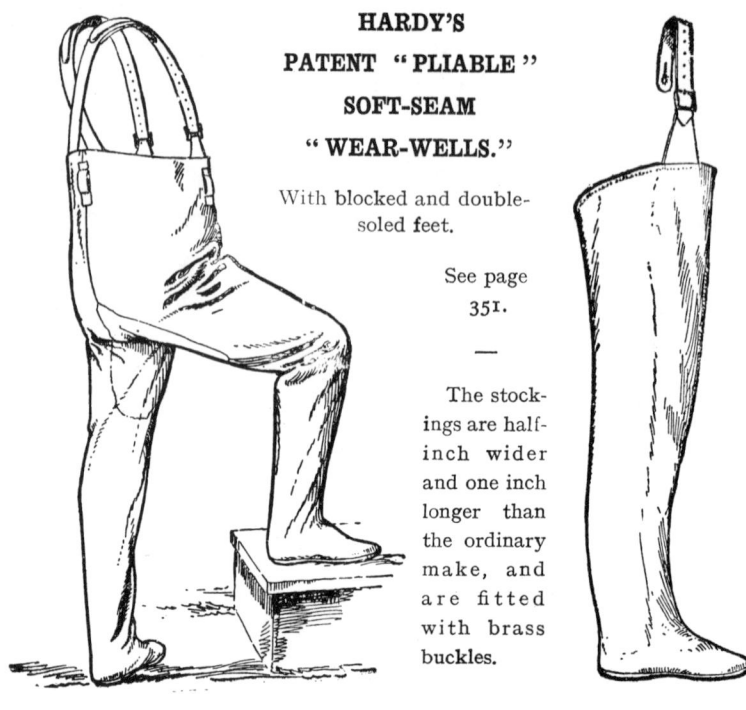

**HARDY'S
PATENT "PLIABLE"
SOFT-SEAM
"WEAR-WELLS."**

With blocked and double-soled feet.

See page 351.

—

The stockings are half-inch wider and one inch longer than the ordinary make, and are fitted with brass buckles.

The Improved "Invincible" Fishing Brogues

Fig. 1.

696—

CANNOT SLIP

ALL HAND-MADE, BLOCK TOES, WIDE WELTS.

PRICE **27/6** PER PAIR.

Hardy's " Between " Waders

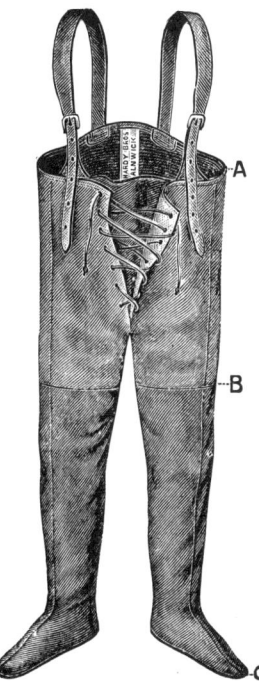

These are neither stockings nor breeches. We have designed them to avoid that cupful of water which is occasionally shipped when using ordinary wading stockings.

The feet and legs are of full-strength material from B to C, but from A to B of fine light texture. The large gusset in front of the long braces permit the garment to be worn very loosely and so keeps one cool in warm weather, especially when walking. They are not intended to take the place of trouser waders, but only for wading thigh-deep, where the light tops provide the necessary margin of safety.

Length of
foot, ins. 10 $10\frac{1}{2}$ 11 $11\frac{1}{2}$ 12
Prices -   **85/-** **87/6** **90/-** **92/6** **95/**
Weight about $3\frac{3}{4}$ lbs.

Hardy's Knee Waders

These were designed during the war for troops when in the trenches, but are also useful for those who only require to wade knee-deep. They are made of our best quality cloth, thoroughly proofed, and are worn over the usual socks or stockings with a pair of large shooting boots. Price **27/6** per pair.   10, $10\frac{1}{2}$, 11, $11\frac{1}{2}$ ins. Weight 11 oz.

Wristlets

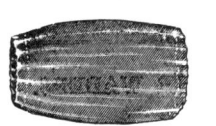

For fitting over coat sleeves to prevent midges biting the wrists or arms, and wet or wind blowing up the sleeves. Very useful for sportsmen or cyclists.

Price **6/6** per pair.

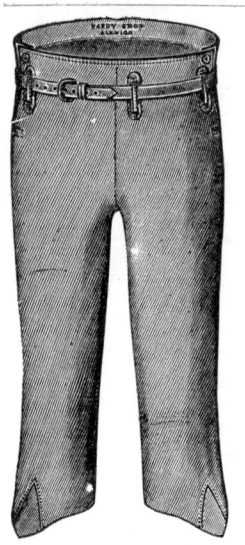
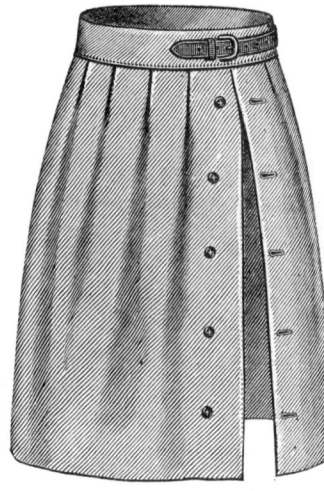

Boating Garments

Fishing from a boat in wet weather, Boating Trousers or Aprons are indispensable.

These garments are designed by us with a view to comfort in wear, in which respect they will be found very superior.

Price—**Boating Trousers,** extra quality, with double seat, **27/6** per pair. With single seat, **20/-** each.   **Boating Aprons, 30/** each.

Mosquito Veil and Gloves.

Anglers fishing in Newfoundland and other mosquito and insect infested countries will find these gloves and veils a great boon. The gloves have long sleeves and so perfectly protect the wrists. The veil covers the head and neck. It is provided with a fine hair window which does not affect the sight. In this window is fitted an automatic closing hole in a convenient position for the pipe.

Veil 5/-, Gloves per pair 6/-

ANGLERS' RECORD. A neat well bound pocket record book, in which can be recorded date, fish, weight, lure, water and remarks. Size $5\frac{1}{4}$ ins. $\times$ $3\frac{1}{4}$ ins. Price 2/6 each.

Rod Rest for Trolling or Sea Fishing.

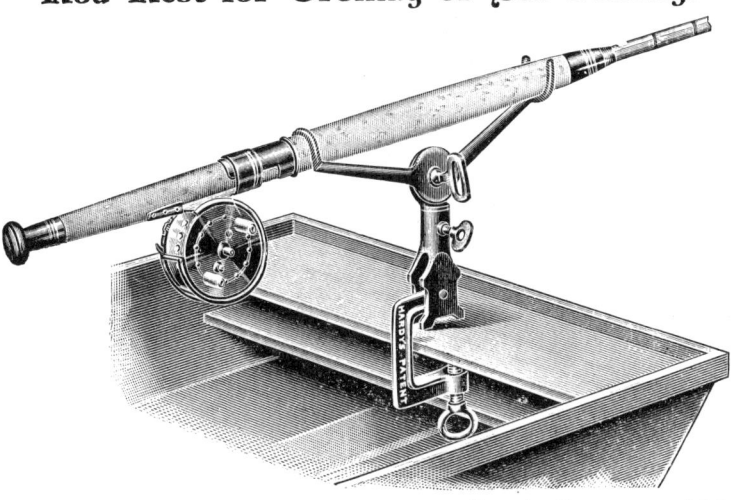

An excellent holder for rod either when trolling, harling, or sea fishing. It has a socket and spindle with pinching screw, which permits the direction of the rod to be altered to suit circumstances, while the arms are so arranged that the angle of the rod can be adjusted as desired. When trolling with two rods a pair may be used. They clamp firmly to the side of the boat in any position. Price **10/6** each.

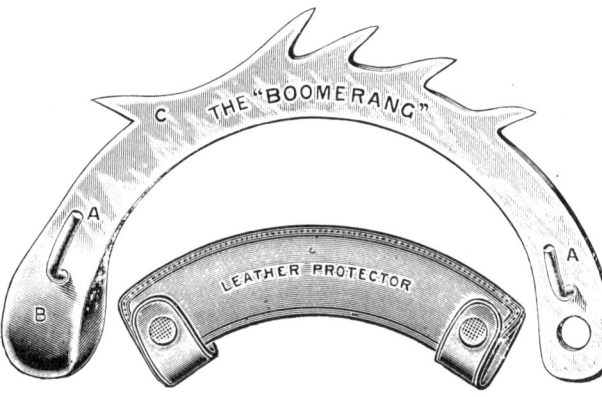

Registered.

A most useful article for the salmon, pike, or sea angler. It is used as a gag by forcing spike C into the mouth against the lower jaw, and pressing any of the other spikes against the upper, until the mouth is opened. The bulb B is a priest, hooks at A A are used to carry a fish, head and tail being tied together. The cord is carried on the pegs, using the " Boomerang " as a handle. Price **3/6**.

Registered.

A unique combination of priest and balance. The balance (to weigh 40lb. by ½lb.) has a metal cover, which is screwed off when about to weigh a fish. The cover is weighted at the end, and makes an excellent priest. Price **10/6**.

1908

HARDY'S REGISTERED CLEARING RING.

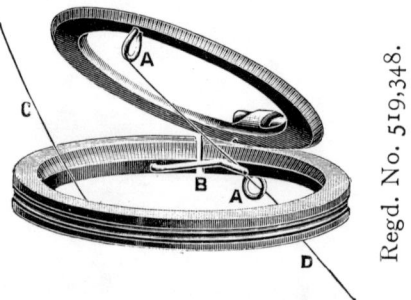

Regd. No. 519,348.

One of the most useful contrivances an angler can add to his kit. The system is quite new, and as may be seen from the illustration, consists of two rings hinged together.

The illustration shows the clearing ring open, a cord D is attached to eye A and operates as a grip. The reel line is inserted at slot B, and the ring manœuvred down to the "fast." Then by pulling on the cord the rings close and grip the tackle or obstruction, which is then either released or broken off close to the hook. The size of the opening in ring permits it to pass over a pike float. It is easily carried, and may save no end of valuable tackle.

Price **5**/- each.

Very stout tanned cord to attach to clearing ring, **9**d. per 30 yards.

Hardy's Clearing Knife.

Made of Steel, Silver Plated, and fitted in Pigskin Pocket.

2s. 9d. each.

A most useful little tool for releasing tackle, size 3in. by 1¾in. Can be screwed by putting hook at back through top ring, a cord being tied through the hole, into the landing net to cut down small branches or weeds, or placed on top of and when placed on the branch and the rod removed will generally clear the tackle. The end is also made as a screw-driver.

Eel Spears.

Best Quality Steel	3	4	5	6	7	9 prongs.
	3/3	4/	4/9	5/9	6/6	7/6

Fitted with long and strong bamboo shafts, 3/6 to 4/- each extra.

Patent
WITH TERRY'S

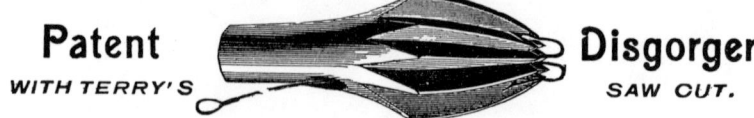

Disgorger,
SAW CUT.

Price 1s. each; by post, 1s. 2d.

Open the mouth of the fish as wide as possible, and fix it with a gag. Pass gut or gimp into the saw cut of the Disgorger; hold the gut or gimp taut, and pass the Disgorger down to the hook. To release the hook, press it downwards into the fish and then draw out. In drawing out, be careful to keep the gut or gimp tight against the handle.

WATER TELESCOPE   ...   .   37s. 6d.

"Silver Devon" Tackle Releaser

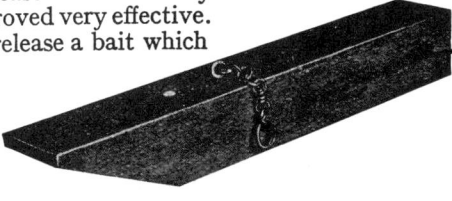

A new form of tackle releaser introduced by "Silver Devon" which has proved very effective. It practically never fails to release a bait which has become "snagged." When "snagged" do not pull—pay off a few yards of line and let it float past the bait, then give a smart jerk with the rod. This very often releases the bait; if not, attach the tackle releaser to the line through the split link A, launch the releaser disc just when it will swim out to and below bait; now give a good pull either with rod or hand, when the tackle should be released.   Price **2/6** each.

Tackle Releaser

Made of wood, concave in shape and with a lead keel. In the majority of cases it will retrieve a bait or tackle from the bottom of the river without breakage to hooks, etc.

To use : Lay down the rod ; draw off a good length of line (coiling

it evenly on the bank at the rod point) ; attach releaser by threading the line through the spiral eyes. Throw the releaser as far as possible beyond or above the " fast." Raise the rod to clear the line off the water and to work releaser beyond or below the tackle, so as to get a pull on it in the opposite direction to that in which the tackle caught up. When in such a position raise the rod and give a smart pull on the releaser.

Price **3/9** each.

HUDDERSFIELD, 6/10/36.

May I congratulate you on the splendid way your 9 ft. 6 ins. De Luxe Rod has stood up to hard work since you repaired it for me ? Fishing for sea trout last week I got three salmon with this toy, and the last one 19½ lbs. tried out the rod, which is no worse.   M. S. H.

Price **24/-** Each

In Chamois Leather Case

Exact Size

The Dry Fly Angler's Knife

This is the acme of all Anglers' Knives. It contains no less than eight essential and useful Tools. In designing this pattern, our object has been to fit all the really necessary Tools for a Dry-fly man, and yet keep the knife as light and handy as possible. We are glad to say that our object has been successfully accomplished. The knife is very substantial, the steel the very best, and each Tool is of the correct strength to give lasting wear.

LARGE BLADE.	LANCE.
SCISSORS.	STILETTO.
DISGORGER.	TWEEZERS (see fly attached).
FILE.	SCREWDRIVER.

Fitted with Shackle (at opposite end to that shown) to which a Chain may be attached. Suitable Chains with Spring Clip, 2/6 each.

Made in Sterling Silver at Proportionate Price.

196

Hardy's Sportsman's Walking Stick Seats

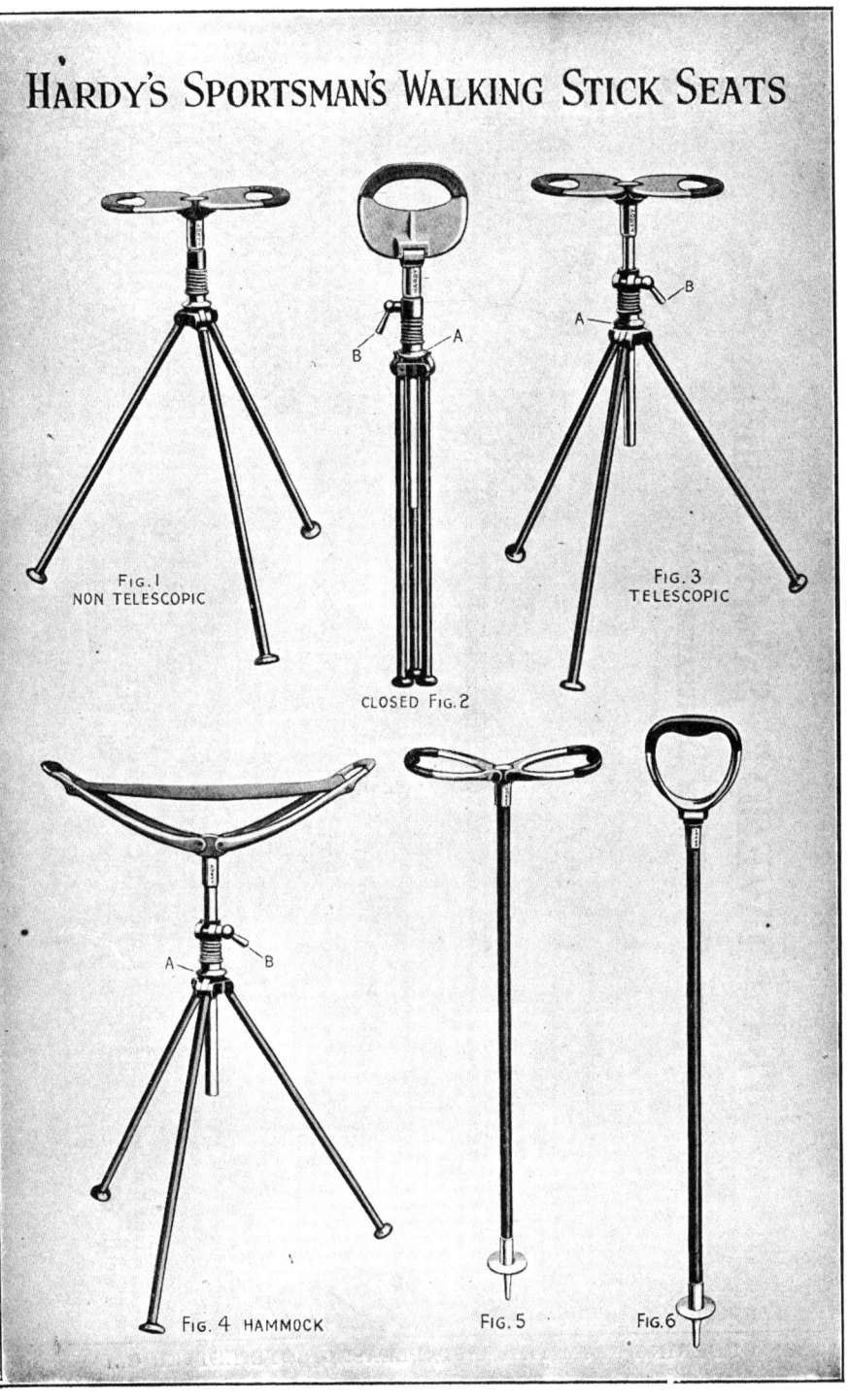

FIG.1
NON TELESCOPIC

CLOSED FIG.2

FIG.3
TELESCOPIC

FIG. 4 HAMMOCK

FIG. 5

FIG.6

Hardy's Sportsmen's Walking Stick Seats

PAT. NO. 4164/22 and U.S.A. PAT. 1502629.

THE illustrations, Figs. 1, 2, 3 and 4 on opposite page, show our patented design of Walking Stick Seat, convertible into a veritable revolving *three-legged* stool. It is suitable for use at the riverside, shooting butt or covertside, and has the great advantage that it may be left standing and resumed at leisure. The revolving seat allows the shooter to swing round, follow his bird, and shoot without rising; while when boat fishing the angler may turn in any direction for casting.

For the **Dry Fly Angler** it is invaluable. When waiting for a rising fish, let him open his seat, adjust it to the height desired, sit down, light his pipe, and be grateful " that his needs are at last provided for."

For the **Tourist** who desires to rest after climbing a hill, etc., it provides a walking-stick and a comfortable seat, not a mere support. Pattern Fig. 3 makes an excellent adjustable camera rest for time exposure photographs. They are also handy as an extra seat in a car.

Each pattern has a leather hand grip for comfort when used as a walking stick.

To fix for sitting, grip any two of the legs, and hold horizontally with the seat pointing away from the body ; pull legs apart as far as possible, when they will automatically lock by ring **A**. In the **Telescopic** design, adjust to desired height, and lock by lever **B**.

To close :—hold seat vertically and pull up **A**, close legs and then release **A**.

Fig. 1. " Non-Telescopic," height from ground 19½ ins. Price **52/6**.

Fig. 3. " Telescopic," height adjustable from the ground 20½ ins. to 30 ins. Price **63/-**.

Fig. 4. " Hammock," Non-Telescopic, **55/-** ; Telescopic, **63/-**.

Figs. 5 and 6. Polished wood stick, aluminium head with leather-covered hand grasp. The hand may be passed through the seat head so as to hang on the arm. The disc at the bottom is permanently fixed. Price **25/-**. This type can also be supplied with Hammock Seat as in Fig. 4. Price **30/-**

The Angler's Third Arm
FOR ONE-ARMED ANGLERS.

Fig. 1.

Fig. 2.

Made in two sizes to suit Trout and Salmon rods respectively. The attachment is adjustable and can be very comfortably fitted to the body. The bracket, Fig. 1 A which holds the rod when the angler is winding in, is locked back close to the chest so that it is well out of the way when casting Fig. 2 A. In the Trout size attachment, it, is automatically brought back into the holding position, as soon as the butt of the rod is inserted into the socket B.   Price **£2 17s. 6d.** each.

Hardy's Pocket Dynamometer

For testing the breaking strain of lines up to 6 lbs.

This small pocket line tester is a very useful adjunct to the Thread Line Angler.

Can be easily carried in the waistcoat pocket. Total length $3\frac{1}{2}$ ins.

Price **7/6** each.

The Angler's Pocket Thermometer

The Thermometer is enclosed in a very strong frame which is fitted with a spring clip to hold it in the pocket.

Price **7/6** each.

Hardy's " Angler's and Sportsman's " Pipe

Patent No. 274365.

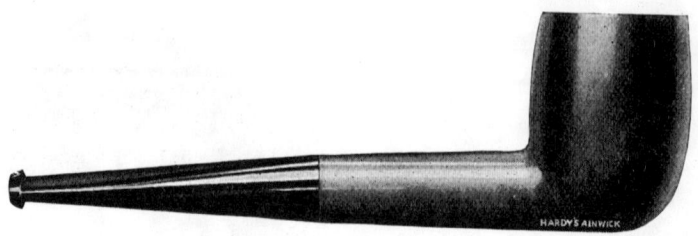

Illustration is ¾ size of the Medium Pipe.

Most Anglers and Sportsmen smoke a pipe. A good pipe—i.e. one which does not get foul or bitter—is one of the greatest joys of life. What can be more enjoyable ?

In Hardy's " Angler's and Sportsman's " Pipe you have the ideal.

Some years ago, we realised the necessity for a dry pipe, so determined to find out if it could be made. After many experiments and burning of much tobacco, we decided that we had at last achieved our object. We made at our Works at Alnwick, several pipes, and with our friends have smoked them for years with much satisfaction.

We have now resolved to make and offer them to our Angling and Sporting friends. We claim that it is the cleanest, driest, sweetest and most hygienic pipe that has been made. It smokes evenly and practically without moisture, burns its tobacco to the very end, leaving nothing but a little white ash at the bottom.

What happens when a pipe is lighted ? The tobacco immediately below begins to exude moisture which is nicotine.

It occurred to us—Why not destroy this nicotine by burning it as it is produced ? As the tobacco burns this moisture increases, and works its way to the bottom of the bowl, where in an ordinary pipe it is partly drawn into the tube and so into the mouth.

Our design of destroying it by burning is clearly shown in the diagram. The flat bottom of the inside of the bowl in conjunction with a mouthpiece projecting over it, traps the nicotine. This mouthpiece fits tightly, and so prevents any moisture from the bowl getting into the pipe stem. When the tobacco is about three parts consumed, the nicotine trapped at the bottom is drawn into the fire by capillary attraction, and burnt up. No other pipe has this feature.

The line DD denotes approximately the position of the fire where it commences to consume the nicotine.

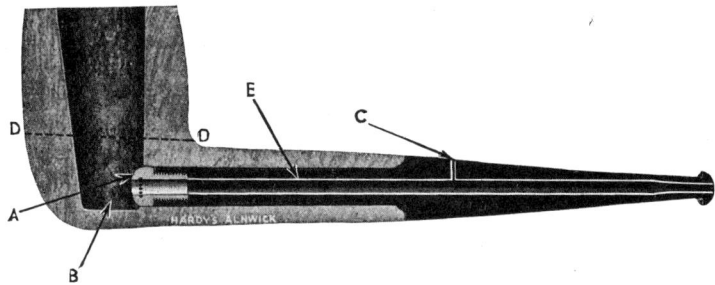

This illustration is a section of Hardy's " Angler's and Sportsman's " Pipe.

THE COOLEST AND SWEETEST SMOKING PIPE MADE
(Designed and Manufactured by Messrs. Hardy Bros. Ltd.)

The advantages and improvements are :

A cool smoke, as the perfectly straight taper of the bowl burns the tobacco evenly and with decreasing fire area.

An economic smoke, as the tobacco burns freely to the very bottom of the bowl.

Moisture lying on the bottom of the bowl cannot get into the mouthpiece as IT IS TRAPPED and consumed by the burning tobacco, owing to the end of the mouthpiece ' A ' projecting into the bowl with the smoke inlet just raised above the inside bottom of ' B.'

No check to baffle the smoke and cause condensation, as the hole of tube ' E ' from the bowl to the mouth is straight.

Easily cleaned as the hole is straight.

Free and easy draw, as the metal end of the mouthpiece has several inlets.

A cool and sweet smoke, as the small hole ' C ' drilled into the smoke tube permits a certain calculated percentage of pure air to mix with the tobacco smoke.

Can be placed on a table, etc., without fear of the ashes or cinder falling out, owing to the bottom being flat.

It is the most hygenic pipe made and recommended by Doctors.

All are made from the finest selected and seasoned bruyere.

Large—Medium—Small   -   12/6 each.
Soft Leather Case, 2/6 each.

Obtainable from all our branches.

Special straight grains marked blue star in leather covered case, 55/-

---

INDIA, 20/10/29.

For the last twenty-eight years I have been searching for my Ideal pipe ; now I have found it and at a moderate price, too.

With Hardy rods, Hardy reels and tackle, and a Hardy pipe what can any man want more—only the skill of the Hardy family in catching fish—alas, I can never attain that.

Please dispatch two more No. I pipes.   NEE-KEE.

REAMERS FOR HARDY'S ANGLERS' AND SPORTSMEN'S PIPE

As it is desirable to retain the tapered shape of the inside of the bowl—an important feature—we have designed and registered the Reamer illustrated here to clean out the bowl of the pipe.

Nos. 1, 2, and 3 (pipes are marked with size). Price **6d.** each.

Reg. No. 746403

Remove mouthpiece before reaming to avoid cutting nozzle 'A.'

KAMLOOPS, B.C., 6/9/29.

The pipe in question is every bit as good as you claim and then some. It's on a par with all things stamped " Hardy's." H. L. FEWINGS.

HANTS., 9/12/29.

I feel that I must inform you that, thanks to you, I have at last found the perfect pipe, which you really should call the *Perfect (Anglers')* *Pipe*. Although I got my first pipe from you less than a fortnight ago, I have already had four for myself and friends. G. F. L.

LONDON, E.1, 6/5/29.

I have been tempted to smoke one of your pipes although I have always been prejudiced against Patent Pipes and have never smoked one before.

To my astonishment I find that your Pipe smokes most excellently in every way. Although I am a wet smoker I find that my pipe will keep dry inside and does not want to be cleaned out.

It certainly does what you claimed for it and certainly should have a brilliant future. P. C. DE G.

MONMOUTH, 16/9/29.

I have been smoking one of your " Angler's " pipes for some time now, with considerable satisfaction. I find them cool, sweet and having less effect in irritating the throat than other pipes. S. W. B. S.

ONTARIO, CANADA, 12/7/29.

It is a revelation to me in Pipe construction and it has added a new pleasure and contentment to my use of the Pipe when smoking in moments of ease and rest, while the magnificent material, design and craftsmanship and freedom from tinsel adornments, are an additional pleasure to look upon. W. H. PRETTY.

DERBY.

I feel that I must write and congratulate you on the excellence of your " Angler's " Pipe, two examples of which you supplied me with a few weeks ago. They are without a doubt the finest pipes I have ever smoked (for over twenty years I have smoked ——'s and ——'s exclusively) and fulfil in every respect all the claims you make for them. J. HARRISON WATSON.

26/9/29.

At last, after many years of vexation and much expense, I have found the perfect pipe. It is all you claim for it and a boon to mankind. I did not think it possible to produce a pipe which would smoke so dry and yet be cool and sweet. May I congratulate you. L. C.

COVENTRY.

Many thanks for the No. 2 " Angler's " Pipe to hand yesterday. It smokes like an old pipe already, and is the only Patent pipe I have ever come across that is any good. May I congratulate you on the design, the materials, and the execution of the job generally. Please send me another just like it ; I have never seen a better bit of bird's-eye grain. No more ——'s for me ! RICHARD CALDICOTT.

MALVERN, 20/4/29.

Thanks for the " Angler's " Pipe. Although I have had it so short a time I can unhesitatingly say it is all you claim for it. It is a joy to smoke and its only disadvantage is that I shall have to scrap my other pipes, several of them more expensive ones than yours. Yours will save its cost in tobacco in a few months. It is the nicest and sweetest pipe I have ever smoked in over forty years of devotion to a pipe. F. R.

BIG GAME FISH SECTION
Giant Tahitian Striped Marlin
(New Species—First One Caught)

Length, 14 ft. Girth, 6 ft. 9 ins. Weight, 1040 lbs.

Caught on " Hardy-Zane Grey " Rod and "Hardy-Zane Grey " Reel. Time, 7 hours.

After being brought up this fish was attacked by sharks that tore off from **150** to **200 lbs.** from the tail and one side. Normal weight would have been near 1300 lbs.   ZANE GREY.

The "Sea Silex" Reels

(1914 MODEL.)

FIG. 1.

FIG. 2.—Interior of Reel.

FIG. 3.—Line Drum.

A.—Controlling lever.

B.—Pressure lever through which Spring C exerts pressure on hub and prevents overrunning.

D.—Lever carrying ratchet F.

E.—Lever for throwing check out of or into gear.

G.—Main spring.

NOTE.—This reel is specially designed as an all round sea reel, either for casting out bait from a pier or shore, as well as general boat work.   For special boat reel, see the "Farne," page 367.

Hardy's "Tuna" Reels

(Prov. Pat. No. 32450'20).

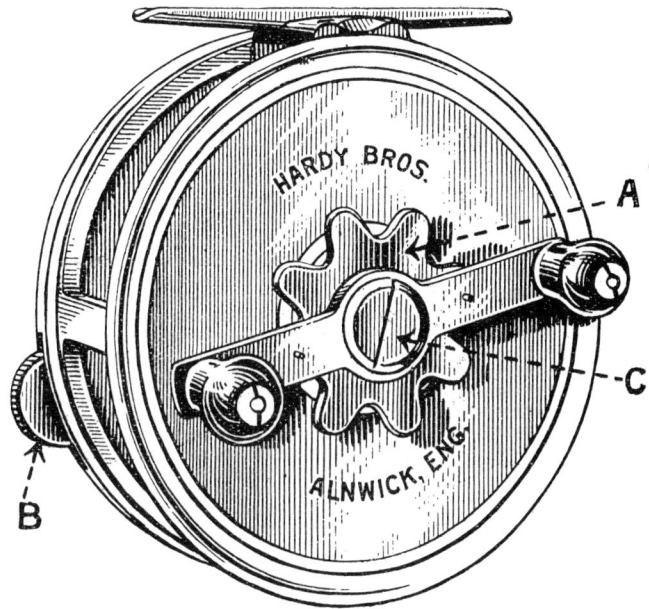

These reels are designed for very heavy sea fishing and are made of a special aluminium alloy which withstands the corrosive action of salt water.

The special features are :—

1. The handles remain stationery when playing a fish, consequently there is no liability of injury to the hands, while they are at once available for winding.

2. The breaking mechanism is very accessible and can instantly be applied. By turning the star shaped washer A to the right increases the pressure, while to the left decreases it. Brake pressure to 24lbs. can be applied.

3. By throwing over the disc shaped lever B the reel is made free running.

4. The bearings have been carefully designed to prevent "Seizing." When a fish is taking out line at a very high speed, the line drum revolves on almost frictionless ball bearings.

5. Lubrication of all parts can be applied from the outside of the reel.

To dismount the reel, unscrew centre screw C, remove the handle bar and unscrew star shaped tension washer A, when the drum can be taken out. When assembling care must be taken to see that the locking keys in the sleeve (which fits over the spindle) engage correctly with the keyways cut in the ball races.

Sizes -	-	-	5 ins.	6 ins.	7 ins.
Prices -	-	-	**144/-**	**160/-**	**179/6**
Line carrying capacity			200 yds.	250 yds.	350 yds.

The "HARDY-ZANE GREY"
Big Game Fish Reel

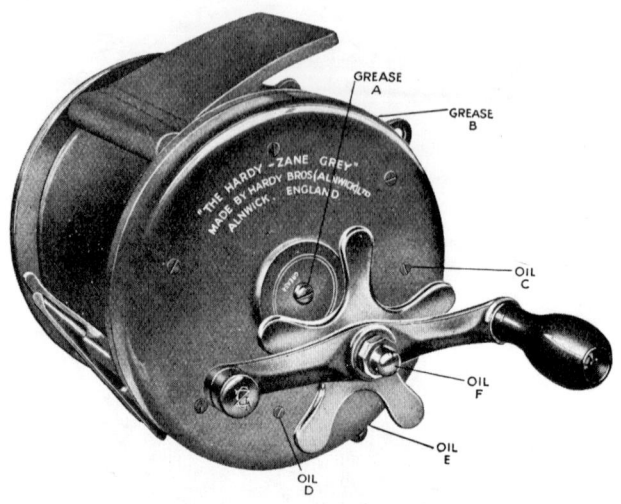

Designed and manufactured to meet the requirements of the famous angler and author, Mr. Zane Grey.   It is used and recommended by him, Mr. R. C. Grey, and Captain Mitchell.

In associating his name with this reel, Mr. Zane Grey stipulated that it must be the best Big Game Fish Reel in the world.

It is constructed of genuine Monel Metal, the strongest non-ferrous metal known, and guaranteed to be absolutely immune to the action of sea water and air in any part of the world.

The multiple gear is single helical, the teeth of the involute type, running silently, and has a ratio of $2\frac{1}{2}$ to 1.

The line spool spindle runs in encased high grade ball bearings, eliminating any possibility of the bearings seizing.

All details of design and materials selected for their various functions, have been given exhaustive tests before being finally accepted.

This Reel will stand up to the very hardest and most strenuous tests a reel can be subjected to.

As with everything Hardys make their guarantee goes with it.

LUBRICATION :

All bearings are lubricated from the outside. A, A1 (In centre of plate on side not shown) and B are for grease. Remove the screws (screwdriver provided), screw in the grease gun (provided) and give two or three turns to Charge.

C, D, E and F are oil holes—squirt in oil (Squirt provided) after removing the screws.

Sizes	Line Carrying Capacity		Prices
6″	600 yards	39 thread	£30
5½″	500 ,,	36 ,,	,,
5″	500 ,,	24 ,,	,,

Hand-made solid leather reel case, containing two turnscrews, grease gun and spanners, **70s.**

HARPOONS

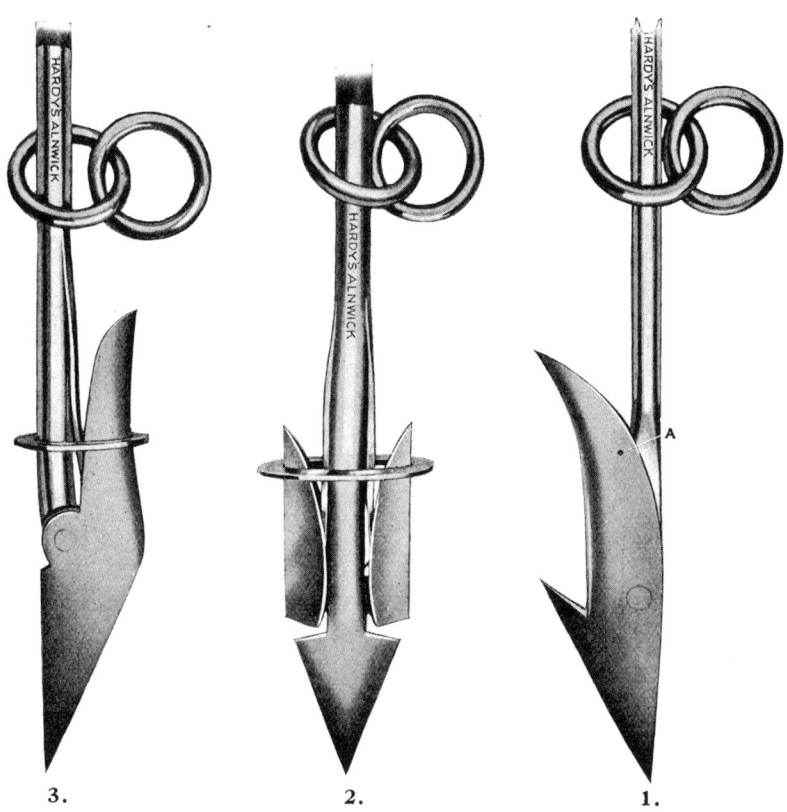

3.　　　　　　　　　**2.**　　　　　　　　　**1.**

1. The " Cook," same design as old whaling harpoons ; shank of best Swedish iron to stand bending. The point and barb of best tempered steel. The barb is set by a small wooden peg " A," and after entering the fish, releases itself, to engage.

As used by Mr. White Wickham.　　Price, **37/6.**

2. Double barbed with setting ring which slips off when driven into fish.　Price, **27/6.**

3. Single barbed with setting ring which slips off when driven into fish.　Price, **22/6.**

INDEX

Lessons Given in Fly and Bait Casting

Mr. F. TILTON, the Scientific and Quick Teacher, Coaches
his Clients the following Casts.

SALMON FLY CASTING

1 The Overhead Cast
2 The Wind Cast
3 The Loop Cast
4 The Spey Cast
5 The Double Spey Cast
6 Prevent a Drag Cast
7 Back Fishing in Steady Pools
8 Dry Fly Casting for Salmon

SPINNING WITH THE "SILEX MAJOR"

For Salmon
For Trout
For Mahseer
For Pike, etc.

TROUT FLY CASTING

1 The Overhead Cast
2 The Short Cast
3 The Wind Cast
4 The Underhand Cast
5 The Backhanded Cast
6 Casting into the Wind
7 The Loop Cast
8 The Spey Cast
9 The Double Spey Cast
10 The Up-Stream Cast
   (with high weeds at the edge)
11 Picking the Line off the Swift-Water and
   Looping up-stream
12 Preventing a Drag

For Terms Apply—

Mr. F. TILTON, *The Wimbledon Park Golf Club Ltd.*
Wimbledon Park, LONDON, S.W. 19

Phone: Wimbledon 1250.

Anglers read the "Fishing Gazette."

From the]   **"FISHERMAN'S LUCK."**   *["Fishing Gazette."*